Ancient China

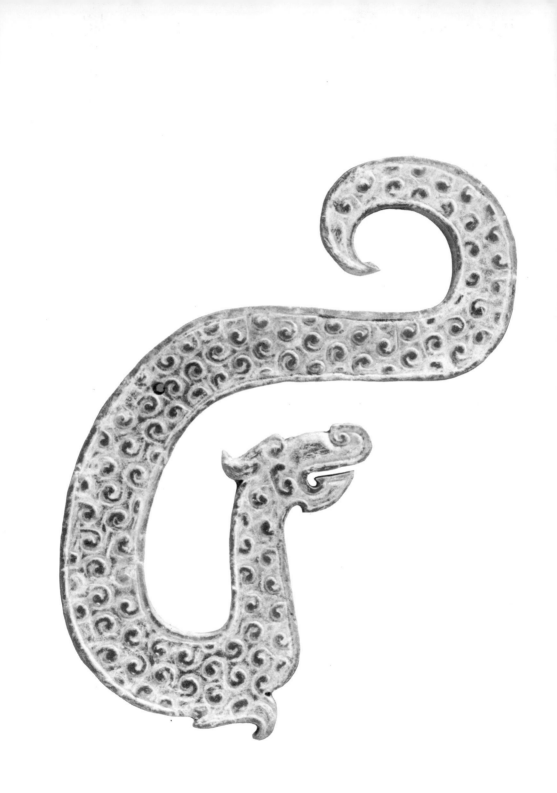

Ancient China

Art and Archaeology

Jessica Rawson

Book Club Associates
London

Cover: The Great Wall of China north of Peking
Frontispiece: Jade dragon pendant, Eastern Zhou

© 1980 The Trustees of the British Museum

British Library Cataloguing in Publication Data

Rawson, Jessica
    Ancient China, art and archaeology.
    1. China — Antiquities
    I. Title II. British Museum
    931'.0074'02142 DS714

ISBN 0 7141 1415 4 cased
ISBN 0 7141 1414 6 paper

This edition published 1980 by
Book Club Associates
By arrangement with British Museum
Publications Ltd, 6 Bedford Square, London WC1 3RA

Designed by Humphrey Stone

Set in 10/13pt Monophoto Photina
Printed in Great Britain by W. S. Cowell Ltd, Ipswich

Contents

Acknowledgements

The archaeology and history of ancient China is at present a field of great intellectual activity. We all owe an immense debt to the dedicated work of Chinese archaeologists whose excavation and reports are the foundation of work in these subjects. Both in Japan and the West this activity has generated many detailed scholarly studies. All of these I gratefully acknowledge. The reader is referred in particular to the works of scholars mentioned in the text. No such reference would, however, adequately record my debt to William Watson, Max Loehr, and Hayashi Minao who have, through their writing and in person, directed and moulded my understanding of ancient China.

At different stages, the text of this book has been read and commented upon by friends and colleagues: Sarah Allan, Robert Bagley, David Keightley, Michael Loewe, Lawrence Smith, Jenny So, Mary Tregear and Angus Walker. I am grateful for their advice and criticism; the errors and omissions that still remain are, however, my responsibility. I owe especial thanks to Roderick Whitfield and Penelope Hughes-Stanton for their help in the preparation of the manuscript for the press. Roderick Whitfield has written the Chinese characters and Penelope Hughes-Stanton has compiled the bibliography and the indexes. Without their help and encouragement, and the unfailing support of Celia Clear of British Museum Publications, this book would not have been so easily completed.

Introduction

This book is intended as a companion to the collection of early Chinese art and archaeological material in the British Museum. It describes the period from the Neolithic c. 5000 BC to the Han dynasty (206 BC–AD 220). Although many items in the collections will be discussed in some detail, this book is not a catalogue or handlist of important objects. Instead the collections in the Museum will be used as a vantage point from which to consider the general development of early Chinese art and its historical context.

Although, as we shall see, the Chinese had an elaborate literary tradition, written sources relating to early China are limited. For China, as for many other early cultures, the surviving artefacts are important because they are the only evidence we have for some of the preoccupations of Chinese society. Moreover the Chinese, more than any other people, exercised their greatest artistic talents in the manufacture of ceramics, bronzes, and jades. They diverted valuable materials and much labour to these ends, and the enduring monuments of the ancient Chinese are the fine painted bowls and the intricate ritual bronzes that they made. Indeed the high level of accomplishment they achieved, and the large scale of production, are astounding. Unlike many ancient civilisations, the architectural remains are limited. From what still exists, however, it is evident that here, too, large numbers of men were deployed in monumental tasks. Little graphic art has survived. A collection of three-dimensional artefacts of the size of that in the British Museum is therefore one of the best available sources. Very few items in the collection come from known archaeological sites. They will therefore be compared with recently excavated material. References to excavated finds, similar to those illustrated in this book, are given in the appendix.

China is also a country with a long and rich literary and historical record. The Official Histories alone, which were modelled on the great pioneering work of Sima Qian (c. 145–86 BC), writing in the Han dynasty, set out a wealth of historical fact. Sima Qian was the official historian under the emperor Wu (141–87 BC). His was the earliest attempt to produce a comprehensive account of past and current events. Other earlier official or semi-official records survive.

Of these the earliest are the oracle bones of the late Shang period, *c.* 1300 BC. These are the bones and turtle shells used for divination, on which were inscribed the matters to be divined. Inscriptions on bronze and the first bare chronicles of the ancient Chinese states became important in the succeeding Zhou period. Other texts recorded the rites and practices of the state.

The official nature of such documents is pronounced. This special character of early Chinese writing can be counterbalanced to only a limited degree by considering the works of poetry and philosophy which have also survived. By and large, philosophy in China, especially in ancient China, was concerned with questions about the nature of the state. A similar concentration was implicit in the histories. Philosophical writings of the Confucians or their opponents, the Legalists, were prescriptive, while historical works were formally descriptive; but both were the work of officials or scholars concerned to suggest proper modes of government or action in the context of their society.

Early Chinese poetry can also be related to this official tradition. In the first collection of Chinese poetry, the *Shi Jing*, brought together *c.* 600 BC, there are a number of love songs and other lyrical poems of an intimate character. But prominent in this collection are also poems setting out the history of the Zhou peoples before their conquest of the earlier Shang dynasty: they are concerned with the foundation of a state and its antecedents.

Later poetry, whether formal or personal was, along with all the other literature mentioned, the work of the class of educated men who controlled the country, namely the officials. Poets, philosophers, and historians were one with the official. This gives the written culture of China great unity, a unity inevitably obtained at the expense of varying perspectives and traditions.

Archaeological field work is the other major source of evidence for the periods covered by this book. Since 1949 excavations have continued steadily in most parts of the country. Many digs have been carried out as rescue operations in conjunction with construction projects. Others are part of an on-going programme of investigation of the major ancient sites long known. The results of the researches are regularly published in Chinese. Such evidence can to a certain extent make good some of the omissions in the literary record, but the marriage of the two types of evidence is by no means easy.

This book will attempt to make use of both types of evidence. As the objects in the collection will be related to those recovered from excavations, they can serve as an introduction to the archaeology of China. At the same time it will be shown that notions about ancient China gained from the written record can be supplemented and extended by the archaeological evidence. To sum up, the aim of this introduction is to examine the objects of the collection in the context of the other available evidence, and in this way to show what kind of information about ancient China can be provided by artefacts.

The collections

Collections of Chinese art and artefacts in Europe are relatively new. In the West, attempts to understand man's past were founded upon the teachings of Christianity and the surviving texts and monuments. A serious approach to antiquity began with an examination of classical texts and buildings, leading in turn to the study of the ancient Near East.

The Far East was a different matter. Despite the descriptions provided in the thirteenth century by such travellers as Marco Polo, or by the Jesuits in the seventeenth and eighteenth centuries, the Europeans had little interest in China or Japan for their own sake. Distant lands with curious habits provided the raw material for the presentation of utopias or alternatively lands inhabited by fabulous beings. Only in the late nineteenth century did Europeans start, as missionaries, traders and soldiers, to travel extensively in China in any numbers, and to require and acquire a more realistic understanding of the country. A small section of the Museum's collection of Far Eastern material came with the founding collection of Sir Hans Sloane, whose formidable assemblage of curiosities, brought together in the eighteenth century, made up the original British Museum. The bulk of the collection of Chinese antiquities, however, arrived only later, as a consequence of the close contact which European businessmen, soldiers, and travellers came to have with China in the early years of this century. The great exhibition of Chinese art held in Burlington House in the winter of 1935–6 was a turning point. It is from that time that the widespread interest in Chinese art in this country, and indeed in many others, is to be dated. Those years too saw the growth of great private collections of early Chinese art and artefacts. Chinese porcelain had always been prized and collected in Europe, but the bronzes, jades, and tomb figures were unknown before the beginning of this century. The British Museum is heir to the enthusiasm and generosity of the British collectors of the early twentieth century.

The subject matter of this guide is the bronze ritual vessels, bronze weapons, jades, pottery vessels, and other tomb furnishings which came out of China and entered Western collections between the wars. A collection formed in this way cannot be comprehensive. In the first place, the major discoveries of the subsequent years cannot be represented. Secondly the items on display all come from some sort of burial, mostly from tombs but also to a lesser extent from ritual deposits or from hoards buried in times of trouble and unrest. As a record of the variety of the Chinese past, such a collection inevitably has limitations. As a study of these objects can broaden and balance the view of China as gained from the literary records, so in turn this literary record must at times be invoked to make good some of the deficiencies of an understanding of China founded entirely upon artefacts.

The physical aspect of the country

For the purposes of this guide China will be taken to include three main areas: first the Yellow River area; then the great steppe and forest region to the north and north-west; and finally the south from the Yangtze River southwards. The importance of the first area, both archaeologically and culturally, generally outweighs the other two.

Within these larger regions several significant subdivisions can be noted. The southern bend of the Yellow River marks the centre of one such area. One of the most important neolithic cultures, the Yangshao, developed here. Subsequently several of the major dynasties, the Zhou, the Qin, and the Western Han established a base in this region, consolidated their power, and from here extended their conquests. The area lies at the heart of the primary loess, that is, the thick deposit of soft soil blown from the Gobi desert over north-west China in the Pleistocene period, from about a million years ago. In places this deposit is hundreds of feet thick and, because it is soft and porous, great ravines have been cut through it by the rivers and the weather. In the loess cliffs, caves could be hollowed out for dwellings, and the soft soil supported agriculture because it was rich in minerals brought to the surface by capillary attraction. Southwards and eastwards this area of loess reaches into the Huai River valley and Anhui province, an area that forms an important zone between the Yellow River and the Yangtze.

Along the east coast, Hebei province in the north is linked by way of Shandong to the central coastal provinces of Jiangsu and Zhejiang. In the neolithic period, in particular, these geographical links probably account for the similarities in the important cultures of this long coastal region. Fujian and the southern part of Zhejiang form an independent area cut off from the main body of China by mountains.

Along the extreme west are the great mountains of Tibet. Despite the harsh terrain of this western area, there were important north-south communications by way of Sichuan between Gansu province in the north and the far south-west, what is now Yunnan province. But this western area lay on the periphery of the main developments in Chinese culture that are to be the subject of this book. In central southern China was a further distinct area, comprising southern Henan, Hubei, and Hunan provinces, in which a notable variant of the main Chinese culture developed during the Eastern Zhou period in particular.

Chronology

The existence of a comparative wealth of written material should make it possible to set out an absolute chronology rather than a relative chronology based on excavated material. There are, however, difficulties. The first arises from the absence of written evidence for the neolithic period and for part of the first dynasty, the Shang. This deficiency is to some extent made good by recent work on radiocarbon dating. Next, for the succeeding period, up to mid-ninth century BC, there are several conflicting chronologies to choose from. These chronologies all provide different dates for the Zhou conquest of the Shang, an event of great historical significance. Two chronologies, deriving from different documents, are more important than the others. The first is based on a text known as the *Bamboo Annals*, said to have been buried in a tomb during the third century BC. It was found again in the third century AD. Judging from dates which had been copied from this work and quoted in other surviving early Chinese texts, the Zhou dynasty would appear to have been founded in about 1027 BC. The other system of dating, known as the 'traditional chronology', is based on another historical work, the *Han Shu or History of the Former Han Dynasty*. From this work a date of 1122 BC is derived for the Zhou conquest. In the present guide, 1027 BC is taken as the date of the Zhou conquest merely because this date has gained wide currency; it may very well be that revision to a date nearer 1100 BC will some day become necessary. Therefore, although specific dates will be assigned to particular objects, in general it is best to think in terms of late Shang or early Zhou, i.e. relative rather than absolute dates.

There is less difficulty in establishing the dates of the other major political changes important to a consideration of the collection. The first part of the Zhou period, known as Western Zhou, is taken to run until 771 BC, when the capital was moved from the west, near the present day city of Xian, eastwards to Luoyang. The second part of the Zhou is known therefore as Eastern Zhou. This second part is divided into two further sections, the Spring and Autumn period, and the period of the Warring States (see p. 128). With the victory of the Qin in 221 BC, the Eastern Zhou came to an end. The Qin dynasty was relatively short-lived, and was succeeded by the Han dynasty (206 BC–AD 220).

Plan of the book

Thus there are five major periods dealt with in the five chapters of this book: the Neolithic, the Shang dynasty, the Western Zhou period, the Eastern Zhou period and the Han dynasty. These chapters will attempt to trace the origin of the main aspects of Chinese material culture. Although this book is only concerned with the early phases of Chinese history and goes no later than the third century AD, it covers the formative periods of China's past. By the close of the Han period many of the distinctive features of Chinese civilisation had come into existence: the language with its ideographic script, the main philosophical schools, and some of the most important literary forms. Among the arts, however, painting and sculpture were still to come to the fore. But most of the other important aspects of the material culture had made their appearance, including a unique architectural style, a unique form of bronze casting, and the methods of exploiting or working jade, silk, lacquer, and high-fired ceramics, all arts which are peculiarly Chinese.

A note on transliteration

The Chinese phonetic alphabet, or 'pinyin' as it is known, has been used throughout the book. On 1 January 1979 the Chinese government officially adopted pinyin for the romanisation of the names of Chinese persons and places to replace the 'Wade Giles' spelling system in use previously. All Chinese words have therefore been romanised by the pinyin system with the exception of English book titles that incorporate Chinese words. A few names of cities, notably Peking, are given in a non-pinyin form.

In general pinyin is pronounced as one would expect from the English values for the alphabet. A few letters are exceptions: *c* is pronounced as *ts*; *q* stands before words with an *i* or a *u* vowel sound to make *ch*; *x* is approximately equivalent to *sh*; and *zh* to *j* or *dj*.

In their full form Chinese place-names have three parts: province, county, village. Each part usually consists of two or more syllables. In the pinyin system these are run together to make a single word. Where the last part of a name is the term *xian*, county, or *cun*, village, it has been separated from the rest of the name.

A name likely to cause difficulty is that of the city Sian here written Xian. It has two syllables which are separately pronounced, and it should be distinguished from the word for county *xian* which has only one syllable. The transliteration of the provinces of Shensi and Shansi is now given as Shaanxi and Shanxi.

1 The Neolithic

The term 'neolithic' is used to describe early societies in which the use of metal is as yet unknown, but which have mastered and come to be dependent on the deliberate cultivation of plants and the domestication of animals. Before the Neolithic, men subsisted by hunting and gathering. Hunters had by and large to adopt a mobile way of life, its comings and goings governed by the movements of animal populations and the availability of plant foods. Farmers, inevitably drawn to a more settled form of existence, had a greater measure of control over a food supply that was capable of supporting much larger populations. The introduction of farming and animal husbandry was a momentous change in human history, so that it is no exaggeration to call it, in the words of Gordon Childe, the 'neolithic revolution'.

This chapter will, however, describe more groups of people than just those who belong to neolithic societies within this definition. It will include some peoples who were hunters and gatherers, and refer to others who were able to work metal. The upper limit of this chapter will be the beginnings of the full-scale casting of bronze. As writing was not widely used until the Bronze Age was well advanced, the chapter will be concerned with peoples who left no written record, and whose names are not known. The different groups are therefore defined and described by the material remains they left behind: pottery and kilns, stone tools, buildings, and tombs. From these the skills and preoccupations of the peoples can be inferred. The complex of traits associated with any one group is known by the term 'culture'.

The identification of the exact place and time when the neolithic revolution took place in China has been a subject of much debate. Techniques of radio-carbon dating together with extensive excavations have considerably revised our ideas about the process. First, the date when agriculture became significant in China has been reassessed and shown to be not later than the fifth millenium BC. This is earlier than had been supposed. Secondly, it has been shown that the development of neolithic societies took place in several centres at much the same time, and that they probably arose quite independently of each other; the older view that the neolithic way of life evolved only once is firmly contradicted by the evidence of archaeology. Two major groups are now known: those defined by their painted pottery, which will be considered under the general heading of the Yangshao culture; and the east-coast cultures. A third and less well explored group of cultures is found in southern China, and is characterised by pottery decorated with cord or incised markings.

The antecedents of the Neolithic

The precursors of the Neolithic are best considered in two territorial groupings, corresponding to the two major divisions of the ensuing neolithic phase.

While remains of neolithic date are now known to be very extensive in northern China, those of the immediately preceding hunting and gathering peoples have proved more elusive. The presence of such societies in northern China is inferred from finds of microlithic tools. Microliths are small chips of flint, chert, or any other hard stone, made by flaking from a hard core. They often have a cutting edge sharpened by further or secondary chipping. Microliths are found at what were probably the sites of hunters' camps. It has recently been suggested that stone tools found at sites of the palaeolithic period include prototypes of the microliths, and therefore that north China was one, if not the major, eastern Asian source of the microlithic tradition. This view would replace the earlier theory that the origins of this tradition are to be found outside China.

Microliths have been found at only a few sites in China proper, notably the very early site of Shuo xian Zhiyu in Shanxi province, and the later sites of Shayuan in Shaanxi province and Lingjing near Xuchang in central Henan. Microlithic sites are far less common in China proper than on its periphery, in Manchuria, Mongolia, and Siberia, and no direct connection between these latter sites and the early neolithic cultures of northern China has yet been traced. This gap notwithstanding, the peoples who inhabited this area and lived by hunting must have been the precursors of the neolithic farmers. They were either the ancestors of the Yangshao peoples, or were ousted and replaced by them.

The situation is different in the south, but here again it is difficult to establish clearly defined stages leading continuously from hunters and gatherers to the Neolithic. South-eastern coastal China falls within a large area, including parts of south-east Asia and possibly New Guinea and Japan, where highly developed pre-neolithic societies were found. These groups not only pursued animals but to a limited extent cultivated roots and fruits. It should be added, however, that in semi-tropical climates fruits and roots can be grown quite easily, with little forethought or planning. Their cultivation is, therefore, rightly regarded as much less significant than the systematic

cultivation of grain crops on which neolithic societies depended. But the peoples living in south-east China, in Thailand, and in Japan in particular, had another important skill, that of making pottery. This is a rare and unexpected technological achievement among peoples living by hunting and gathering. The characteristic feature shared by pottery from these areas is a decoration of incised lines or cord-markings. Simple designs found on sherds from Hong

Kong relate them to sherds from Taiwan sites (Dapenkeng and Fengbitou). The sherds come from sites with radiocarbon dates in the fifth millenium BC. These very early dates raise the possibility that the cultures of the south-east coast contributed to the formation of the Chinese Neolithic.

A recent excavation at Hemudu in Zhejiang province confirms the special importance of the coast, as distinct from the southern continental area of China, as a centre for the development of neolithic society. The site at Hemudu, south of Hangzhou Bay, has yielded the remains of an ancient village. Its two earliest strata predate all the eastern neolithic cultures known so far. Although the bones of deer, turtle, rhinoceros, and elephant indicate that hunting was still important during the early occupation of Hemudu, the extensive remains of rice and of bone tools for tilling show that rice cultivation was well established. Bones of domesticated dog, pig, and water-buffalo have also been found. The transition from dependence on hunting and gathering to the full-fledged Neolithic of the east coast was clearly well under way at this site.

The Yangshao and associated cultures

Yangshao is the name applied to groups of people who lived first a semi-settled, and then a fully settled life in Shaanxi, Henan and later in Hebei province, from around 5000 BC. The extension of the same cultural tradition westwards into Gansu province will be treated separately below (see p. 24). The first remains of Yangshao type were found in 1920 at the village of Yangshao in north-west Henan. Excavation has subsequently shown that this is a relatively insignificant site, and that early stages of the culture are better represented by a settlement excavated at Banpo cun in Shaanxi province. The Museum is fortunate to have acquired by exchange pots, stone axes, and some sherds from the Banpo site.

The earliest phase of the Yangshao culture has been found at sites at Baoji Beishouling and Hua xian Yuanjunmiao. The large fortified settlement excavated at Banpo belongs to the second phase. Like the later Yangshao farmers, the people cultivated fox-tail millet (*Setaria italica*) and domesticated the dog and the pig. Dependence on millet and pigs is characteristic of the Chinese Neolithic.

The village at Banpo was probably not lived in continuously, but used for several occupations. If settlement was intermittent rather than permanent, the agriculture must equally have followed a shifting pattern. Land would have been cleared and planted, then abandoned to be re-cleared at a later date of the scrub that had grown up on the deserted fields. This return from time to time of wild vegetation is shown by the presence of the pollen of wild species at certain points in the stratigraphic sequence. The fertility of the loess soil, however, meant that the times when it was necessary to abandon the settlement were widely separated. The shape of stone axes from this phase would seem to confirm the existence of a system of slash-and-burn agriculture (1). Their oval cross-section and rounded cutting edge are suitable for felling the trees and scrub that had to be cleared whenever a settlement was moved. This axe form should be contrasted with the axe types of the east coast, notably the adze with a ground edge. Such adzes are better suited to working wood than clearing scrub vegetation.

The settlement at Banpo was of formidable size, occupying at least 50,000 square metres, of which only a quarter has been excavated. In plan the village was carefully organised. The living area was surrounded by a ditch and thereby set apart from a kiln area and a cemetery. The foundations excavated within the living area belong to several different types of houses. There was one enormous long house that must have been used communally (2). This latter building was constructed during a late phase of the occupation and

1 *left* Stone axe, neolithic, Henan Yangshao culture, fifth millennium BC. Length 13.7 cm.

2 *below* Reconstruction of a large house excavated at Banpo cun. The excavators argue that a house of this size, about 160 square metres, with its central position, would have been used by a large number of people, possibly as a meeting place.

3 *right* A group of sherds of fine
earthenware decorated in black
slip and burnished, with triangle
and net designs. Neolithic,
Yangshao culture, fifth millennium
BC. These patterns are related to
the fish design shown in (5).

4 *left* Amphora of red earthen-
ware with cord markings, neolithic,
Yangshao culture, fifth millennium
BC. Excavated at Banpo cun.
Height 31.7 cm.

may indicate changes of some significance in the structure of society. The
areas specially reserved for ceramic manufacture seem to anticipate the
creation of separate workshop areas, a feature of great importance in the later
cities of the Bronze Age. Further, the special attention given to kilns and to
ceramic manufacture at Banpo underlines the central role of ceramic techniques in early Chinese society. Space and status were clearly accorded to
pot making, and particularly fine wares must have served some special
function beyond the mere utilitarian. The vessels were shaped by hand, sometimes made in moulds or by coiling. It seems likely that a turntable was used
for finishing the rims. The pottery falls into several categories. Some pots of
rather coarse clay were decorated with cord, mat, or basket impressions (4),
but the finest bowls and cups were made of well-levigated clay, burnished and
painted (3). Although it is this finer pottery that dominates any discussion of
the Yangshao culture, it made up only a very small percentage of the wares
produced and cannot have been intended for daily use. The painted pots have
been found chiefly in burials and would appear to be primarily mortuary items.

The location of Banpo near a river probably accounts for the popularity of
the amphora, a shape suited to carrying water (4). The fish from the river,
caught with finely made bone hooks, provided the main decorative motif
painted on the pots. The most complex designs appear inside a few shallow
bowls. These are composed of human faces or masks combined with fishes.
The three triangular projections from the mask, fringed with short strokes, are
also given a certain resemblance to the bodies of fishes. The fish reappears as
the favourite motif for decorating the exteriors of bowls with vertical sides.
From the fish motif abstract patterns were derived, culminating in compositions
of triangles. The development of these designs is clearly illustrated in a diagram

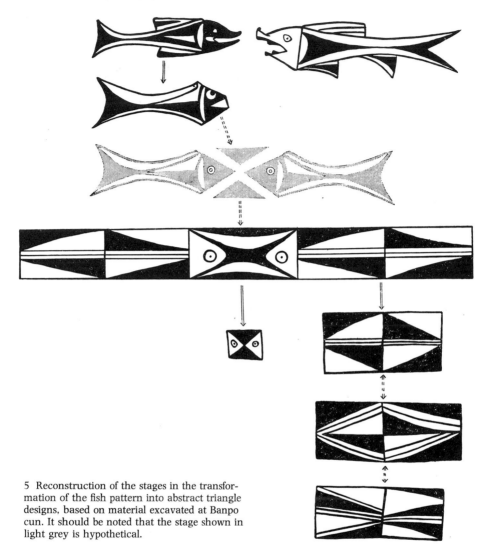

5 Reconstruction of the stages in the transformation of the fish pattern into abstract triangle designs, based on material excavated at Banpo cun. It should be noted that the stage shown in light grey is hypothetical.

given in the excavation report of the Banpo site (5) and on sherds in the Museum's collection (3).

The later phases of the Yangshao are characterised by new pottery designs. The most important of these come from the site of Miaodigou, which on archaeological evidence can be securely dated later than Banpo. In establishing this succession the most important factor has been the stratigraphic sequence brought to light by excavations at Xiameng cun in Bin xian, where remains of Banpo type lie below those of the Miaodigou category. Secondly, radio-carbon dates for sites of the Banpo phase show them to be appreciably earlier

6 Earthenware bowl and jar, neolithic, Yangshao culture, fifth millennium BC. Excavated at Banpo cun. The bowl is decorated around the rim with red slip and burnished. Diameter 19 cm, height 16 cm.

7 Drawings of bowls with painted decoration excavated at Miaodigou, neolithic, Yangshao culture, fifth-fourth millennium BC. *Top left*, round dots or nuclei are the focus of the swirling lines; likewise the 'flower' pattern on the bowl (*lower left*) consists of black dots and arcs outlining triangles. The 'flower' shape is an incidental product of this design in black.

than sites of Miaodigou type. Finally, analysis of some general features of the two cultural groups has shown that while the people of the Banpo phase relied as much on hunting and gathering as they did on farming, those of the Miaodigou phase were predominantly occupied with agriculture, and belonged therefore to a more advanced and presumably later stage of the Neolithic.

There is nonetheless a close connection between Banpo and Miaodigou. This is most clearly visible in the pottery shapes, especially in those of the highly decorated ritual or ceremonial wares. The hemispherical bowl and the bowl with a contracted base, both important shapes at Banpo (6), are also prominent at Miaodigou. Painted pottery is found at both sites, but the designs used differ considerably. The patterns seen at Miaodigou are particularly elegant and inventive (7). Although at first sight the complex of arcs and spirals on these pots might suggest some sort of repeating floral motif, as proposed by Chinese archaeologists, it is more convincing to regard these designs as generated by a concern with abstract pattern. Thus Louisa Huber has put forward a sequence of designs that would derive the Miaodigou patterns from spirals punctuated by nuclei. However, an emphasis on the importance of spirals in creating the Miaodigou designs inevitably calls for an argument connecting them with the painted pottery culture of Majia, in which spirals were the main form of decoration on pots (see p. 24 below), while the stratigraphic evidence known at present does not support such a direct causal connection. The possibility cannot be ruled out, though, that the spiral designs, which flourished particularly in the painted pottery cultures west of Shaanxi, made a contribution at some stage in the development of the Miaodigou pottery.

The two fundamental elements of the Miaodigou designs are the arc and the dot. Pottery excavated at a site in Shanxi Ruicheng Dongzhuang, suggests that the origin of these design elements need not be sought in the spiral (8). The excavators assign the Ruicheng site to the Banpo phase of the Yangshao, but point out that in certain respects the pottery shows important differences from standard Banpo types. A few clumsy examples of Banpo fish designs are seen together with the usual abstract arrangements of triangular shapes. Another abstract design is formed of curved segments or arcs that derive from the outline of the fish, together with a ring or dot taken from its eye. There are also a number of geometric patterns which elaborate on this combination of eye and arc.

The variety of painted sherds from the Ruicheng site may not be merely accidental or the result of local stylistic aberrations. The examples illustrated seem rather to document a continuous evolution leading from the Banpo fish designs to the more abstract patterns typical of Miaodigou. Given the quite evident similarity of Banpo and Miaodigou vessel shapes, an evolution of

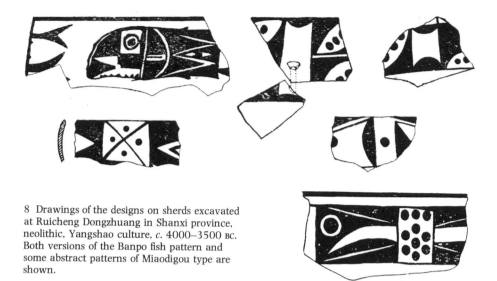

8 Drawings of the designs on sherds excavated
at Ruicheng Dongzhuang in Shanxi province,
neolithic, Yangshao culture, *c.* 4000–3500 BC.
Both versions of the Banpo fish pattern and
some abstract patterns of Miaodigou type are
shown.

designs linking the two phases would not be surprising. Many varieties of the
Miaodigou arc-and-dot design are known. Some are visibly related to spiral
designs, and may have been influenced by Majia pottery. In others, for example those with semicircular arcs in layers alternating with a net pattern, the
spiral element is completely absent. This net pattern seems to be a direct
inheritance from Banpo pottery. Such pronounced resemblances, together
with the pervasive influence of the Banpo fish designs, illustrate the unity, or
rather the close inter-relationship, of several groups of neolithic peoples
within the central China Yangshao, while distinguishing them from the Majia
people further west, whose artistic traditions, despite rare similarities, set
them apart.

There are, however, several other closely related regional variants of the
central Yangshao, notably those found at sites in Henan and Hebei provinces.
Of these Hougang is the earliest, being roughly contemporary with the second
part of the Banpo period, that is, the second half of the fifth millenium. The
vessels from this site are rather plain, being decorated only with simple
painted bands or striations. More elaborate painting is found on pots from
Dahe cun which have neatly divided bands filled with arcs, sometimes symmetrically paired, or with vertical lines and cross-hatching. Dahe cun has
close affiliations with Miaodigou. Further to the north, extending into Hebei
province, there occurs a variety of pottery named after the site of Dasikong cun.
Its decoration is made up of pairs of shallow arcs, or of hooks and commas.
In such designs the vigorous traditions of Miaodigou seem drastically
attenuated.

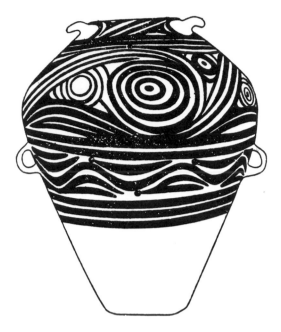

9 *left* Large jar with spiral design, neolithic, Majia type, latter part of fourth millennium BC. Excavated at Hua xian Yangzizhenchuan, in Gansu province.

10 *below* Earthenware jar with birds in a configuration of spirals. Neolithic, Majia type, latter part of fourth millennium BC.

The painted pottery cultures of western China

To the west of the main area of the Yangshao culture a separate group of painted pottery cultures has been found. Despite their recognisably distinct character, these cultures still fall into the Yangshao division of the Chinese Neolithic. The meeting point of the main part of the Yangshao and the western group lies along the Wei river.

In the west the Majia culture is the most important and produced the most admirable pottery. By contrast with the designs already described, which are composed largely with solid areas of colour, the pottery of the Majia phase was painted with fluid linear designs. Spirals, occasionally centred on dots or nuclei, cover the vessels with lively movement (9). A further element, which seems to be peculiar to the region, is a drawing of a bird that appears together with early forms of the spiral pattern (10). As in the case of the Banpo fish designs, this representational motif seems to have been overwhelmed by its surroundings and transformed into dynamic abstract patterns.

The Majia spiral designs appear to be related to arc-and-dot designs of the Miaodigou type, as already mentioned, and the general similarity of the Majia and Miaodigou patterns has been noted by Chinese archaeologists. The affinities have even led some scholars to suggest derivation of the Miaodigou culture from the Majia. However, since the finds from Ruicheng discussed earlier seem to show Miaodigou growing out of a culture of Banpo type, it

seems more likely that the two cultures arose from separate sources but subsequently came into contact and shared features of design. This view is given
support by the particularly well-defined characters of the two artistic traditions,
both of which are highly sophisticated and sharply distinct. Next to the signal
differences of character, the similarities of a few motifs and shapes seem to be
of secondary importance. Among the Majia pots are some spectacular jars, a
shape rarely seen at Miaodigou (9). These distinctive shapes appear together
with a wide repertory of unparalleled painted designs in which the dominant
decoration of branching spirals and eyelike nuclei often combine to give an
uncanny, rather disquieting effect. The inventive brilliance of the designs
and the calligraphic flair of their execution make even small patterned sherds
interesting and instantly recognisable.

Although the Majia style is not represented in the Museum, wares from
contemporary or at least overlapping cultures in the same western area can
be well illustrated from the collection. Bold spirals reminiscent of Majia designs
occur in new and splendid versions on large urns of the Banshan culture. The
forms are simplified but the range of colours much enriched, now including
black, red, brown, and purple. In place of the loose, fluid painting of the Majia
spirals these are firm, dense, and notched with teeth (11). Where the Majia

11 Earthenware jar painted
in red and black, neolithic,
Banshan type, third
millennium BC. Many jars
of Banshan type have been
excavated from Guanghe
Tibaping, in Gansu pro-
vince, and like this one are
often large and imposing.
Height 38 cm.

spirals had been centered on small whorls, the nuclei of the Banshan spirals designs are often large panels, lozenge-shaped or circular, filled with striations or hatching.

A second culture related to Majia, known as Machang has traditionally been associated with Banshan. Indeed for a long time Banshan and Machang pottery wares were thought to come from the same culture, the large Banshan urns being reserved exclusively for burials, the Machang pots being the everyday ware of the same people. This confusion was resolved when excavations of houses showed that Banshan pots similar to the mortuary urns were also meant for daily use; in the same way Machang burials were found to be provided with typical Machang pots. Both stratigraphic and stylistic evidence suggests that Machang is a late offshoot or variant of the Banshan culture. The large urns characteristic of Banshan are less prominent at Machang sites, but do occur. The main distinction between the two traditions lies in the comparative plainness of the Machang decoration, which is simplified, bolder, and rather more careless in execution.

A common Machang pottery form, and one that had an important later history, is the waisted jar with two bow handles (12). This persists well into the Bronze Age successor cultures of the same region, notably Qijia and the

12 Three earthenware jars, all with similar bowed handles. *From left to right*: neolithic, Machang type, *c*. 3000–2500 BC; Lifan type, Han period (206 BC–AD 220), so named because similar pieces have been excavated at Lifan; neolithic, Xindian type, *c*. 1500 BC. Height 10.2 cm, 29 cm, 22 cm.

still later Xindian. The Qijia versions are particularly important, as the sharp lines of the flat handles and the clearly articulated angles of the body appear to imitate a metal prototype. Although no examples in sheet metal have yet been found, many of the Qijia pottery types may have been derived from metal vessels, as pointed out by M. Bylin-Althin in an exhaustive study of Qijia pottery. A few copper implements have been found at Qijia sites. The pervasive evidence for metal working in this culture has recently assumed special importance, since radiocarbon dates indicate that Qijia cannot be a late and provincial derivative of the bronze-using cultures of central China, but actually precedes the earliest documented metallurgy in the central area. Here and elsewhere there are signs that further excavation will push the beginnings of the Chinese Bronze Age back to rather earlier times than hitherto assumed.

The urns from Xindian are less impressive than those of Qijia or the earlier Yangshao styles. Xindian is contemporary with advanced Bronze Age societies in central China, and its material culture, including pottery, looks distinctly impoverished. Elaborate painting and trim shape have given way to slack forms and schematic drawing. Both here and in the Qijia culture this dwindling of the painted pottery tradition is at least in part due to the impact of the Longshan traditions of east China, which spread gradually westwards in the two millennia or so preceding the Bronze Age. The conspicuous lack of painted decoration in the Qijia pottery, and a number of the vessel shapes as well, provide convincing connections with the undecorated Longshan pottery, and indeed Longshan influence may have contributed to the formation of the Qijia culture (see p. 36 below). It is, therefore, all the more remarkable that a few shapes of the Yangshao tradition survived for the full duration of the Qijia culture to become standard types in the Xindian culture, thus continuing in use well into the Bronze Age. The waisted jar with bow handles in fact survives in western China still later. It reappears in an especially attractive form in an urn from Sichuan province, made probably as late as the Han period (second–first century BC). In this case the shape of the urn can only be explained as an isolated survival of an earlier local pottery tradition, as it is quite distinct from other contemporary forms. Such continuity illustrates above all the somewhat isolated and conservative character of the western region.

The east-coast Neolithic: Longshan cultures

The fundamental division between the neolithic groups of western China and those of the east coast was first recognised and defined in terms of pottery types. The contrast is pronounced and the distinction remains a useful one. While in the west the first pottery has elaborately painted decoration, applied normally to rather simple curvilinear shapes, the pottery of the east coast is characterised by complicated, highly articulate shapes with little or no surface decoration. There are many other distinctive cultural differences, the east-coast cultures showing in particular certain special burial practices, divination by scapulimancy, and a highly refined jade-carving industry. It is significant that these same traits later appear as defining features of the Bronze Age culture of the Shang when it emerges in central China early in the second millenium BC.

The distinctive traits just enumerated have a long history on the east coast, but the highly developed phase in which they were first observed at the Long-shan site in Shandong province represents only a late stage of the east-coast Neolithic, one perhaps even surviving into the Bronze Age. It is therefore somewhat arbitrary, but none the less convenient, to use the established term 'Longshan' in a more general sense as embracing also the antecedents of this late, so-called 'classic' Longshan culture. It is these antecedents that are of particular historical importance, not only on their own account but also because of their impact on the neolithic cultures of west China, and for their eventual indirect contribution to the formation of the first Bronze Age civilisation in China.

The earliest neolithic culture now known on the east coast must ultimately be ancestral to the well-developed Longshan, but the distinctive features of the latter only appear in the course of time and are not present in the earliest stages. A very early rice-growing culture, that found at Hemudu in Zhejiang province, has already been mentioned as an important recent discovery. The Qingliangang culture of Jiangsu province was uncovered in earlier excavations. The lowest strata at both these sites belong to an unmistakably early stage, in the vicinity of 4,500 BC, before the sharp increase in activity that marked the appearance of cultures recognisably Longshan in character. It has been tentatively suggested that the difference between the Hemudu and the Qingliangang cultures reflects a geographical division that persists in later phases. Thus southern Jiangsu and Zhejiang, represented in succession by Hemudu, Songze, Majiabin and Beiyinyangying, are viewed as belonging to a sequence to some degree independent of developments further north, which were to lead eventually to the classic Longshan phase. The northern group, which seems to have centered first on northern Jiangsu and to have moved gradually northwards into Shandong province, is represented by the sites of Qingliangang, Liulin, Huating, and Dawenkou. It is this latter sequence that is best established, and it is from this area that Longshan culture spread westwards to influence and largely supplant the Yangshao Neolithic in central and western China.

Among the favourite vessel shapes of the Longshan cultures, three are

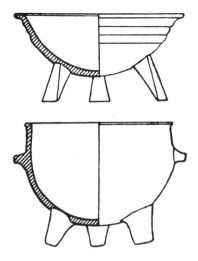

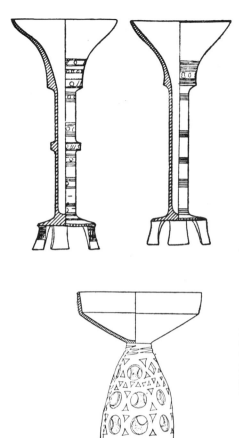

13 Drawings of the characteristic vessel shapes of the Longshan cultures, mid-fourth millennium BC: *above left, bei,* drinking cup on a tall foot; *above right, ding,* tripod vessel; and *left, dou,* platter on a high foot. These examples were excavated at the site of Dadunzi in northern Jiangsu province, and belong to the Huating culture. Similar vessels are found at Dawenkou (see 15).

particularly prominent: a tall drinking-cup, called a *bei*; an offering bowl on a high stand, called a *dou*; and a bowl on three legs, called a *ding* (13). The tall cups are found in a variety of impressive forms. The exaggerated fragility of the slender pierced stands seen on both the *dou* and the *bei* must have challenged the ingenuity of the potters, and no doubt presented special problems in firing. Cups of such eccentric form and delicate construction were presumably devoted to some special purpose: the decorative character of the pierced stands is more appropriate to ceremonial than to everyday use. With no written evidence it is impossible to do more than speculate about the ceremonial function of these very striking pottery forms. The importance of wine sacrifices in the Bronze Age Shang culture, which seems to have so many important connections with the east-coast Neolithic, perhaps encourages the supposition that already in the Longshan cultures religious exercises centered on sacrifices of wine.

The evolution of the main Longshan pottery shapes has been well documented by excavation. Although these were special ceremonial wares forming only a small percentage of the ceramic production of the area, they have proved a useful means of identifying the different cultures in the Longshan sequence, and of charting their relationships.

Ceremonial pottery tells us little directly about daily life, but this is by no means to dismiss it as uninformative. On the contrary, differences between peoples are most clearly revealed in the material objects that touched their central preoccupations most closely. One of the major innovations in the Longshan sequence was the introduction of a fourth distinctive vessel shape, a pouring vessel on legs that was particularly popular in the Dawenkou culture. The earliest versions of this vessel, known as a *gui* (not to be confused with the later bronze form with the same romanised name), had solid legs. At a later stage the legs were made hollow and bulbous (14). The tripod with hollow legs is a peculiar and important invention that was transmitted from the east-coast Neolithic to early and middle Shang ceramics and bronzes, and revived still later in early Western Zhou bronzes. Few features of early Chinese bronzes betray neolithic antecedents so clearly as this hollow leg later seen on the *li, jia* and *he* shapes (see p. 62).

It is significant that, mixed together with the wide repertoire of highly refined Longshan vessels shapes, a handful of finely painted bowls and jars has been found in a few graves at east-coast sites, especially at Liulin, Huating and Dawenkou (15). Both in shape and decoration these painted wares are derived specifically from designs originating within the Miaodigou culture, although there are signs that some at least are local imitations rather than imports. Their appearance on the east coast is distinctively intrusive, and is confined to a relatively short interval within the Longshan cultural sequence. This transient influence of Miaodigou on the east coast provides an important clue in the relative dating of the two major divisions of the Chinese Neolithic, as Louisa Huber has noted.

In addition to specialised ceramics, other features of material culture can be singled out as characteristic of the east-coast Neolithic, notably the highly

14 White pottery tripod jug, *gui*, Longshan culture, mid-third millennium BC. Excavated from Shandong Weifang. Height 29.7 cm.

15 Plan of tomb no. 4 at Dawenkou together with the artefacts found in it. Neolithic, Longshan, fourth-third millennium BC. In addition to the tripod and the platter on a high stand, both typical eastern neolithic forms, there is one painted pot, decorated with a spiral design, adopted from the western neolithic cultures; stepped and ground-edge adzes are also found, compare (18).

16 Polished hardstone axe, neolithic, Qingliangang type, mid-fifth-fourth millennium BC. Similar axes have been excavated at Huaian in northern Jiangsu. The rounded cutting-edge and the slightly inward-curving sides are characteristic of the early date. Later axes had parallel sides and, in the latest examples, a straight cutting-edge. Length 14 cm.

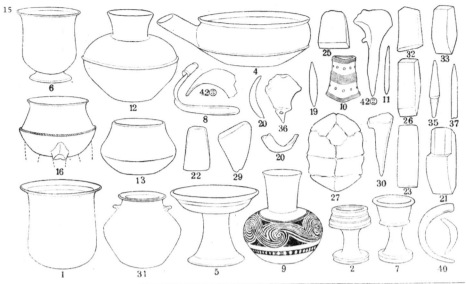

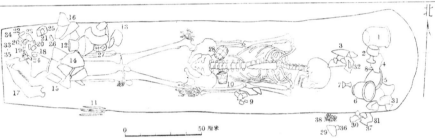

developed lapidary industry (16). A variety of fine hardstones were worked and polished, the most precious being jade. Of the two minerals nowadays referred to as jade, only nephrite was of importance in antiquity in China. Nephrite was evidently prized for its durability, subtle colour, and for the fine polish it would take. It is extremely tough and difficult to work; it cannot be cut even with steel tools, so that still today it must be worked with abrasives.

The jade industry of the east-coast Neolithic, like the manufacture of highly elaborate pottery shapes, implies a complex organisation of society and developed ceremonial practices. No source within China has yet been found for the jade worked at east-coast sites. Although it is not impossible that some source existed in China in neolithic times, on present evidence it seems more likely that the stone was imported over long distances from Baikal in the north, or even from Central Asia, the major source of jade in historic times. Methods of exchange must therefore have been well established. The expense of the material itself, even more than the labour invested in working and finishing it, ensures that objects made of jade were reserved for use in ritual or as mortuary offerings, even when they are replicas of axes or other tools of daily use. Patronage by restricted groups within the society, a religious or political élite, would have been necessary to support the highly specialised jade craft and to use its products; and the skill required to work this intractible material represents in itself a major technological achievement.

Besides the superbly finished replicas of axes, the jades found at east-coast sites include a considerable number of highly polished arc-shaped pendants, frequently of lustrous pale green nephrite. Like the pottery drinking-cups meant for ritual use, jades continued to be important in Shang times, especially as mortuary items.

So far only the artefacts made for ritual use have been mentioned. Other forms of archaeological evidence provide information concerning daily life. Excavation of several large settlements has shown that villages were occupied continuously for longer periods than were the Yangshao settlements. Many sickles in stone and shell testify to well-established agriculture. The use of ground-edge adzes (17) and stepped adzes (18) suggests that there was widespread activity in woodworking and carpentry. These adze forms are found the whole length of coastal China and illustrate the cultural links between the peoples inhabiting this region, with their similar practices and skills.

On the east coast the cultures just described culminated in the classic Longshan culture of c. 2500 BC and later, first discovered at the very late sites of Chengziyai and Liangchengzhen in Shandong province. The classic Longshan is best known for its exceptionally fine black pottery, wheel-made and turned to an incredible thinness (19). Although the potter's wheel had been in use since the middle of the Huating phase, here the technique was brought

19 *above* Two black earthenware vessels, neolithic, Longshan culture, *c.* 2500–2000 BC. Excavated at Shandong Weifang. Height 12.5 cm, 16.1 cm.

17 *far left* Ground-edge adze. Neolithic, mid-third millennium BC, from Lamma Island, Hong Kong. Length 6 cm.

18 *left* Stepped adze, eastern neolithic cultures, mid-third millennium BC, from Lantau Island near Hong Kong. Similar axes are found at sites in eastern and south-eastern coastal China. Compare an adze from a tomb at Dawenkou (15). Length 11.7 cm.

to new levels. Once again high drinking-cups with narrow and often waisted stands are prominent. This pottery is represented in the Museum by only a few sherds. The most common shape was the *gui* tripod, already remarked on in connection with the Dawenkou culture (14). A fine polished axe of green jade (20) reflects the high level attained in jade working by this time.

It was not, however, this final phase of the east-coast Longshan, with its refined jades and distinctive black pottery, that brought Longshan influence to bear on neolithic cultures further west. The westward movement of Longshan cultural influence began at a rather earlier stage and gave rise, as has been noted, to the successors of the Yangshao cultures in the provinces of Henan,

20 *left* Green jade axe, neolithic, Longshan culture, *c.* 2500–2000 BC. A similar axe has been found at Rizhao Liangchengzhen in Shandong province. Length 15.1 cm.

21 *right* Vessels excavated from Henan Xichuan Xiawanggang, third millenium BC. Henan Long-shan type. Several tripods are shown, together with a lobed pouring vessel and one which appears to have a flat bottom.

22 *below* Hardstone disc, *bi*, neolithic, Liangzhu type, third millennium BC. Discs of this type of rough stone have been found in Zhejiang province. Diameter 19 cm.

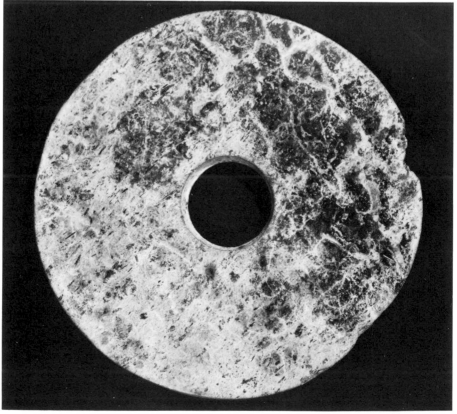

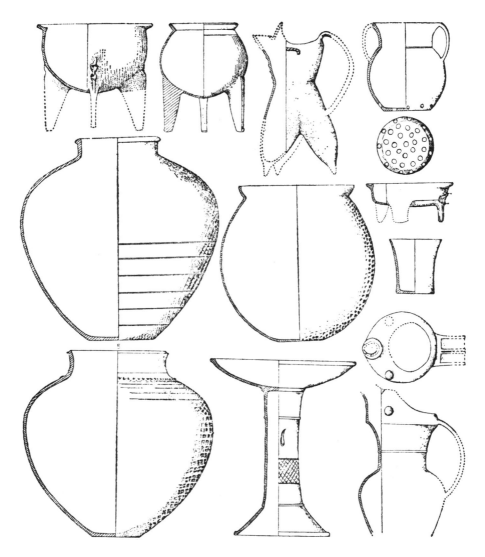

Shaanxi, and still further west. Although the cultures in question are referred to as the Henan Longshan and the Shaanxi Longshan, it must always be remembered that this nomenclature cannot be taken to imply a wholesale transfer of traits from the east coast. The interaction of the east-coast Neolithic with the painted pottery cultures of central and western north China gave rise to distinctive new cultural entities different from either of the two antecedents.

The typesites of the Henan and Shaanxi Longshan cultures are Hougang II and Kexingzhuang II respectively. At both sites the prominence of lobed vessels with hollow feet represents the Longshan inheritance, but the vessel shapes are distinctive. The lobed pouring jug called *gui* was made with a neck rising directly over the fairly slender hollow legs (21); in the earlier east-coast versions, on the other hand, the lobes are bulbous and spreading and the neck and spout are off-centre, pushed forward away from the handle behind (14).

The confluence of western and eastern neolithic traditions can be examined in detail at the Henan site of Xichuan Xiawanggang, where finds within a single stratum include both tripod vessels of east-coast origin and shallow painted bowls derived from the Yangshao culture (21). The Bronze Age culture of the Shang was the beneficiary, if not indeed the product, of this cultural mixing. Early Shang remains overlie the Longshan level at Xichuan Xiawanggang, and in general are found to lie stratigraphically above remains of Hougang II type; the continuity into the Bronze Age of Henan Longshan cultural traits, and in particular of pottery shapes, is quite clear. Lobed vessels are thus typical early Shang pottery types. On the other hand, the presence of pottery vessels that reflect metal prototypes in some of the western and central Longshan neolithic cultures is a trait of obvious importance in connection with the rise of Shang metallurgy, and one that so far cannot be traced to the east-coast Longshan. At Xichuan Xiawanggang, for instance, there was found a pottery pouring jug with a flat bottom instead of hollow tripod legs. The shape is reminiscent of vessels from the Qijia culture of Gansu, where the influence of wrought-metal prototypes is pervasive. It is thus of particular interest that, while some of the early Shang bronze shapes are smooth, rounded and lobed — all typically ceramic features — others, like the *jue*, have hard, angular shapes and attached spouts and handles that appear to be derived from wrought metal (43). The existence of two forms of one particular early bronze vessel type, the *jia*, one with lobes and the other with a flat bottom (31), confirms that there were two different sources for the one vessel type.

In assessing the neolithic contribution to the civilisation of the Bronze Age, the later jade-working traditions of south-eastern and southern China deserve special consideration. Throughout coastal China, jade working is found in the context of cultures with Longshan features. Jades are particularly prominent, for example, in the Liangzhu culture in Zhejiang. Disks with a large central perforation from Liangzhu sites, a shape later known as a *bi*, are among the items derived from the east coast that became popular with the Shang (22).

A jade with even greater influence was the *zong*, a tubular object with square outer and round inner perimeter (23). Excavations in the area of the lower Yangtze and at Shixia in Guangdong have shown conclusively that this jade form originated in neolithic times. Like many ceremonial items, it seems to have been important within a restricted, fairly well-defined area, being associated particularly with south-east China. The fullest reports, which come from Shixia, show that the *zong* is found in the context of a culture with a pro-

23 Jade *zong*, neolithic,
from south-east China.
A very similar piece has
been excavated from Shixia,
Guangdong. The faces on
each corner are simplified
versions of those seen in
(24). Height 20.3 cm.

24 Part of a jade *zong*
showing the face across
one of the corners;
neolithic, from south-east
China. The fine incised lines
and the form of the nose
can be compared with
those on the ring shown in
(25). Width 8.2 cm.

25 Jade ring with incised
designs of faces, neolithic. Rings
of this shape are found at
neolithic sites along the eastern
and southern coasts of China.
Diameter 7 cm.

26 Drawing of the two different
faces on the jade ring in (25).
The face with simple round eyes
is seen on many jade *zong*, e.g.
(24); that with the more
elaborate eyes, on pendants and
weapons. The two faces are
arranged with one right way up,
the other upside-down.

27 Drawing of the design on a
stone axe, neolithic, Longshan
type, late third millennium BC.
Excavated at Rizhao Liangchengzhen in Shandong province. The
oval eyes of the two faces and
the swirling lines around them
can be compared with the more
elaborate of the two faces on the
ring (26).

28 Bronze ritual vessel *ding*,
from Panlongcheng, middle
Shang dynasty. The oval or
almost square eyes can be
compared with the central portion
of the eyes on the axe from
Shandong (27). Around the
eyes the hooked ends on the
meanders filling the horizontal
borders resemble the plumes
around the faces on the axe.

vincial variant of Longshan pottery: the repertory of shapes includes a variety of tripods and also the lobed pitcher called a *gui*.

The most important feature of the *zong* is the design of simple faces arranged in tiers that decorates each corner (24). The two eyes of each face lie left and right of the corner of the *zong*; they are sometimes carefully drawn, formed of concentric circles with pointed projections. In other instances the eyes are more rudimentary, consisting merely of single small circles. Set in relief above the eyes are a pair of parallel horizontal bars embellished with fine incised lines. The only other feature regularly shown on the face is a short bar with incised scrolls standing for the nose.

The *zong* is only one of a group of jades decorated in this way. The others include several varieties of pendant, one of semilunar shape and another with a fluted or scalloped outline. Both types are most often plain, but on occasion they are decorated with versions of the face design, having either simple circular eyes, or more elaborate oval eyes surrounded with swirling lines. The latter version, which is of particular importance, is well represented by a bangle in the collection (25). Here it alternates with the simple eye-form, demonstrating that the two designs were contemporary. Both are executed in the same incised line; on the more elaborate face, the potential of this fine linear execution has been exploited to great effect in the swirling pattern around the eyes (26).

The bangle made of hard stone – not necessarily jade – was current throughout coastal China, undecorated examples having been found at Shixia in Guangdong in the south, and at Dawenkou in Shandong in the north. This north-south connection was the means by which a species of jade ornament originally peculiar to the south came to be used in northern China. The motif transmitted to the north was apparently not the simple face that appears regularly on the *zong*, but the more complicated version with oval eyes. These compelling eyes are the focus of the design on a stone axe excavated at Rizhao Liangchengzhen in Shandong province (27), and related patterns occur on pottery sherds excavated in the same area. These sites fall very late in the Neolithic, if not indeed still later, in the succeeding Shang period. However, there is no doubt that the origins of the Liangchengzhen designs lie in the Neolithic proper. The faces on the stone axe, like those on the southern bangle, are executed in incised line, but the patterns have been elaborated. The eye-forms are altered, and the surrounding embellishments have taken on a spiralling movement. The carefully hooked spirals and plumes have an ornate, florid richness that compares interestingly with very early designs on bronzes, for instance on a *ding* from Panlongcheng (28). If the jades did not simply inspire the bronze designs directly, there must at least have been a definite relationship between designs in the two materials. Discussion of this point will be resumed in the next chapter. At present it suffices to single out the Liang-chengzhen axe as providing a link between a species of Neolithic jade orna-ment on the one hand, and the major art form of the succeeding Bronze Age on the other.

Conclusion

This chapter has shown that the earliest Neolithic cultures of China belong to two principal groups: the Yangshao (painted pottery) cultures in the west of China, and the sharply distinct cultures of the east coast. There was also a third major area of development in the south, characterised by pottery with corded or incised designs which has been mentioned only briefly. These three divisions correspond to at least two and possibly three separate occur-rences of the Neolithic revolution in China. Within each of the main groupings, however, several major cultural subdivisions are important and it cannot be argued that there was a single line of development within any one of the three. At a later stage, a mixing of the Yangshao and the east coast Longshan cultures occurred in central China as the latter spread its influence westward, giving rise to essentially new Neolithic traditions in Henan and Shaanxi. The Henan branch of the resulting culture is particularly important, since it seems to have provided the substratum out of which the first Bronze Age culture grew.

The emphasis given in this chapter to the principal Neolithic art forms, ceramics and jade, is not disproportionate. These crafts must have taken up much of the surplus resources of the societies described and were carried to a very high artistic and technical level. Moreover, although the purposes of the dishes, cups, and *zong* are as yet little understood, they must represent im-portant social habits and beliefs of the people who made them. They were central to Chinese Neolithic culture and contributed significantly to the suc-ceeding Bronze Age.

2 The Shang Dynasty

The use of bronze is taken as the defining characteristic of the period which is the subject of this chapter. Its exploitation in China was the achievement of the Shang dynasty. The peoples known as the Shang appear to have dominated north China from *c.* 1700 BC to *c.* 1100 BC (or to as late as *c.* 1027 BC if the revised chronology described above is used, see p. 11). The centre of their power lay in the middle reaches of the Yellow River valley.

Some features of the Shang culture can be traced back to the Longshan cultures of the east coast. These include burials in stepped pits with wooden chambers, the use of ox scapulae or turtle shells for divination, and jade working. The manufacture of bronze, on the other hand, hints at connections with western China, since the earliest metal-working tradition so far known seems to be that of the Qijia culture in Gansu province. Lastly, the Shang culture has a demonstrable continuity with the immediately preceding Neolithic culture in the same area of central northern China, most clearly visible in the retention of certain pottery types.

The Shang are central to any discussion of early Chinese culture because they had a writing system: in the latter part of the dynasty, they regularly inscribed the bones and turtle shells used for divination. These oracle bones have been excavated from the late Shang sites near the present-day village of Anyang, and their use is described in more detail below (see p. 55). The inscriptions on the bones are written in a highly developed system of Chinese characters that is clearly related to those still used today. This writing system appears already perfected in the Anyang period, and its origins are as yet obscure.

The records of the divinations name all the Shang kings, and include references to military campaigns and to the organisation of the state under different officials. From these it is possible to construct an outline of the events of the period and to investigate certain aspects of Shang life and belief. The contents of the inscriptions have also made it possible to substantiate the list of Shang kings given in the *Shi Ji*, written by the Han historian Sima Qian in the second century BC. Indeed the importance of the inscriptions on the oracle bones for the understanding of the Shang is emphasised by this correlation with the *Shi Ji*. Without the oracle inscriptions it would be difficult to give credence to the account of Shang history given in the *Shi Ji*. Sima Qian's mention of an earlier dynasty, the Xia, should also be taken seriously, but this people did not leave any written records. It has therefore not been possible to identify Xia remains with any certainty, and the description in the *Shi Ji* cannot be confirmed archaeologically. It seems possible that one of the groups of Neolithic peoples described already, or a group living at a time contemporary with some part of the Shang period, will prove to be the Xia.

The excavations of Shang dynasty sites

The surviving oracle bones with inscriptions all belong to the late Shang period. To discuss the Shang period as a whole it is therefore necessary to consider first the excavated evidence. The most important excavations are those made at Erlitou, Zhengzhou, Panlongcheng and Anyang. Among the data on the Shang given in the *Shi Ji* are the names of many different capitals occupied by the Shang. It is tempting to associate these large sites with the named capitals but they are not always easy to match.

Of the sites found so far, the one at Erlitou is the earliest. If not a capital, it was undoubtedly an important settlement. A large platform has been excavated — 108 metres from east to west, and 100 metres from north to south. This was the base for at least one building, a palace or a ceremonial complex. House floors, storage pits, and the remains of workshops have also been found, the latter including kilns, bronze-casting moulds, fragments of crucibles, and remains of stone and bone artifacts. This lay-out is common to later urban sites. The pottery with incised designs, the primitive bronze vessels, the more numerous bronze weapons and jades found here were the antecedents of those of the later Shang, which are better represented in the Museum's collection. The grave furnishings already include the special ritual vessels, *jia*, *jue*, *gu*, *he* and *gui*, used in sacrifices.

Radiocarbon dates for some strata at the site fall within a probable period of occupation in the vicinity of 2000 to 1500 BC. The third phase is the most important, and to it belong the palace foundations, kilns and other workshop remains, the burials with jade and cinnabar — a red powder of mercuric sulphide — used as mortuary decoration, and, most important of all, the metallurgical remains. The period to which Erlitou belongs will, for the purposes of this handbook, be described as early Shang. However, in the light of research in progress at the present time, it seems possible that this phase precedes the Shang period proper and should be known by another name.

A later important Shang settlement has been discovered in a fruitful series of excavations carried out at Zhengzhou. Numerous sites have been found in this area. Stratigraphical evidence both at Erlitou and at other sites, together with an analysis of the artefacts, has established that the early phase of the site of Erligang, in the Zhengzhou area, succeeded the Erlitou phase and belongs to the period here described as middle Shang.

An earlier Shang settlement may already have existed here, but during the Erligang phase the Shang city at Zhengzhou expanded in size and activity, and workshops, burials, and a city wall dating from this time have been found. The immense size of the wall implies a city of wealth and importance, if not a capital. It had a perimeter of 7195 metres and enclosed a roughly rectangular area of 3.2 square kilometres. One scholar, An Jinhuai, estimates the original wall to have been approximately ten metres in height, with an average width of twenty metres. Archaeologists have calculated that a wall of these dimensions, built of *hang tu* (compressed earth), would have taken twelve and a half years to build if the Shang had been able to deploy 10,000 men working 330 days a year on the task. This alone suggests that the Shang had great reserves of labour. The mobilisation and feeding of this vast labour force would have required complicated organisation. Not only would skilled management of labour have been needed, but also a large surplus of grain to maintain, at least for large portions of the year, those employed on such vast non-agricultural works. Some labourers would have worked both on construction projects and in the fields; others, notably the bronze casters, would have devoted most if not all their time to their specialised trade. Further excavations show that within the city different functions were separate and subdivided. In addition to houses with compressed earth floors clustered in groups, a large building with lime-plastered floor and substantial post-holes has been excavated. Adjacent to it were sections of a ditch in which about a hundred human skulls were buried, mostly sawn off at the level of the eyebrows and ears. This seems to have been a sacrificial offering that made use of skulls from which bone had already been taken to carve in the workshops. To the north of this building was a platform of compressed earth which, by analogy with other platforms at the late Shang site at Anyang, is thought to have been a large altar. Outside the city wall were further houses and, most important of all, workshop sites. These included bone workshops, kilns, and two bronze foundries, one associated with stamped-earth houses of substantial size.

Two bronzes in the collection resemble those cast and excavated at this site: a small *jue* (29, 30) and a much larger *jia* (31). The thin walls of the vessels, the slightly awkward shapes, the reference in the case of the *jia* to ceramic as well as bronze forms, are all characteristics of the Zhengzhou bronzes. They differ considerably from the heavier and more highly decorated bronzes from Anyang (48, 54), the late Shang capital.

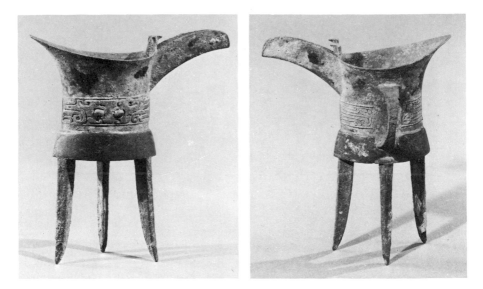

29 *left* Bronze ritual vessel, *jue*, middle Shang dynasty. This vessel is decorated with Style II designs of a *taotie* with two oval eyes and scroll extensions on either side. On the other side of the vessel, the bronze is decorated with the thread relief of Style I (30). It is similar to other pieces of middle Shang date from Zhengzhou, Panlongcheng, and Liulige. Height 14.6 cm.

30 *right* Bronze ritual vessel, *jue*, middle Shang dynasty. The other side of the vessel in (29), showing an abstract design in Style I. The fragile legs are characteristic of early vessels. Height 14.4 cm.

31 *opposite* Bronze ritual vessel, *jia*, middle Shang dynasty. The posts and the handle are slight in relation to the volume of the vessel and have not, at this early stage, been fully integrated into the design of the bronze. The decoration is of very forceful Style II: on the side opposite the handle, a face is seen from the front, with two eyes; behind the curling side extension of the body on each side is another creature, in profile, facing forwards (49). Height 22.5 cm.

Historical texts describe the Shang as moving their capital from one place to another. Certainly the Zhengzhou area became less important after a time, and attention turned to Anyang. However, this change is not clear cut, and for a period at least the two areas may have been occupied simultaneously. Indeed there is ample evidence for a good many middle and late Shang urban centres, so that while Anyang may have been the focus of ceremonial and governmental activities, it was by no means the only important city of its time.

Nevertheless, the importance of the Anyang site cannot be overestimated. If the capital status of Erlitou and Zhengzhou remains to be established, the records of royal divinations found in the Anyang area leave the primacy of the site in no doubt.

The fifteen seasons of excavation at Anyang, started in 1928, were the first major excavations to be undertaken in China. Since 1949 work has continued, producing an impressive body of information about the late Shang period. The remains found in the Anyang area, in or near several different

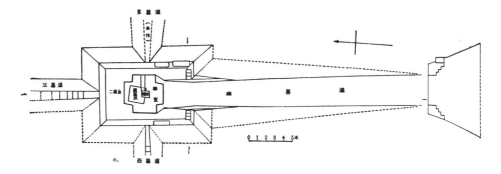

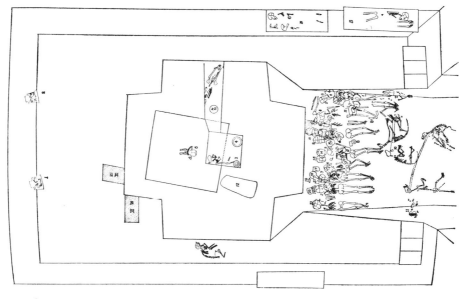

32 Plan of a late Shang dynasty tomb excavated at Yidu xian Sufutun, Shandong province.
Above, the whole tomb, showing the cruciform shape and long access ramp; *below*, a detail of
the central area with sacrificial victims at the entrance to the main burial pit, and two axes in
the outer trench similar to (33). The tomb with its ramps is approximately 70 metres in length.

present-day villages, fall into three main groups: buildings; foundry sites and
other workshops; and immense tombs, which are now regarded as royal
tombs. The city consisted of a network of specialised centres. Its connections
extended into the surrounding countryside, reaching towards the source of
the food needed to support a large complex of royal, ceremonial, and manu-
facturing areas.

    The most important buildings in the complex, found near the village of
Xiaotun, are assumed to have formed part of the royal dwellings. They share
two characteristics with the important buildings found at Zhengzhou: the use

of solid stamped-earth foundations, in other words *hang tu*, and the extensive sacrifice of human beings. The sacrifice of men is a recurrent feature of the Shang period. Human sacrifices are found in large numbers of foundations of buildings, in sacrificial pits and trenches, and also in the royal tombs.

A recently excavated tomb in Shandong province is a typical example of the burial of a great man accompanied by large numbers of human victims (32). Men were sacrificed along with many animals as part of the rituals performed to ensure the success of the king in his activities. One type of weapon, a heavy axe (33), is particularly associated with the sacrifice of humans at burial. Axes of this type were found in the outer trenches of the large tomb in Shandong already mentioned, and at most other Shang cemetery sites, both at Anyang, and in Hubei and Hebei provinces. The same axes, poised to decapitate victims, are depicted in bronze inscriptions.

Many of these victims were probably prisoners of war. Considerable forces, numbering 1000–5000 men and occasionally even more, were involved in warfare. Campaigns were conducted against neighbouring tribes and clans, including the Zhou, the future conquerors of the Shang. The main weapon of war was the dagger-axe, or *ge*, a knife-shaped bronze blade mounted at right

33 Bronze axe, late Shang dynasty. The demonic face on this axe is that of a man rather than a *taotie*, as it has the angular eyebrows seen on jade figures of men. The flared outline and hole in the centre are ultimately derived from jade prototypes. A middle Shang axe excavated from Panlongcheng has the more slender proportions of a jade axe (compare (20)), and also a large round central hole taken from a jade or stone example. In the late Shang, such axes were made with the broader form seen here. Height 24.8 cm, width 19 cm.

34 Three bronze *ge* halberds, late Shang dynasty. The central one has a jade blade in a bronze tang inlaid with turquoise. These weapons illustrate the variety of shapes that might be in use at any one time. A similar range has been excavated from the tomb of Fu Hao at Anyang. The weapons from that royal tomb include halberds with blades of jade, a material which cannot have been employed in warfare but can only have been intended for ceremonial use. Length 27 cm, 18.5 cm, 36.5 cm.

35 Five bronze arrowheads, illustrating changes of shape from the Shang to the Eastern Zhou period. *From left to right*: Shang dynasty, length 6 cm; Western Zhou, length 7.3 cm; Eastern Zhou, seventh century BC, length 3.5 cm; Eastern Zhou, fourth century BC, length 5.6 cm; Eastern Zhou, third century BC, length 4.7 cm.

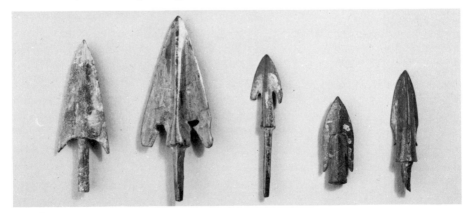

angles to a long wooden shaft. Several different forms of the *ge*, all comparatively simple, have been excavated at Erlitou. By the late Shang period the
weapon had been greatly elaborated and diversified, and a wide range of forms
and decorative elaborations are known (34). Bows and arrows were also
standard weapons (35), and at a late date chariots were introduced.

As mentioned above in connection with Zhengzhou, the scale of Shang
construction work at Anyang suggests that in peace, as in war, the labour of
large groups of men was at the disposal of the Shang kings. Vast quantities of
earth had to be moved, both to make the foundations of the royal palaces and
temples, and to dig the great tombs. Work on the compressed-earth structures
had to be subdivided into different operations. This required hundreds or even
thousands of men, regimented and organised in a flow of repetitive tasks.
If the remains of Shang buildings are no longer impressive, this is because the
material used for the light superstructures was not stone but wood and thatch.

In the context of the Museum's collections, the royal tombs are the most
important constructions. The bronze and jade objects in the collection must
have come from these or similar graves. Tombs of this period were of the shaft
or pit form. The burial goods and sacrifices were arranged in and around the
wooden chamber containing the coffin with the body of the dead man. The
great Shang tombs had the added refinement of four access ramps, usually
two short and two long in the shape of a cross (32). However, one of the most
recently excavated, that of Fu Hao, consort of the king Wu Ding, was more
modest in scale and without ramps.

Chariot burials: communications with western Asia

There is one further type of site excavated at Anyang and other parts of north
China that provides important evidence for the late Shang period, the chariot
burial (36). The chariot itself and two bronze items associated with it, a 'jingle'
and a particular knife or dagger (37, 38) raise the question of outside influence.
Although contacts between China and western Asia were rare in the early
period, the introduction of the chariot suggests that the issue cannot be ignored.

Chariots were apparently not known in China before the beginning of the
Anyang phase of the Shang dynasty, *c.* 1300 BC. The chariots of that date,
which were evidently buried in connection with royal funerals, bear some
resemblance to those found in burials in the Caucasus. They are similar in
three distinctive respects: both types have a low open-fronted box in which
to ride, wheels with a large number of spokes, and felloes, or wheel rims, made
of two bent pieces of wood. Even the burial of the chariot is a shared practice.
The origin of this type of chariot cannot be decided until the date of the Caucasus
chariots has been clarified. As yet it is not certain that they pre-date the Shang

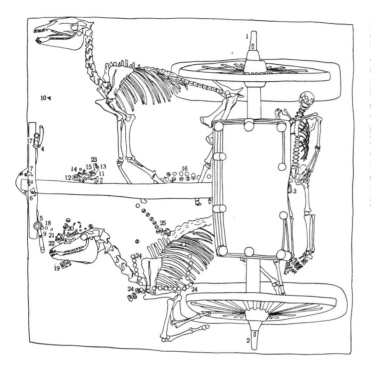

36 Plan of a late
Shang dynasty chariot
burial excavated at
Anyang. Details of the
structure of the chariot
are identifiable: the
low box in which the
charioteer stood; the
wheels with many
spokes, and axles with
long axle-caps; shaft
and various harness
fittings. A rectangular
cheek-piece for the bit
lies below the horse's
jaw.

chariots. On the other hand the chariot was undoubtedly a new addition to the armoury of the late Shang period.

The arc-shaped jingle (37), which frequently accompanies buried chariots, was once thought to be a chariot ornament. However, the weapons found regularly with chariots, as in a burial at Anyang, are also distinct in character. It seems likely that this strange bow-like object belongs with the weapons rather than with the vehicle. However, it is still not agreed that it is part of the composite bow carried by a warrior in a chariot, or an ornament of some other item of equipment. The composite bow, characteristic of eastern Asia, is constructed in three parts, of which the outer two parts are bent back in use. The jingle is thought by some scholars to be part of the mechanism for straightening the bow. Whatever its function this jingle, like the chariot, can be associated with areas further west. Pieces of similar shape are found in south Siberia at the time of the Karasuk culture (c. 1200–800 BC). The close parallels between the jingles from different areas must be the result of contact, and the jingle seems to illustrate cultural influence from east to west.

The small animal-headed knife belongs to the same category (38). It too has frequently been excavated from chariot burials and belongs to the group of bronzes associated with the chariot. Because such knives are found on sites in the north-western periphery of China and in Siberia, and because they are

38 *right* Curved bronze knife inlaid with turquoise, late Shang dynasty. The knife is decorated with an ibex head, a design not seen on the bronze ritual vessels of the same date. Such knives have been excavated both from chariot burials and from royal tombs, for example that of Fu Hao. Length 24.7 cm.

37 *below* Bronze bow-shaped jingle, late Shang dynasty. The fine design on the curved central section consists of *taotie* faces doubling as pairs of dragons. While the designs on each side of the boss can be read either as dragons or as faces, those at the curved ends are more easily seen as dragons. This fissuring of the mask is typical of this advanced form of relief decoration (Style v). In this example the raised areas, as well as the background, are decorated with *leiwen*. Length 34 cm.

decorated with schematic animals similar to those used by the peoples of the border areas, they are often thought of as an import from these areas arriving with chariots in China. However, the small curved or S-shaped knife with a ring handle, rather than an animal head, has been found in early Shang sites predating the introduction of the chariot. Typologically such knives have two descendants: a small group of greatly enlarged ceremonial knives; and a very large and diverse group of small knives which were used throughout the Shang, Western and Eastern Zhou periods, and which in due course gave rise to the single-edged ring-handle sword (see p. 168). The curved knife with ring-handle thus appears to be a Chinese invention, and was probably transmitted northwards from China. However, the realistic animal heads seen on the handles of many examples from Anyang, some of them especially fine, are un-Chinese in style. As this motif was clearly more popular in the peripheral regions, where the knife was elaborated in quite different forms, it is likely that this substitute for the ring-handle originated outside China. Two further weapons, the socketed axe and the leaf-shaped spearhead are found both in China and Siberia. The source of these artefacts has been much disputed in the past, but as William Watson has argued the shared characteristics again seem to reflect transmission from east to west. The less civilised people of Central Asia seem to have provided an avenue of communication for the advanced settled civilisations on their borders, from which they adopted weapons and technology. However, the role of such contacts was relatively unimportant in the general development of Shang civilisation.

Shang sites outside the central area

The two previous sections have concentrated on sites in central north China. In addition to the site at Zhengzhou, a middle Shang site has been known for some time at Hui xian Liulige, also in Henan province. However, new discoveries have shown that the middle Shang state was far from being confined to the vicinity of these two sites. Indeed, on the contrary, the evidence of recent excavations suggests, as Robert Bagley has argued, that middle Shang was the period when the geographical extent of Shang power was at its greatest. A large settlement has been excavated at Panlongcheng in Hubei province, far to the south of Zhengzhou. Here there were found large ceremonial buildings and elaborately furnished tombs similar to those revealed at other large settlements of the Shang period. Bronzes excavated from the tombs are decorated in the style of the middle Shang period, i.e. the Erligang phase at Zhengzhou. They thus demonstrate the direct influence of, and possibly control by, the Shang dynasty at this period. Remains of crucibles, malachite, charcoal, and baked clay used for bronze-casting moulds are evidence that the bronzes were made at Panlongcheng. Bronzes of the same period have also been found at sites in Shaanxi, Shanxi, Hebei, Jiangxi, Anhui and Shandong, following in the main the metropolitan style current at Zhengzhou.

After the middle Shang, the importance of Panlongcheng declined. Shang influence and control appears to have contracted in the late Shang or Anyang period. Finds of Anyang period bronzes in other areas, such as Shaanxi province (see p. 88), support the same conclusion. The peripheral areas apparently acquired some degree of skill and independence. Bronzes in pure Anyang style have been found in widely scattered areas from Peking in the north to Hunan in the south. Unlike the Panglongcheng bronzes, they appear to be imports rather than local products. At the same time some very unusual bronze vessels have been found in such provinces as Shaanxi, Anhui, and Hunan. These latter have convincingly been shown to be the products of local bronze-casting centres making their own somewhat idiosyncratic bronzes, influenced but not ruled by Anyang taste. The power of the Shang state was no longer so pervasive, and its metropolitan culture was less influential. New and possibly competing powers had established themselves.

None the less, the spread of Shang cultural influence was scarcely hindered by the decline of the political power of the dynasty. Pottery with geometric designs from Jiangsu province, contemporary with the Shang dynasty, shows

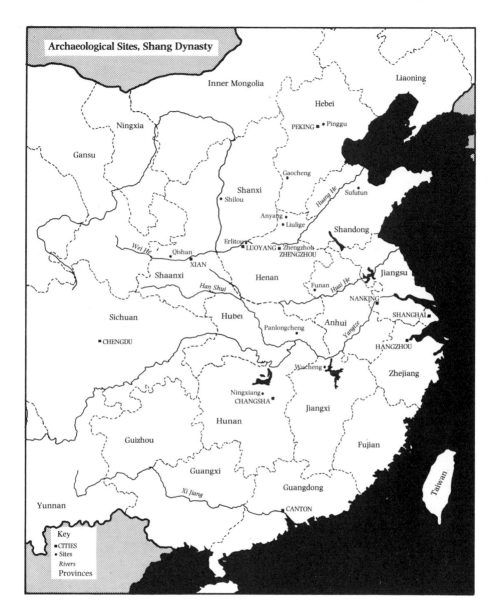

Archaeological Sites, Shang Dynasty

clear connections with the Shang bronze styles; and from Wucheng in Jiangxi province there has come pottery incised with signs clearly derived from the Shang script seen on the oracle bones. The political rivals of the Shang power must have owed their very existence to adopted Shang technology. The range and nature of the influence of the Shang state is only gradually being revealed by excavation.

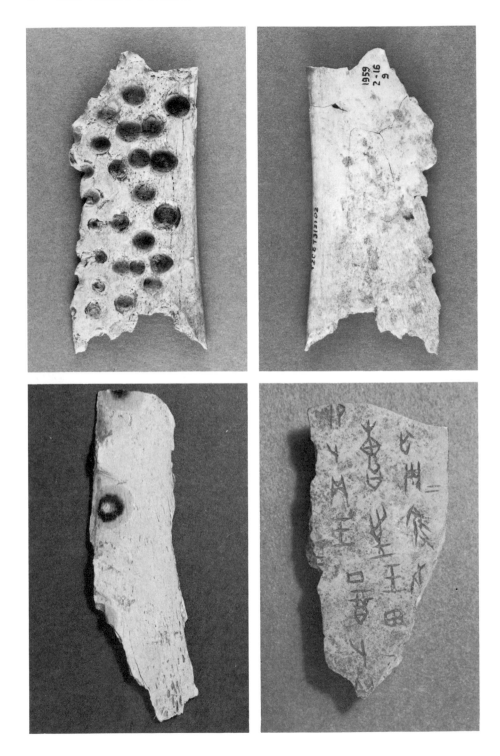

Oracle bones

The use of bones for divination was a widespread custom in the ancient world. But only in China were the bones specially prepared by drilling hollows and applying hot brands to create cracks. Skilled practitioners used the configurations of cracks to interpret the wishes of the spirits, to predict the outcome of events, and to determine courses of action. Scapulimancy was one of the many practices that the Shang took over from the eastern Neolithic cultures. The earliest evidence for divination by the burning of bones has been found in Liaoning province, where it dates from the fourth millenium BC, and the method was widely used in the later eastern Neolithic cultures.

In the late Shang period several important modifications of technique, which have been examined in detail by David Keightley, were made. First the hollows, which in the Neolithic and early Shang had apparently been drilled at random (39), were arranged in orderly rows; secondly, in the Zhengzhou period, turtle shells or plastrons came into use as alternatives to scapulae; and thirdly, it became the custom to inscribe many of the bones or plastrons used for divination.

The inscriptions followed a standard arrangement. Marginal notations were put on the shells before the hollows were drilled; these stated where the shells came from, and who had been involved in their preparation. The formal record of the actual divination consisted of a preface (and occasionally a postface) and the charge, which gave the main topic of the divination; the crack number; the reading of the crack (favourable or unfavourable); the consequent prognostication; and sometimes a later verification of the accuracy of the oracle. The preface gave, in cyclical form, the day on which the divination was performed, the name of the diviner, and occasionally the place where it was done. The inscriptions tend to be rather abbreviated, and relatively few include all of the separate parts just enumerated.

The subjects of the divinations touched on all facets of Shang life. As the divinations were performed on behalf of the monarch, all matters of state were subjects of inquiry: military campaigns, commands to officers, building of settlements, mobilisation of labour, and tribute payments. So too were most aspects of daily life: hunting expeditions, excursions, the weather, and agriculture. Finally, the private life of the king and — most important of all — his relationship with his ancestors were subjects of divination: sickness, child-

39 *opposite* Fragments of oracle bones, Shang dynasty, illustrating different aspects of the process of divination. *Top*, back and front of a section of a bone from Zhengzhou, the back with irregular pitting, the front showing the crack. *Bottom left*, a fragment of bone from Anyang with the regular burn marks typical of the late Shang period. *Bottom right*, an inscribed fragment recording a divination about hunting. Length 10.5 cm, 7.9 cm, 3.5 cm.

bearing of consorts, dreams, and the sacrifices needed for ancestors, especially the periodic sacrifices made in accordance with a complex system of inter-locking calendrical cycles.

The nature of the crack indicated whether the divination had proved auspi-cious, and this was noted beside it. From this reply the outcome was predicted. Afterwards a statement might be given to record what actually happened concerning the event or subject of the divination. In the long history of scapu-limancy in China, these inscriptions are an unusual feature, being confined to the Anyang period. The Anyang kings must have felt a great need for this method of reinforcing and proclaiming their authority. The inscriptions recorded the king's success in day-to-day affairs and were in effect statements confirming the legitimacy of his power. No pains, therefore, were spared in carrying out the necessary procedure correctly. Divination was a lengthy process, particularly as at any one session a set of plastrons was used, usually five in number, each drilled with many hollows. On many the topic of the divi-nation was phrased in both positive and negative forms.

The inscribed oracle bones of the Anyang phase were divided by Dong Zuobin into five periods according to characteristics of calligraphy, detailed references to persons and events, and particulars of idiom. Definite changes have been noted in the content and style of the divination between periods I and V. The divinations became briefer and more generally optimistic in interpretation over time. The complementary pairs of charges, the marginal notations, and the use of diviners' names had virtually disappeared by the last period. These features suggest that the process of divination had to some extent become a matter of routine.

Oracle-bone inscriptions are fundamental to the understanding of Shang religion and the nature of Shang kingship. The process of divination was used to consult the ancestors of the monarch, indeed the ruler alone could consult and offer sacrifices to his ancestors. This access to the ancestors and other spirits was presumably one of the essential sources of the power of the Shang ruler. The importance of particular ancestors depended on the closeness of their relationship to the reigning monarch. Within this ordered group the most important, if also the most impersonal, was the High God known as Di. Di, or Shang Di, ruled the world of spirits in parallel with the Shang monarch who ruled the earthly state. Next in importance came two groups of ancestors: those who had lived in the distant past, and those who had lived more recently and could be reliably fitted into a generational scheme. Cyclical characters denoting the ten days of the week were used to designate the members of this second group. Because these ancestors were figures of history rather than of myth or invention, the attitude of the Shang people to them probably resembled their view of living people. Religion and everyday life were clearly allied, and the forms of worship and of daily organisation appear to have shared common features. A concern for rank and relative position was a characteristic found both on earth and in the hierarchy of the spirits. The offering of sacrifices was deemed to be part of a reciprocal system of obligation. It was thought that the right offering would secure the desired response; the right response from the spirit world in turn created the need for an appropriate offering.

Bronze vessels: techniques

The most outstanding products of the Shang dynasty are undoubtedly the bronze ritual vessels. A knowledge of their method of manufacture is essential if their appearance is to be understood, for they were made by a complex and highly unusual form of casting.

Although China has a remarkable tradition of casting bronze, metal working began, in the view of some scholars, not with casting but with wrought copper and bronze. Evidence is fugitive: a few worked bronze plates have been found in the late stages of the Longshan culture in Shandong; copper implements associated with Qijia sites in Gansu province of c. 2000 BC also belong to a wrought-metal tradition.

More important, pottery vessels from the early Shang site at Erlitou have attached spouts and handles that imitate riveted metal, and imply the existence of metal prototypes with such worked details. Indeed, the development of one vessel, the *jue*, may record some of the changes which occurred in the transition from the use of sheet metal to casting. A *jue*, with a spout emerging from the side of the body and a symmetrical opening at the top, has been excavated in Zhejiang province. This spout was clearly difficult to cast and, it must be presumed, had been copied from a sheet-metal vessel. In some early cast vessels, this still closed, tubular spout was moved from the side to the lip, as in a primitive *jue* excavated at Panlongcheng. As a last stage, the spout at the lip was opened in the classic vessel shape (29). This last form was much better adapted to casting than the early one with the spout attached to the side. The early *jue* in the collection shows another feature possibly remaining from a sheet-metal technique. The line around the inside of the lip seems to indicate the folded lip of a wrought-metal prototype. This detail was of no interest to the bronze caster and disappeared in later vessels.

However, if such metal-working methods did exist on any scale, they were soon abandoned in favour of a system of casting vessels in ceramic piece-moulds. The few bronzes that have so far been excavated at Erlitou, including several *jue* vessels, were made by casting in such piece-moulds assembled from closely fitting sections of clay. Large groups of clay moulds have been excavated at foundry sites at Zhengzhou and Anyang, a few with traces of

40 Fragments of pottery moulds for casting bronze vessels, late Shang dynasty. The upper fragment would have produced decoration with flat plain areas of Style IV, while the right-hand piece would have been used for a vessel with relief designs decorated with *leiwen*. Average length 5 cm.

41 Reconstruction of the assemblage of pottery moulds used for casting a rectangular *ding*. The four-legged vessel was cast upside-down.

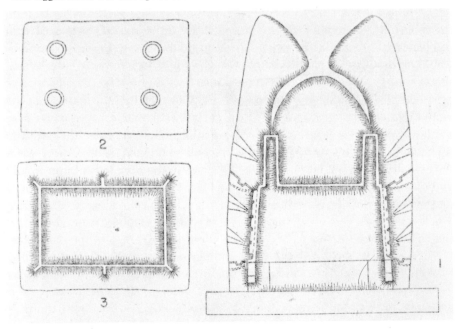

metal remaining in them from the casting (40). The moulds are small and fragmentary, but this technique did not place any restriction on the size of the vessels produced. Some of the surviving bronzes are enormous, and very large crucibles for heating metal have been found (41).

A casting process in which ceramic piece-moulds were used can be contrasted with the *cire-perdue* method that was used in the ancient world in the West. In the *cire-perdue* system, a model of the object to be cast was first prepared in wax or some similar substance. The clay for the mould was modelled around it, and the whole was heated. The molten wax then ran out, leaving the mould firm and ready for the liquid bronze to be poured in. In the *cire-perdue* method much effort and care had to be put into making the model, but the mould was relatively easily produced. In addition, as the wax was melted out, there was no problem in detaching or releasing the mould from the model. The method is thus suited to casting objects of irregular shapes; there is in theory no constraint placed on the shape of the object, since a mould can be made for anything that can be modelled in wax.

The use of a ceramic mould composed of tightly fitting sections poses greater problems and produces a completely different result. Here the care and attention went into making the mould rather than into a perfect model. A model was probably used, but often only as an outline or a guide. It would, even with a releasing agent, have been extremely difficult, if not impossible, to remove the mould from a model had it been fully prepared with complicated designs, and with the significant degree of undercutting required for the more elaborate Shang bronzes. The over-all form of the moulds would have been taken from the model. They would then have been detached in sections and the detail completed by further work on each piece. In this system greater attention would naturally be given to the surface decoration, which was easy to produce, than to intricate shape, which was difficult. In addition to the moulds, cores were needed to ensure that the vessels were hollow and thin-walled. To keep the mould and core separate, and to allow the bronze to flow between the two, small metal spacers were set between them. In a few instances the clay core itself had small extensions used instead of metal spacers to create a gap between the core and the mould. This practice left holes in the bronze wherever mould and core touched, as in the foot of the *yu* (45). The cross-shaped holes seen in most *gu* apparently have the same origin. Such holes would have been formed if a cross-shaped section of the clay made a bridge between the mould and the core and held them apart at the required distance.

The use of moulds assembled from fitted sections had the disadvantage that small seams of bronze might leak between the parts, leaving traces of the vertical joins. For this reason projecting flanges were elaborated to turn this particular characteristic into a decorative feature. Further, because the moulds were made in pieces, there was a tendency for the vessels to appear to be built up of sections, even though in the Shang period the bronzes were usually poured as single unit. Most early bronze vessels from Zhengzhou or Panlongcheng follow closely the rounded forms of pottery vessels, but by the early Anyang stage the use of section-moulds had created a new aesthetic character. The vessels became architectonic in form, with symmetrical parts organised in tiers. A few small elements, such as three-dimensional heads, were sometimes cast in a separate stage.

The use of so complicated a method of casting bronze came easily to the Chinese because they had already developed a very high level of competence in ceramic manufacture during the Neolithic period. In a process based on complex clay moulds, sophisticated kiln techniques and the control of different consistencies of clay were indispensable. The same mastery is equally to be seen in the Shang ceramic industry, which produced a high-fired ware, approaching stoneware in fabric and covered with a deliberate glaze made from feldspar, the essential constituent of stoneware glazes (42). The intimate relationship between ceramic technology and bronze casting is seen again in the manner in which designs were applied to both bronzes and pots, and in the sharing of the designs themselves. Decorated pottery sherds from Erlitou that predate the earliest decorated bronzes show elegantly drawn linear configurations done in fine sunken line. Unlike a pot, a bronze vessel was not decorated directly; decoration was instead applied to the mould. As the mould was of clay, the natural first step was to apply to it linear patterns like those done on pottery vessels. Since a line cut in the mould appears in relief on the bronze cast from the mould, the earliest bronze decoration is executed in thread relief.

In such ways, bronze casting developed from an indigenous Chinese ceramic tradition. As this method of bronze casting is relatively complicated, it was not a matter for a semi-independent smith with an assistant. It had to be under-

42 Fragment of pottery with feldspathic glaze decorated with a stamped S-pattern, middle Shang period. This type of pottery is remarkable for its sophisticated glaze and relatively high firing temperature. It is a forerunner of stoneware. Fragments with impressed designs have been excavated at Zhengzhou, but this sherd resembles more closely sherds with exactly the same designs found at Shang period sites in southern central China (Jiangxi province). Impressed pottery had earlier been characteristic of this area, and it may be argued that it was introduced into Henan from these regions. Length 10 cm.

taken in workshops producing large numbers of moulds to feed the foundries. Large-scale production, and the subdivision of a process into a number of different closely organised stages, are features which will be even more evident in the working of other materials at a later stage (see p. 206).

Bronze vessels – decoration

The shapes of the bronze ritual vessels are very distinctive, and belong to well-defined categories. The forms of the vessels within each category changed over time; certain shapes fell out of use, while others were introduced. The names of most of the vessel shapes are known from inscriptions found in late Shang and Western Zhou bronzes. The inscriptions may vary in length, but a common formula is 'Person X cast this precious [vessel name] for Ancestor Y'. A few vessel shapes are not named in any inscription, and in those cases the vessel is known by a name assigned to it by later antiquarians. The names and the shapes to which they refer are set out in the table in figure 43.

Vessels of the Shang period differ greatly in the degree of complexity of their shape and decoration. An example of a fully decorated but not unduly elaborate bronze in the collection is a bowl, known as a *yu* (44). It has a shallow rounded body drawn in below the neck. This neck is almost equal in height to the curved part of the body, and it flares smoothly outwards. The bowl stands on a re-latively high circular sloping foot. These three horizontal divisions of the vessel are emphasised by three separate friezes of decoration, each of which consists of a single unit of design repeated three times around the vessel.

This slightly unexpected scheme is dictated by the use of three mould sec-tions for the outside of the vessel; the divisions between mould sections are seen as vertical seams separating adjacent repeated units of the decoration. Small holes in the foot ring are seen on the line of the mould divisions. Such holes were left by the small bridges of clay used to keep the core of the foot ring and the outer mould at the correct distance from each other.

Within the area of each mould segment the design is divided centrally. In the lower two registers the axis of the symmetry is marked by a neat raised ridge, which could have been produced quite easily by a deep score or incision in the mould. The ridge lies along the centre of the nose of a creature, the main element in the ornament of both bands. This creature is given the name of *taotie*, for which there are two very obscure Chinese characters. The term was certainly not used by the Shang themselves. It gained wide currency in the writing of the Sung antiquarians, who had taken it from a late Zhou dynasty text, the *Lü Shi Chun Qiu*, and the name has remained a convenient term.

The *taotie* in the central band around the body is the focus of the decoration of the whole vessel. It can most easily be identified by a pair of large eyes with

Food vessels

ding   fang ding   li   xian

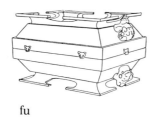

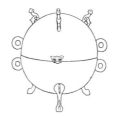

gui   yu   xu

fu   dui   dou

Wine vessels

jue   jiao   jia

43 Ritual vessel shapes

Wine vessels continued

he

gu

zhi

zun

lei

pou

hu

you

fang yi

guang

Water vessels (the yu is sometimes included in this group)

yi

pan

jian

prominent raised pupils at the outer corners. The inner corners of the eyes are exaggerated and pulled down near the central ridge. On either side of the ridge, between the eyes, are vertical quills divided by sunken lines with scrolls. Two scrolls, turned outwards on either side of the bottom of the ridge, call to mind nostrils, but this resemblance may be fortuitous. Running in a broad shallow U-shape from just below one pupil to the other is a double line suggesting the mouth of the creature. Above each eye rises an angular S-shaped plume that serves as a horn. The pronounced horizontal band, on a level with the eyes either side of the central axis, can be interpreted as the body that belongs to the face. This band is enlivened at one end with coiled scrolls near the eyes, and with fins at the other end near the tail, which rises in a high curl. Between the horn and the tail is a broad vertical quill, while below it is a foot, bent backwards through a right angle, with a claw on the end. Two fine quills hang down on each side. Tucked in below the tail of the *taotie* is a small dragon, with a large eye fringed by hooks and quills (45). As the features of the *taotie* are all arranged symmetrically about the central axis, the body and tail are shown twice, once on each side of the face.

The dragon, and the additional quills along the *taotie* body, are devices for dividing and organising the background of fine rectilinear spirals, known as *leiwen*. Although the creature is decorated with sunken meanders, which vary and elaborate its features, there is no possibility of confusing the main figure with the ground. Each strand and quill of the *taotie* and the dragon is broader and therefore more conspicuous than the background spirals.

The same creature can be discovered again in the ornament of the foot. Here the two eyes, essential to the interpretation of the pattern, are much more rudimentary than those in the upper design. They consist of raised oval or squared pupils with rounded corners, and are slightly pointed at the lower inner corner. The rest of the face is a smooth solid area, relying on the apparently chance development of scrolls of sunken meander to outline the nostrils and the C-shaped horns. On either side are two extended quills with slight hooks above and below. In the area around the quills, the neat rectilinear spirals are again organised within limits set by the hooks.

44 *opposite above* Bronze ritual vessel, *yu*, late Shang dynasty. The fine designs on this vessel are excellent examples of the flat decoration of Style IV. Around the middle is an elongated form of the *taotie* with S-shaped horns. Above and below are designs which were to be very influential in the Western Zhou period: the cicada border of triangles; an eye with long spiralling quills; and, at the foot, a *taotie* face with long horizontal quills. Height 14.3 cm, diameter 22.4 cm.

45 *opposite below* Side view of the *yu* (44) showing the mould seam. The line between the two panels of decoration and the small hole in the foot mark the junction of this section of the mould. A small dragon, composed of an eye surrounded by quills, is shown in the main panel of the decoration on either side of the mould seam.

The upper band of decoration is divided horizontally. In the lower part the familiar elements of eyes and quills recur, but in a different configuration. The new motif consists of an eye with four quills, two long and two short, extending horizontally to fill the band. It is paired with an identical motif facing it symmetrically. Between the two is set a small three-dimensional animal head. Above this, and running in a continuous band around the vessel, is a border of triangles. These are filled with sunken V-shapes with scrolled ends, above a further pair of scrolls, and the pattern so formed is related to the cicada motif found on many vessels. The zig-zag line of the triangles shows well that all of the ornament rises in relief above the level of the plain surface of the vessel. To achieve this effect the design must have been cut into the smooth mould, rather than being derived from a model. Had the design been cut into a model, the line of the triangles would have been flush with the plain area of the neck on the model and therefore on the vessel as well.

The complexity of the ornament of the *yu*, and its neat organisation in relation to the shape, show it to be the product of an advanced and highly sophisticated design tradition; it is far from being a primitive or experimental venture. Vessels of similar character have been excavated at Anyang, providing evidence that they belong to the late Shang period. The sources of this advanced stage lie much further back in the primitive vessels cast in the early Shang period and known from a few pieces excavated from Erlitou. Indeed the shapes, regarded as peculiar to the ritual vessels, have yet more ancient antecedents, some deriving from neolithic ceramics. Tripods and containers with hollow lobes are descended from Longshan prototypes. Others with spouts and handles incorporate features which seem to have been developed within a tradition of sheet-metal craftsmanship, possibly in the west of China. A variety of features taken from several sources were thus altered and standardised by the constraints imposed by the mould-making process. Modifications, introduced at first to facilitate casting, unified and reshaped the prototypes.

Although the shapes show consummate skill in casting, it is the surface ornament which demonstrates most vividly the inventiveness of the bronze workers. The use of section-moulds, which facilitated detailed working directly on the mould surface, gave the caster a special opportunity to elaborate this particular aspect of the bronze art. Divisions of the moulds separated units within the ornament. Thus the decoration of the bronzes was closely tied to the shape of the vessels. The designs on the bronzes have been the subject of much study. Among the many approaches, the one which has proved most revealing is the scheme of five styles proposed by Max Loehr in 1953. As this particular interpretation has proved seminal it will be set out briefly, and then elaborated with further comments.

STYLE I   Decoration in thread relief, confined to narrow bands, is the characteristic feature. Vessels with this decoration are slight and thin-walled, and only a limited number of shapes are known. The designs either side of the handle on a *jue* (30) are in the thread relief of Style I.

STYLE II   The most important feature of this style is the use of broad lines of varying width to produce the designs. These are still confined to horizontal bands, some of which show a hint of vertical divisions in the centres of the frieze units in addition to the vertical seam lines due to the mould assembly as in *jia* (31). In shape the vessels are more varied and bolder than those with the pure Style I designs, but the castings are still very thin.

STYLE III   The designs are now dense, fluent, and curvilinear, with many feather-like or quilled extensions. On some vessels they are still confined to narrow bands, but on others they occupy large areas. The repertory of vessel shapes with these designs is much wider than that of the previous style. A late version of this style is seen on a *pou* (47); a slightly earlier one on a *li* (46).

STYLE IV   The important new element is the separation, within the ornament, of the main motifs from the background. In place of quills are rectilinear spirals, distinct from the main elements of the ornament. As on the *yu* (44) described above, the main design and the spirals, with the exception of the eyes, are flush with the surface. The use of flanges to mark the mould seams is an important innovation made at about this stage or a little earlier.

STYLE V   On bronzes of this group relief is used for the main motif, as on a *you* (48). In some cases the Style V design imitates Style IV exactly, the only alteration being the elevation of the principal motifs in high relief. In other instances the relief effects are more varied; sometimes the background of spirals was eliminated altogether. Many different versions of relief were cast (colour 1).

These five styles delineate the principal artistic changes made in the methods of producing decorative effects: they are not tied to any content of the decoration. Hence the importance of the five styles lies in the elucidation of the sequence in which the bronze casters discovered the possibilities of their medium. The changes chronicled by the styles can be summarised as follows: as a first step, simple linear designs were cut into the mould, generating thread relief (Style I); more elaborate designs were produced by cutting broader lines into the mould (Style II); the patterns of Style II were then elaborated to a high degree, especially with quill elements (Style III). With greater complexity came the need to accent the principal features of the ornament, at first still in the single plane flush with the vessel surface (Style IV), then with high relief for the motifs (Style V). The changes are changes in mould-making technique as well as in design. Cumulatively the effect was to develop the patterns from relatively abstract embellishment, in which the principal focus of attention was either a pair of eyes or a single eye, to motifs that were specific and differentiated.

46 *left* Bronze ritual vessel, *li*, middle Shang dynasty. The *taotie* face is barely visible among the hooks and quills of the Style III decoration. The upper band around the neck, executed in the thread relief of Style I, is an abstract pattern and can be compared with examples excavated at Panlongcheng. Height 24.7 cm.

47 *below* Bronze ritual vessel, *pou*, late Shang dynasty. This vessel is covered in the fine quills typical of Style III. These fill the space between the horns of the main *taotie* to either side of the central flange and its tail. The upper band shows dragons in profile, all following in the same direction around the neck from left to right. This is a late version of Style III, and can be compared with bronzes from Anyang. Height 20.3 cm, width 28.9 cm.

48 *opposite* Bronze ritual vessel, *you*, late Shang dynasty. The body is oval in cross-section with the handle across the short axis. The decoration is in relief (Style v), showing a standard version of the *taotie* with C-shaped horns complete with body and claw. The notched teeth and horn can be compared with the jaw and ear respectively of a tiger in jade (64). Small dragons in profile are the precursors of many later dragon designs. Height 22.5 cm.

The thread relief of Style I was technically the easiest form of decoration to execute. The very earliest decorated bronzes from Erlitou and Zhengzhou are embellished with rows of raised circles, dots, and criss-cross lines, all very easily cut or impressed into the mould surface. The introduction of the face design, the *taotie*, was a new departure. Possible origins of this face will be discussed later in the chapter. It too was first executed in thread relief, both in rudimentary forms and in more complicated versions. Thus, within Style I, several successive degrees of refinement are to be seen, ranging from ornament consisting of little more than a pair of eyes outlined in thread relief, as on a *jue* from Panlongcheng (56), to highly elaborate symmetrical patterns of scrolls and fins centred on two solid, nearly square eyes, as on the *ding* from Panlongcheng, already discussed (28). In both cases the decoration was confined to narrow bands around the vessel.

The ornament of Style II was a natural progression from Style I, and in it the expressive use of line was carried a step further. The fine thread relief was transformed by cutting broad lines of varied width in the mould that, when cast, provided a more interesting surface than the earlier thread relief. Advances in the vessel shapes are also evident. A comparison of the shape of the *jue*, with a primitive version of Style II (29) with that of the *jia* (31), with the more advanced decoration, is instructive. The slight almost unstable legs of the *jue* are awkwardly placed in relation to the body, and the two elements have not at this stage been fully integrated with each other. On the *jia*, on the other hand, the legs are larger, splayed, and contribute to the over-all balance of the piece.

The first two styles predominate among early bronzes, and account for the decoration of all but a few of the most advanced bronzes found at the middle Shang sites of Zhengzhou, Liulige, and Panlongcheng. Styles I and II are, therefore, generally to be associated with the earliest bronzes. However, as noted above, once invented the styles survived, at least for a time, alongside one another. Styles I and II are, for example, seen on the same *jue* (29, 30). The use of the styles in establishing the dates of particular examples is not always straightforward. None the less, earlier and later versions of the same style can, with experience, be reliably distinguished. As with the shapes, the Style II designs on the *jue* are much less advanced than those on the *jia*, and this reflects its earlier date.

Crucial to the understanding not only of the development of the five styles, but also the evolution within any one style, is the recognition that the bronze decoration is an art which saw the development from simple, almost abstract designs, to more complex and increasingly explicit patterns. In this the bronzes can, for example, be contrasted with the Neolithic pottery of the Yangshao cultures in which the changes in the ornament went the other way. The decor-

49 Details of the decoration of the *jia* (31): *above*, the *taotie* face on the front of the vessel, with two eyes with pointed corners, and a jaw with scalloped inserts as teeth; *below*, creature in profile, behind the *taotie*, with a long pointed nose and jaw to the left, and, behind the eye, a tail with hooks above the claws below.

ation of the bronzes is to be understood as an ornamental rather than a representational art. Elaboration of pattern, rather than the development of any system of depiction, accounts for most of the changes that can be observed between the designs on the *jia* and those on the earlier *jue*. On the *jia* the solid areas around the eyes have been given additional hooks and lines, and the horizontal side plumes on either side are vigorously elaborated (49 top). Such additions in no way directly contribute to the creation of an image. Only the details of teeth, shown by scalloped inserts, are additions which can be seen as having a representational quality. Behind the *taotie*, on either side of the handle, are creatures with single eyes (49 bottom). The use of a single eye as a focus of a pattern, suggesting a creature in profile, was an innovation of Style II. On later bronzes such patterns were to coalesce into dragons or birds.

At this early stage their attributes are hardly specific enough to make such identifications possible. It is more relevant to observe that, when a design is presented without an eye, it lacks interest. Such an eyeless pattern is seen around the neck of the *li* (46). So important is the eye that the viewer here is

likely to try to read one of the scrolls in each of the repeated elements as an eye – with little prospect of success. The eye appeared even in designs which could never be interpreted as a creature, for example, with pairs of diagonal lines. As they encourage the viewer to try to interpret the patterns organically, eyes add essentially to the tension of the patterns. They thus animate the bronze ornament, not by making it representational, but by persuading the viewer to try to penetrate the ambiguity of the pattern and to find some organic interpretation for it.

A related interest in the potential of the ornament is much in evidence in the next stage, Style III. In early versions of this style, as for example on the *li*, the relative solidity of the face on the *jia* has been dissipated in a series of vertical hooked quills; the designs have not moved in the direction of increasing definition. The interest in ornament is seen in the conflict between those quills that are simply elaborate patterning, and those lines that appear to indicate parts of the creature. Among these latter elements are the coiled tail, shown on either side of the lobe, and the broad hooks hanging down behind the eye, which appear to form the corners of the jaw, while rows of hooks suggest teeth.

A similar ambiguity is seen, in a much more advanced form, on a *pou* (47). This is quite a late version of Style III, with each fine quill being a miniaturised replica of the broader ones seen on the earlier *li* vessel. Some details of the *taotie* now seem quite concrete, with a certain amount of differentiation between the horizontal elements of the body and the narrow quills that all but form a background. But a new complexity comes with the addition of a small dragon in profile below the coiled tail of the *taotie* (50). The hooked nose of the dragon can be read both as belonging to the dragon or alternatively as the claw of the *taotie*. Likewise the tail of the *taotie* also does service as the tail of the dragon, and the horizontal quills at the end of the frieze belong to both creatures. The

50 *left* Detail from the side of a *pou*
(47), showing the side of the *taotie*
with another small dragon below
its tail.

51 *right* Detail from the inside of a
pou (47). The design of a turtle
shows how a depiction of a creature
was put together from geometric
elements. This motif occurs in the
interiors of *pou* and *pan* vessels, and
is occasionally shown in *zun* vessels.

overriding feature of this decoration is the ornamental detail, expressed particularly in quills, that tempts the spectator to follow the design line by line, in
the hope of deciding to which creature each belongs.

In so far as it is possible to divide the quills from the horizontal body of the
taotie on the *pou*, this is indicative of its relatively late date. Earlier versions of
Style III are seen on bronzes from middle Shang sites, and this decorative style
also seems to have been widely influential in other areas of China, for example
in Hebei. By the Anyang period, to which the *pou* can be assigned on the basis
of excavated comparisons, this style seems to be in the process of being superseded by other ornamental schemes which allowed for greater definition of
the different motifs.

Such definition was the purpose of Styles IV and V. On the *pou*, the quills
threatened to overwhelm the face. Therefore, on some pieces, a *jia* for example
(52, 53), certain quills were thickened to outline the elements of the design.
A more satisfactory device was to replace the background of fine quills so
achieved by a background of spirals, or *leiwen*, as seen on the *yu*. High relief
used for the main designs – the *taotie*, dragons, and birds – was a yet more
effective technique. This innovation followed rapidly on the introduction of
the *leiwen*, and both Styles IV and V were in use at an early stage of the Anyang
period. One effect of the clarity of design so achieved was to stimulate the differentiation of the many types of faces, dragons, and birds now in use. The motifs
used in many late Anyang bronzes are indeed very specific.

A standard example of the use of relief is seen on a wine bucket with lid and
handle, known as a *you* (48). The *taotie* face is clear and coherent, its eyes
shown with round pupils; it has two C-shaped horns, jaws, ears, and on either
side claws and a tail rising in a plume. Small dragons are set in the narrow
borders around the neck and foot. The use of high relief notwithstanding,

52 *left* Bronze ritual vessel, *jia*, late Shang dynasty. Height 31.2 cm.

53 *below* Detail of a bronze ritual vessel, *jia*, late Shang dynasty (52). The conspicuous outline of *taotie* faces among fine quills is an important form of decoration transitional between Style III and Style IV. The quills inherited from Style III (47) were replaced by spirals or *leiwen* in Style IV (44). Height 31.2 cm.

54 Bronze ritual vessel, *li ding*, late Shang or early Western Zhou. The two halves of this beautifully balanced design are completely separate, and can be read equally well as a *taotie* face, or as two dragons. Height 26.6 cm.

the bronze casters could not resist the temptation to exploit the interest of ambiguous ornament. On a square vessel with a lid, known as a *fang yi* (colour I), each of the raised elements of the face is enhanced with a tight sunken meander that draws it once more into close association with the background *leiwen*. Moreover, some details are used that are capable of two interpretations: the horns of the *taotie* can equally well be read as two independent dragons with bottle horns.

A different and important example of such ingenuity is seen in the occasional division of the *taotie* into two parts, so that it can be read either as a face or as two confronted dragons. A *li ding* shows a clear example (54). At the centre of each lobe the *taotie* nose is separated from the eyes and the horns. The eyes can be taken as either belonging to the *taotie*, seen from the front, or to the dragons, one on each side of the lobe, seen in profile. Such puns are late phenomena, and most *taotie* faces cannot be interpreted in this way.

Along with greater definition of the designs came a pronounced attempt to bring the decoration and the shape of the vessel into an exact correspondence. The more elaborate Style III designs had covered the surface of the vessel evenly. Given a clearer definition of the motifs within the pattern unit in Styles IV and V, the sections of the design could be more forcefully outlined. As a result, instead of allowing the sections of the decoration to join unobtrusively at the mould seams, the junctions, frequently found between the tails of two *taotie*, came to be marked by a flange. Vertical divisions were emphasised by flanges, horizontal ones by angles introduced into the vessel shapes. The effect of the decorative developments of Styles IV and V was to hasten the creation of the many highly architectonic vessels of the Anyang period.

As in earlier periods, eclecticism was at times an important feature of bronze ornament of the Anyang stage. The complex of designs on such a vessel as the *guang* (55) can only be explained by a survival of Styles II and III. On the lower part of the vessel is a dragon in profile, almost obscured by broad quills

55 Bronze ritual vessel, *guang*, late Shang dynasty. The covered wine pourers of the *guang* shape are often elaborately decorated with many creatures. The dragon with bottle-horns on the handle is frequently combined with a snake's body, as seen here. The upper part of the body is decorated in Style IV while the lower part shows a dragon in profile in a later version of Style II. Height 23 cm.

and scrolls, reminiscent of Style II or III. Above, belonging to Style IV, is a pattern of snake bodies with diamonds set against a background of spirals. Flanges and three-dimensional faces on the lid are features to be associated with the fully developed high-relief styles of the late Shang period. Such a combination demonstrates that, with the passage of time, there was an ever-expanding repertory of techniques as well as motifs from which to choose.

Some developments cannot, however, be easily accommodated within the confines of a single Anyang style, or be explained as eclectic combinations. As Virginia Kane has pointed out, recent excavations suggest that there were important bronze-making centres outside Anyang, notably in Hubei, Hunan, Anhui and Shaanxi. By contrast with the middle Shang period, when bronzes made in many regions reflected metropolitan taste, provincial bronzes of the Anyang period sometimes reveal quite separate and individual styles. A *zun*, or wine container, supported by two rams (colour II) is an example of such a provincial bronze. A vessel decorated with four rams, executed in a comparable sculptural style, has been found in Ningxiang, Hunan province. Moreover, the only other double-ram *zun* known to date, and now in the Nezu Museum in Japan, is said to have come from Changsha in Hunan. The rams, shown with such realism on these three vessels, are unparalleled at Anyang. The execution of the *taotie* face between the two rams, on the Museum's example, also departs from metropolitan designs. Meanders on the face and between the horns bear some resemblance to those of late Style II and Style III. The lines, however, lack the tension associated with metropolitan bronzes. The scrolls and fins are on rather a large scale, and have lost the density and tautness of the original patterns. The line of descent of such southern bronzes from Styles II and III is none the less apparent; prominent among them are drums and large bells, artefacts much less important in the north.

The flowering of these provincial centres of bronze casting in the second part of the Shang period greatly increased the range of bronze styles available towards the end of the dynasty. One consequence was the introduction of new features in bronzes cast at Anyang. Among these were vessel shapes that included forms adopted from ceramics, notably the lobed vessels that had earlier been popular in middle Shang. This departure inevitably entailed abandonment of some part of the architectonic style of the high Shang. Another new venture was the use of comparatively long inscriptions cast on bronzes.

Confronted by so rich and powerful a tradition of ornamental art, and in particular by so omnipresent and enduring a motif as the *taotie*, the question of origins becomes especially pressing. This is the more true since we are far from any understanding of the iconography of Shang art. The evolution of the motifs, and their employment in purely ornamental schemes, has suggested to some observers that Shang art decoration is an art of pure ornament, entirely without iconographic meaning. Others have sought to read a meaning into the different motifs. No definite answer to the question seems possible at present. There is no literary evidence bearing on the bronze decoration to offer any foothold for the iconographer. However, one limited but none the less useful line of approach is to examine once again the earliest forms of the *taotie* motif. It is here that a connection with the Neolithic jade designs mentioned in the last chapter seems important.

As noted in the discussion of the five styles, the earliest bronzes have simple geometric designs, among which the face appeared as a conspicuous innovation. It might be expected that early forms of the face would be found with eyes of solid dots, adopted from the more primitive motifs. However, one of the first faces, between borders of such dots, seen on a *jue* from Panlongcheng, is outlined in thread relief (56). The exact shape of the eyes so delineated is important. The inner line describes an oval, or rather a square with rounded corners, with the lower inner corner being drawn slightly towards the nose. The outer line is not concentric with the inner, and forms a wider oval. This slightly pointed oval outline resembles the outline of the eyes belonging to the faces on the Neolithic bangle (25). The connection between the eyes on the *jue* and the bangle persists in the similarity, already noted, between the face on the axe from Liangchengzhen and the one on the *ding* from Panlongcheng. Not only are the eyes on the axe and the *ding* related, but the hooks making up the plumes around the face on the axe appear to have been an influence on the form of the meanders filling the decorative band on the *ding*.

The next major development in the shape of the eye of the *taotie* on the bronzes can also be traced to jade prototypes. Slanting, rather more realistic eyes, seen, for example, on the *taotie* of the *jia* (31), were anticipated in the decoration of an early Shang jade handle (57) excavated at Erlitou. This handle predates all decorated bronzes. The same eye-form is seen on a fine jade face in the collection (58). Along the top of the head is an incised scroll reminiscent of decoration on many Neolithic jades with the face pattern. It seems likely that this jade too belongs to the early Shang period. Once introduced, this new eye-form existed alongside the older one. Both forms are often seen on the same vessel in the middle Shang period, and the combination survived into the late Shang on such vessels as the *yu* (44).

As both eye-forms are seen in jade at a date before they are found in bronze, it may be presumed that the rudimentary elements of the face were taken from jade on to bronze. The complex of face designs of the Shang period therefore seems to have had its origins in jade motifs particularly associated with the east-coast Neolithic.

Once some elements of a face had been adopted, many elaborations of the bronze designs developed quite logically from the process of carving in the

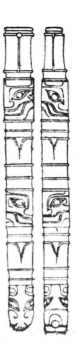

56 *above left* Bronze ritual vessel, *jue*, middle
Shang dynasty. Excavated at Panlongcheng.
This is an earlier form of the same vessel type
as (29). Decoration in thread relief (Style I)
shows eyes of oval form derived from prototypes in jade (compare 27).

57 *above right* Jade handle from Erlitou, early
Shang period. The faces with slanting eyes are
executed in thread relief.

58 *right* Green jade mask, late neolithic or
early Shang dynasty. This jade can be compared with neolithic jades discussed in the
previous chapter. The incised design on the
head-dress is similar to the scrollwork on the
jade bangle from south China (26) and the
flourishes behind the ears to those on the axe
from Shandong (27). The elaborate eye form
which is a new departure, can be compared
with that seen on an early Shang jade handle
excavated at Erlitou (57). Width 5.8 cm.

mould. However, there seems to have been some interaction between bronzes
and ceramics. Impressed patterns on pottery from the Shang sites of Erlitou
and Zhengzhou are similar to those found on the east coast at Liangchengzhen,
and in the south at Jiangxi Wucheng. Repeated S-shapes are, for example, found
on pottery both at Zhengzhou and Wucheng. It might be argued that some
of the designs originated in the east and south rather than at Anyang. Many
of these patterns were influential on the bronzes. As with the jades, the influence
of one material on another was not the product of a single moment of contact,
but rather an intermittent process of long duration.

Jade carving

Shang jade carving was founded on the achievements of the Neolithic jade workers. From the very early stages of the Shang period jade was worked to a high technical and artistic level. Jades excavated at Erlitou are of accomplished design and perfectly finished. By contrast, bronze casting was, at that time, only just about to make an appearance. Among the recent finds from Erlitou are two large knives similar to an equally massive piece in the British Museum (59). The long horizontal form, perforated along the upper edge, was derived from a Neolithic prototype. These knives are enhanced only by a few incised lines, criss-crossed at the two ends. Such ceremonial implements – for items of such a precious material cannot have been intended for everyday use – are impressive by virtue of their large size and simple shape. While the knife in the Museum has a stepped edge, a rare feature, but one which is known from jades from Erlitou, one of the excavated examples has fine notches along the two short edges. The interest of the jades was subtly increased by these details.

The use of notches along the edges of carvings is one of the most important features of Chinese jades, and such notches are found on jades made throughout the Shang period, both on ceremonial weapons and on small amulets (60). This decorative device was the outcome of the constraints on carving this hard material. Even quite simple shapes were difficult to produce, and three-dimensional shapes were especially challenging. The most straightforward method of working the material was to cut a small boulder or pebble into slices or thin slabs by rubbing the stone with a cord and an abrasive sand. The many early jades fashioned from such flat slabs are evidence of the popularity of this technique. With a flat piece of jade, whose surface was easier to polish than to decorate elaborately, much of the interest had to lie in the treatment of the silhouette. A notched outline could be produced with comparative ease by cutting along the edge vertically. Sceptres with notches either side of the butt are one of the most remarkable products of this technique.

While notches and incised lines were relatively simple to produce, thin raised lines, seen on the handle from Erlitou discussed above (57), were very difficult. If a line is to be left in relief, the surface on either side has to be patiently ground away. It was a considerable achievement to render the face designs in this technique. But such carvings represent the most skilful use of

1 Bronze ritual vessel, *fang yi*, late Shang period. The face on the central panel has been neatly subdivided into its constituent parts, each shown in the relief of Style v. The two horns have become independent dragons in their own right. Eyebrows above the eyes are often associated with human figures; the body extensions are here replaced by two small dragons. A similar face is seen on the lid the other way up. The vessel can be compared with a *fang yi* excavated at Anyang. Height 27 cm.

thin relief lines, and later Shang jades were less accomplished in this respect.

The close similarity between the designs on some jades, which include those worked in relief lines, and the patterns on early bronzes has been remarked upon. Such jades, including the handle (57), predate the bronzes. Thus, if the similarity is not fortuitous, it must be the outcome of the influence of the jade designs on the bronzes and not the other way round. However, it was relatively easy to carve quite complicated patterns in the clay moulds used to cast the bronzes. The simple early designs, adopted from the jades, were therefore elaborated on the bronzes. These more complicated designs were then re-worked by the jade carvers in jade.

Beautiful though the material is, jade was not merely a luxury item. It had its own place in the rituals and especially in burial. Jade was rarely worked into vessels, so clearly the function of jade objects was not the same as that of the bronzes. Sceptres of jade, following the shapes normally made in bronze, must have had a special purpose because the same forms were used over a long period. It has been noted that some weapons were made in Neolithic shapes long after the original implement had disappeared from use. Although some sceptres imitated bronze weapons, even these showed much less variety than their bronze counterparts. Most common is the pointed sceptre in the shape of a dagger-axe (61). The bronze dagger-axe was, in the Shang period, made in a multitude of forms. Yet in jade one particular type, with a notched butt decorated with transverse ribs, stands out as all-important. By contrast, the bronze prototype for this jade had been in use only in the early Shang and was then superseded. The jade dagger-axe, in common with the other cere-monial implements, was highly conservative. Presumably the ritual use and the difficulties of carving determined this relatively unchanging shape.

In the many efforts to reconstruct the purposes of these weapons, the ritual texts of the late Zhou period, the *Li Ji* and the *Zhou Li*, have been combed for relevant information. But the names and purposes attributed to pieces more than a thousand years later are not reliable. However, it is possible to relate the use of jades to other notions about the Shang state derived principally from the oracle bones. It has been argued by David Keightley, using this evidence, that the earthly and spiritual worlds formed a continuum in the outlook of Shang peoples. Insignia such as jade sceptres or weapons were probably equally significant both in the hierarchy of the state and in the hierarchy of ancestors. They may therefore have formed part of an offering

---

II Bronze ritual vessel *zun*, Shang dynasty. Only rarely do Anyang vessels approach the sculptural style of this magnificent provincial vessel. A *fang zun* decorated with four rams, square in shape, has been found in Ningxiang, Hunan province. Height 43.2 cm.

59 *above* Jade knife, early to middle Shang
dynasty. This knife can be compared with two
excavated from Erlitou. These early examples
illustrate an accomplishment in jade carving
much higher than the primitive level of bronze
casting in this period. Length 74 cm.

60 *right* Jade bird, late Shang dynasty. The
incised decoration and the notched outline on
the crest and tail are reminiscent of bronze
decoration. Similar birds have been found
among the very rich group of jades in Fu Hao's
tomb. Height 12 cm.

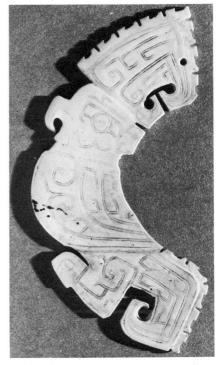

61 *below* Jade halberd, late Shang dynasty.
Such ceremonial jade weapons were modelled on
bronze counterparts (34). Length 28.5 cm.

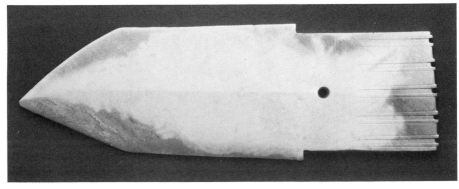

to the spirits, and have been used in the burial of the dead. The discs may be interpreted in much the same way, particularly as some examples have been found buried in the foundations of buildings at Anyang. In this position they took a place similar to that of the sacrificial burials of humans. A simple circle of jade, a *bi* as it is known in Chinese, is a potent symbol, and occurs throughout the period covered by this handbook (62). In the *Zhou Li* it is described as the symbol of Heaven. But in the Shang period the supreme deity was *Shang Di*; Heaven, or *Tian* was not as yet recognised, so the association between the jade and *Tian* could have had no significance. In the same text another jade object, the *zong* is paired with the *bi*. This type of jade, characteristic of Neolithic cultures of the south-east coast, is extremely rare at Shang sites. The only excavated examples are small and plain. They are so rare that any suggestion that they should be paired with the *bi* is entirely conjectural. Indeed, later antiquarians faced by the large and imposing Neolithic examples did not recognise that they belonged to a provincial tradition rather than to the mainstream of Chinese Bronze Age culture.

Apart from a few small decorative items including whip handles and bangles, the other main category of jades was the small animal amulet, particularly popular in the Anyang period (63, 64). The contrast between the large, smooth, and unornamented surfaces of the *bi* and the weapons, and the much more intricate working of the animals, is striking. Weapons were indicated by a simple silhouette, and details derived from stone or bronze originals had a tendency to be reduced by simplification. The outline of the animals was, on

62 Jade disc, *bi*, late Shang dynasty. Both plain rings and those with a collar around the centre were common at Anyang, and have been found, for example, in Fu Hao's tomb. Diameter 21 cm.

63 *left* Jade buffalo, late Shang dynasty. Length 4.6 cm.

64 *below* Jade tiger, late Shang dynasty. The chisel-ended tail is seen on a number of Shang jades, but the purpose for which it was intended is unknown. Length 5.5 cm.

the other hand, elaborate. Realistic form and feature were carefully reproduced. Again by contrast with the weapons, the small animals were frequently worked with decoration on the surface. Most important was a meander similar to that used on the surfaces of the *taotie* on the bronzes. This was either executed in pairs of incised lines or indicated by a narrow ridge. The ridge had been derived from the thin relief lines seen on early Shang jades, but now lacked the fluency of the earlier examples. A few pieces were carved in three dimensions. The jade animals are characterised by a freedom that is quite distinct from the vigour of the bronze patterns. Unconstrained by the ceramic moulds and the symmetry these imposed, the jade carver could explore a different form of expression. Shape rather than pattern was important. The different animals are readily identifiable, and in their execution is none of the play with ambiguity seen on the bronzes. Similar creatures are, however, found: the *taotie*, the dragon, the tiger, the bird, and the buffalo.

Stone, bone, ceramics, textiles, lacquer

These same creatures appear again and again in other materials, in stone, in bone, in ceramics or lacquer. The diversity of the materials which the Shang worked to an extremely high technical level is extraordinary. The ornament shows throughout the motifs and styles seen in bronze and jade decoration. In bone carving, the manner of execution has the same intricacy and detail as the decoration of bronzes. Stone on the other hand was used for animals that resembled the smaller jade carvings in three dimensions. It would appear that the jades were to some extent influenced by the style used for stone sculpture; there is the same block-like rendering of form and the same use of the meander taken from the bronzes (65).

The influence of ceramics on bronzes has already been mentioned but there is another example in which the relationship was reversed. One of the most striking types of Shang pottery is that made of a very white clay with a large proportion of kaolin in it. This is the same material from which, at a later date, porcelain was to be made. But in the Shang period it was fired at a temperature considerably below that required for porcelain, namely 1000 °C rather than 1300 °C. The few fragments in the Museum are decorated with lozenge designs, cicadas and the *taotie* face, derived from the bronze tradition (66). At this stage, this highly refined form of ceramic was still linked to the most important craft of the time, bronze casting. Later it was to be developed independently with the making of true porcelain, one of China's major contributions to the world.

Another peculiarly Chinese invention, lacquer, was also current in the Shang dynasty. Lacquer is the sap of the lacquer-tree, the *Rhus verniciflua* which can be tapped like the rubber tree. The resulting liquid is then applied to a solid surface like wood or hemp, usually with a colouring agent in it. It forms a glossy waterproof coating which can, under certain conditions, prevent the decay of organic materials. Fragments decorated with the ancient bronze designs have been excavated from the northern area of Shang influence, namely Hebei province. It seems likely that some of the painting on wood recovered from the tombs at Anyang was also done in lacquer.

65 Limestone buffalo, late Shang dynasty. Such stone carvings are more solid and block-like than their jade counterparts. A similar sculpture has been excavated from the tomb of Fu Hao. Length 19.2 cm.

66 Fragments of white pottery decorated with bronze designs, late Shang dynasty. Complete vessels in this type of pottery are extremely rare; one has been found at Anyang. Maximum length 5 cm.

67 Detail of jade knife (see 59) showing a 'ghost' of a coarse textile in which the knife was wrapped for burial.

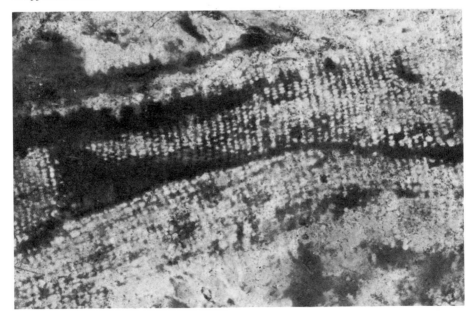

Silk, a typically Chinese material, was also in use during the Shang period. This thread, which has to be wound from the cocoons made by the silkworm, was probably already known in the Longshan period, and cocoons have been found in excavations. In normal conditions textiles rarely survive from the Shang period, but accidental imprints are to be found, mainly on bronze, and occasionally on other materials. One of the most striking examples of such a ghost is to be seen in the staining of the large jade knife (67). This was clearly not a silk fabric but a much coarser cloth, such as hemp.

Conclusion

The Shang dynasty, the first archaeologically identified dynasty of China, has been shown to be directly descended from Neolithic antecedents in the same area. In addition to the survival of such general features as the elaborate settlements, direct connection is established by the transmission of particular traits, namely pyro-scapulimancy, and the ceremonial use of polished jade.

Both extensive excavations and the oracle bones provide evidence of a complex and highly organised society, headed by a king and his family, and supported by officials. A class of craftsmen was of some significance. Slaves or prisoners of war were probably the main group among the many sacrificial victims. Powerful though the Shang state was, other groups of people existed alongside, at times providing competition and even a threat.

The ordering of society, which is known both from excavated evidence and from textual information, is also to be inferred from the bronzes, jades, and ceramics made in such profusion. The scale and high quality of production, the diversity of the materials, and the intricacies of manufacture imply a high degree of division of labour requiring detailed supervision and direction, with specialised uses in mind.

At the same time, neither the wide range of materials in use, nor the numerous items which were made, detracted from the unity of conception of the main stream of Shang art. With the exception of some provincial styles mentioned above, coherence of the style of items of any one period is impressive. The bronzes, jades, and ceramics express in visual terms the forceful and distinctive character of the Shang people.

3 The Western Zhou

Parts of the earliest surviving Chinese historical text, the *Shu Jing* or Book of Documents, were written under the next dynasty, the Zhou. It describes the destruction of the Shang, here referred to as the Yin, by the Zhou peoples: 'Heaven then greatly ordered Wen Wang to destroy the great Yin and greatly received its mandate; its states and people as a result became orderly.' (*Shu Jing, Kang Gao*, translated by Bernhard Karlgren, *Bulletin of the Museum of Far Eastern Antiquities*, no. 22, pp. 39–40). According to the revised chronology this conquest took place in 1027 BC. For the next three hundred years the capital was established in the area near Xian, in Shaanxi province. The period is known as the Western Zhou period because the capital was then situated at a western site.

The Zhou people had lived, for at least part of the Shang period, to the west of the Shang state in the area of the present-day province of Shaanxi. References to the Zhou in the inscriptions carved by the Shang on the oracle bones indicate that they were at different times described as an enemy and as an ally of the Shang.

Something more can be learned about the Zhou by examining the bronzes that they cast. It has in the past been difficult to distinguish bronzes made by the Zhou before the conquest from those made in other parts of China in the Shang period. However, recent excavations in Shaanxi province have made it possible to describe some aspects of bronze casting associated with that area. Bronzes from Shaanxi of the middle Shang period, decorated in Styles II and III, are in most cases similar to those found at Zhengzhou. Shang influence over Shaanxi, as over other outlying areas, for example Panlongcheng in Hubei, must have been considerable; for metropolitan styles were not only imitated, they were accurately copied. However, as in the south, direct Shang control or contact appears to have decreased in the Anyang period. Bronzes of the late Shang and conquest periods, which have been found in Shaanxi, are either rather poor versions of the main forms made at Anyang, or have been cast with unusual and exotic variations in design quite unlike any found at the Shang centre.

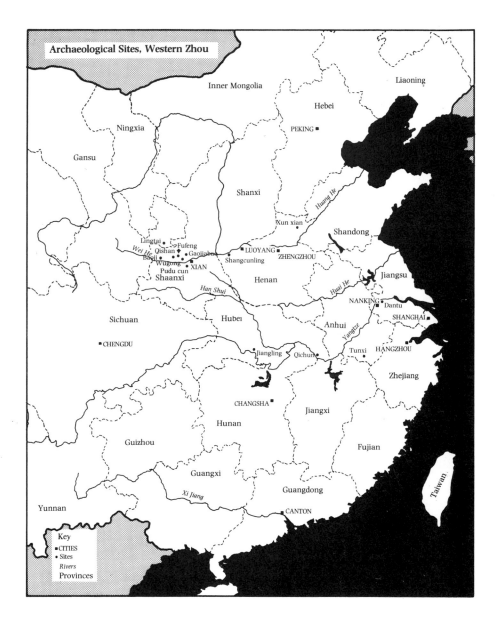

A small basin, or *yu*, is an example of the somewhat inferior Anyang style bronzes found in Shaanxi (68). In shape it belongs to the same category as the *yu* described in the Shang chapter (44). Here, however, although the vessel stands on a moulded foot, the shape is much simplified. The bowl slopes outwards in a continuous line to a slight ridge at the rim. There are only two narrow bands of decoration. Around the foot are designs of birds, and at the

neck the band encloses eyes at the centre of extended horizontal quills. This same pattern was also seen on the Shang *yu*. The use of the Style IV technique on the Shaanxi *yu* is old-fashioned and lacks vigour.

By contrast, other bronzes were flamboyant and eccentric. The design of a bird on a *gui*, excavated at Wugong xian, illustrates this group (69). Birds are seen on Anyang bronzes filling the main areas of decoration, but this bird is different. The Shang birds have broad wings and relatively shorter tails. Their plumes or crest are crisp and jaunty, similar to the horns of dragons. The Shaanxi bird has a long body and tail, rather a narrow wing, and a long, almost straggling S-shaped plume hanging down behind its head. This plume is especially characteristic of the Shaanxi bird. A small dragon pattern borrowed from the repertory of earlier bronzes, seen, for example, on the Shang *yu* (45), is tucked rather uncomfortably over the wing of the bird. In two other respects this bird design does not conform to Shang patterns: the bird is not properly confined to a single register of the vessel, for both the claw and the tail hang down from the central area of the body on to the foot; the beak of the bird is joined to that of another facing it, so that in effect they share a single beak. In this second detail the Zhou casters had adapted the Shang convention, appropriate for showing the face and body of the *taotie*, and used it for the bird. However, the Shang bronze casters themselves had never extended the methods

68 *left* Bronze ritual vessel, *yu*, early Western Zhou, eleventh century BC. The simple decoration of an eye with quilled extensions in the upper border, and of birds around the foot, is in Style IV. A *yu* of this shape has been excavated in Shaanxi. Height 10.5 cm.

69 *right* Rubbing of the decoration on a *gui* excavated in Shaanxi province, early Western Zhou, eleventh century BC. This rather baroque bird is unlike those found on bronzes from Henan.

used for the *taotie* to birds, and indeed only rarely showed creatures other than the *taotie* with two bodies. The Zhou casters, however, not only used conventions suitable for the *taotie* for birds, but also applied the same logic to other creatures including the buffalo — the buffalo is shown with a single head and two bodies on a *lei* from Peng xian in Sichuan, an area in which Zhou styles were also current. The Zhou certainly emulated the Shang, but the inventiveness of such bronzes demonstrates their considerable independence of the Shang tradition at the time of the conquest.

Excavations in the western part of Shaanxi, in the Qishan area, have also thrown further light on the relationship between the Shang and the Zhou during the period before the conquest. A complex of buildings has been found, presumably the royal palace, in what is thought to have been the homeland of the Zhou. Most important of all a large group of oracle bone fragments, some of them inscribed, have been excavated in a storage cellar under part of the main buildings. This is a surprising find in that, after their conquest of the Shang, the Zhou did not continue to inscribe the oracle bones. During this earlier period they must have been sufficiently under Shang influence to follow the practice current at Anyang. Preliminary reports indicate that the divination topics on the bones include many familiar from finds from Shang sites: sacrifices, good fortune, expeditions, hunting, warfare, and harvest. One oracle bone records that King Wen of the Zhou sacrificed to a Shang king, and another records the visit of a Shang king to Shaanxi.

Several circumstances might explain the presence of the inscribed oracle bones at Qishan. The Zhou may indeed have been dependants of the Shang and would have adopted their divination methods. Alternatively the marriage, recorded in a later text, between a Zhou prince and a Shang princess who became the mother of King Wen, might account for the piety that he showed in offering sacrifices to a Shang king. However, it is also possible that the Zhou did not generally follow Shang practice quite so slavishly. The Shang kings, on the other hand, are known from the oracle bones to have travelled extensively, presumably as a means of enforcing their power over their territory and the adjacent areas. The oracle bones, especially those inscribed, may therefore have been a product of the times when the Shang visited these areas or attempted to exert political influence in this region. They may even imply that the Zhou people were becoming assertive and a threat to Shang power. By the time the Zhou conquered the Shang, they had moved their capital from Qishan to the area of Xian. During their dynasty they extended their rule over a wide area, controlling more territory than had the Shang.

Excavations

The archaeological evidence at our disposal, relating to the Western Zhou period, cannot be used to set a framework for the whole three hundred years of this first section of the Zhou dynasty. The textual record is of more importance and offers much detail for the understanding of events of the Western Zhou period. None the less, the excavations of Western Zhou sites are extensive and have provided abundant information. The area around the present day city of Xian has been sporadically excavated. Of the five capital cities which the Western Zhou are said to have established in the region over a long span of time, two, Hao and Feng, have been tentatively identified. Sites near villages on both sides of the river Feng, near Xian have been examined, and remains of houses, burials, chariot-burials, workshops, and bronze hoards have come to light. A complete sequence in the typology of the artefacts and in the forms of tomb construction has been put together from the large number of burials excavated in the area. In so doing, it has proved possible to use the changes which can be observed in the development of the ceramic forms to delineate five main phases of Western Zhou occupation of this area. The different habitation sites and workshops have been dated by comparing the ceramics excavated in these areas with this postulated sequence. These excavations have also shown that, despite the political upheaval, many aspects of Chinese culture remained essentially as before. The use of ritual bronzes and jades in

70 Plan of a shaft tomb, early
Western Zhou, excavated near
Peking. In addition to bronze and
pottery vessels, the grave contained
the body of an attendant or slave
buried with the main occupant.

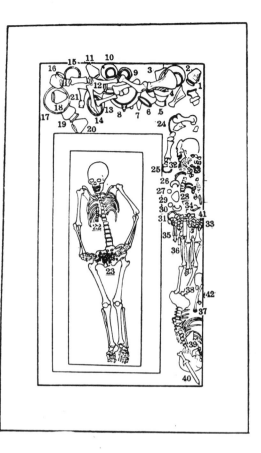

ceremonies, and of the halberd and the chariot in warfare, are examples of
this continuity. The shaft tomb, the main form of Shang burial, continued to
predominate (70).

The influence of the Western Zhou can be followed beyond the main seat
of power across northern China. Both tombs and bronze hoards have been
found, not only in the principal areas of Zhou power in Shaanxi and Shanxi,
but also in the old Shang territory of Henan and Shandong. In Henan, the
construction of a walled city near present-day Luoyang was of administrative
and military importance. Far to the north, bronzes and a chariot burial have
been found near Peking, and several groups of bronzes have come to light in
Liaoning. These remains lie within what was formerly the minor state or
dependency of Yan. In the south, extraordinary types of bronze have been
excavated at sites along the Yangtze valley: at Dantu in Jiangsu, Tunxi in
Anhui, and at Qichun and Jiangling in Hubei.

While the bronzes found in the extreme north are usually related to, if not
imported from, the main metropolitan centres, those found at the southern

sites show important divergences from the main Western Zhou types. The vessel shapes and surface decoration of the bronzes from these southern areas were clearly made with a knowledge of the metropolitan forms, but they have idiosyncratic and individual features which are a result of local interests and inclination. Designs on some show the influence of the local traditions of pottery with impressed repetitive geometric designs. Thus the *taotie*, for example, was modified and transformed as it was submerged beneath the imposition of such geometric motifs (see p. 151). It would appear that the north was firmly under central control, while the influence of the Zhou was less strong in the south and therefore, perhaps, less direct. At the same time, finds of similar high-fired ceramics at Luoyang in the north, and at Tunxi in the south, illustrate that an exchange of techniques, ideas, and trade took place.

Textual evidence

The texts of the Western Zhou period include two of the most important documents of early China: the *Shu Jing*, a collection of historical documents of varying date, and the *Shi Jing*, the earliest anthology of Chinese poetry, brought together *c.* 600 BC. This collection of poetry also includes poems of an earlier date. These two sources, both of a comparatively late date in the Western Zhou, are supplemented by a group of long inscriptions on bronze vessels. Such inscriptions record sacrifices and offerings to ancestors, and describe major acts of war or similar events. An inscription cast on a vessel, known as the *Li gui*, excavated in Shaanxi in 1976, records the Zhou conquest, also of course the subject of much of the *Shu Jing*. It illustrates dramatically the importance of such inscriptions as historical documents. The largest group records the king's charges or commands by which he exercised his authority, and the gifts that were exchanged on such occasions. Among the inscriptions on bronzes in the British Museum, those on the *Kang Hou gui* and the *Xing Hou gui* are particularly important (colour III, IV).

From the *Shu Jing*, the poetry, and the inscriptions, it is possible to reconstruct both an outline of the historical events of the Western Zhou period and a description of some of the main aspects of government, ritual, and belief. To take the historical events first: after King Wu had overthrown the Shang, so the records explain, he divided the lands he now ruled into the eastern and western territories, the eastern comprising the ancient Shang domain and the western the former Zhou lands. Over the east he set up Wu Geng, a descendant of the Shang royal family, together with three of his own brothers. This appointment may indicate a degree of respect for Shang religion, for by continuing to live in this area the Shang descendants were able to continue the Shang sacrifices. To the west he assigned the Dukes of Zhou and Shao.

The reign of King Wu was brief and he was followed by a minor, King Cheng, who during the first part of his reign lived under the regency of his uncle, the Duke of Zhou. In the later Zhou period, when ministers and advisers were of great importance in the administration, the Duke of Zhou was looked to as a model. He was probably not revered in quite this way in his lifetime. The Duke figures prominently in the *Shu Jing*, and the speeches attributed to him set out the principles of government as conceived by the Zhou.

One of the most important events of this period was a so-called rebellion of the eastern counties under Wu Geng. Although this may indeed have been a rebellion, the initial conquest of the Zhou had been far from complete, and a continual and gradual campaign of pacification was necessary in a vast land, unevenly populated, with different centres of power.

One of the two most important inscribed vessels in the collection, the *Kang Hou gui*, can be related to these further campaigns caused by unrest. The inscription (71) mentions the attacks on the Shang and then goes on to record that the Marquis of Kang, Kang Hou, was assigned to the territory of Wei. A relative of Kang Hou, with the office of *situ*, was associated with him in his duties and was instrumental in the casting of the vessel to commemorate the occasion. Since the rebellion of the Shang people took place during the reign

71 Rubbing of the inscription cast inside the bottom of the *Kang Hou gui* (colour III). The bold, elegant, characters are characteristic of the calligraphic style of bronze inscriptions of the first part of the early Western Zhou.

of King Cheng, the vessel was probably cast in his reign and is a significant contemporary historical document. Not only does it record an important historical event, but it illustrates the manner and circumstances in which a great noble was assigned to a particular area, presumably to govern and control it, by means of a 'charge' or command.

The second important event of this period was the establishment of a second capital in the east. This move came about as one of the results of the progressive advance of the Zhou conquest. Control of the area required a seat of authority in the east, the primary seat of Zhou power being in the west near the present-day city of Xian. The new city was founded near Luoyang, and some of the Shang were moved there away from their own base. Such wholesale transfer of large groups of people was used throughout Chinese history, both to control disaffection and to man the frontiers.

The reigns of King Cheng and his successor King Kang saw the consolidation and the high point of Western Zhou power; or so it appears today, for it is to these reigns that many of the documents of the *Shu Jing* refer. From these decades also date the most important of the bronze inscriptions. The reigns of King Zhao and King Mu were noted particularly for campaigns against the eastern and southern peoples. After this period, contact with the southern regions seems to have been drastically reduced, perhaps because the peoples living there were no longer a significant military threat. Of the kings of the later Western Zhou, King Gong's reign is important for innovations in bronze design, and the period of King Li is associated especially with difficulties with the great land holders. After a brief interval followed the long reign of King Xuan and finally that of King You.

The Zhou who thus came to take the place of the Shang had a detailed mythology about their origins. This is mainly to be found in poetry. For example, the distant ancestor of the Zhou, Hou Ji, is claimed as the inventor of agriculture and described in the *Shi Jing*:

> Truly Hou Ji's husbandry,
> Followed the way that had been shown,
> He cleared away the thick grass,
> He planted the yellow crop.
> It failed nowhere, it grew thick,
> It was heavy, it was tall,
> It sprouted, it eared.
> It was firm and good,
> It nodded, it hung,
> He made house and home in Tai.
>
> (*Shi Jing*, Mao 245, translated by Arthur Waley,
> *Book of Songs*, p. 242).

Of his descendant Dan Fu, who is said to have led the Zhou into Shaanxi province, it was written:

> So he halted, so he stopped.
> And left and right
> He drew the boundaries of big plots and little,
> He opened up the ground, he counted the acres
> From west to east;
> Everywhere he took his task in hand.
>
> They raised the outer gate;
> The outer gate soared high.
> They raised the inner gate;
> The inner gate was very strong.
> They raised the great earth-mound,
> Whence excursion of war might start.
>
> (*Shi Jing*, Mao 237, trans. Waley, p. 248).

Indeed it was Dan Fu and his descendants who are thought to have had their capital at Qishan where the recent finds of oracle bones have been made.

King Wen, named in the quotation at the head of this chapter, was venerated as the founder of the fortune of the Zhou:

> King Wen is on high
> Oh he shines in Heaven
> Zhou is an old people
> But the charge is new
> The land of Zhou became industrious
> Blessed by God's charge
> King Wen ascends and descends
> On God's left and on his right.
>
> (*Shi Jing*, Mao 235, trans. Waley, p. 250).

Although the consolidation and organisation of the Zhou may be attributed to King Wen, he was not the conqueror of the Shang. His son, King Wu, the 'martial' king, made the actual conquest. None the less, despite the activities of King Wu, great veneration was accorded King Wen as the founder of the Zhou fortunes, and as the man who gained the approval of Heaven, or *Tian*, the force or power which from this point appears all important. This respect for *Tian* should be contrasted with the Shang veneration of *Shang Di* with which it came to be combined.

The respect for King Wen suggests that the Zhou were intent on emphasising the distinctiveness of their rule, and on keeping it separate from that of the Shang. It would have been possible to claim instead that King Wu took over from the Shang as a legitimate descendant from common ancestors. Such descent could have been emphasised by the perpetuation of sacrifices to the dead Shang kings. The veneration of King Wen, a Zhou ancestor, appears to be part of a general challenge of the Shang right to rule.

The reasons given for the Zhou success under the guidance of King Wen were the depravity of the Shang and their consequent loss of the 'Mandate of Heaven'. This is the most important political concept to be discussed in the texts of this period. A man or people received the mandate only if they were righteous. The Shang, the Zhou claimed, lost their right to rule because they had been dissolute and gone against the wishes of Heaven. It had been lost in the distant legendary past by other rulers, and could in turn be lost by the Zhou.

A new note of morality was here introduced. *Shang Di* and the other spirits worshipped in Shang times appear to have been morally neutral. Once it was thought that *Tian* had adopted the Zhou because of their virtue, a new force had entered into the political calculation. Drink was regarded as the peculiar vice of the Shang. They, the Shang, following the apparent practice among peoples of the eastern Neolithic cultures, may have laid emphasis on alcohol and inebriation as a necessary part of ritual. The prevalence of Shang drinking vessels, the *gu* and *jue* at least suggests, as do the documents, that alcohol was more than ordinarily important:

He [the last Shang king] was greatly excessive in wine. He did not think of ceasing his licentiousness. His heart was malign and he was unable to fear death. Crimes existed in the city of Shang and in the states of Yin, but for the extinction he had no anxiety. It was not (so) that fragrant offerings (made with) virtue ascended and were perceived by Heaven; greatly the people were resentful and the crowds intoxicated themselves, and the rank smell was perceived on high. Therefore Heaven sent down destruction on Yin and had no mercy for Yin, it was due to his excesses. Heaven is not tyrannical, people themselves draw guilt upon themselves. (*Shu Jing, Jiu Gao*, trans. Karlgren, *BMFEA* 22, p. 45).

or again:

'. . . it was that they did not reverently attend to their virtue and so they prematurely renounced their mandate.' (*Shu Jing, Shao Gao*, trans. Karlgren, *BMFEA* 22, p. 49).

This concept of the mandate of Heaven by which the king was charged with the government of the State was paralleled by the charge which the king in turn laid on the nobles and landowners to govern or organise parts of his territory on his behalf. A specific instance of this practice has already been illustrated in the discussion of the *Kang Hou gui* (see p. 95).

The charge or command, from the Chinese *ling*, that a lord laid on his retainer, was the most important element in the method by which the king and below him the great landowners controlled their territory. This charge was two-sided in that it gave both parties obligations. The lord would lay a charge on a retainer to perform some task and give him land, servants, and goods to enable him to finance these duties. In return the retainer had an obligation to carry out the task and to continue to offer his services to the lord, notably in rendering tribute and military aid.

A four-handled basin, the *Xing Hou gui* [also known as the *Jing Hou gui* or the *Zhou Gong gui*] (colour IV), has a famous inscription referring to such a charge. This vessel, cast in the early Zhou period, has been much discussed, and the translation of the inscription is still debated. Its general meaning is clear, and concerns the issue of a decree by the king, by which the Marquis of Xing was granted control of three groups of peoples. In return, the Marquis of Xing offered formal thanks to the king and reiterated his loyalty, commemorating the occasion by casting the bronze in honour of the Duke of Zhou.

This inscription anticipates those on later Western Zhou vessels. Such later inscriptions record the occasions when officials were invested with their offices. They also describe the gifts which formed an essential element in the granting of office. In addition to land and retainers, such gifts might include jade, cowries, spirits, and weapons. Gifts were obviously a necessary part of the transaction, being at one and the same time transfers of land and retainers, the provision of military equipment, and possibly also a form of trade. All gifts created or recognised responsibilities:

You should carefully record (which of) the many princes bring offerings; and you should also record those who do not bring offerings. In the offerings there are many courtesies; if the courtesies are not equal to the objects (offered), it may be said to be no offering. (*Shu Jing, Luo Gao*, trans. Karlgren, *BMFEA* 22, p. 52).

This passage enshrines the concept later known as *li*, the idea that the correct offering will get the correct reward, and that the correct reward demands due return. Under the Shang, such a system of offering and gifts had existed between monarch and ancestor; under the Zhou, the gifts and services were exchanged between ruler and dependant. In many instances this was a relationship between the king and his relatives, and thus the obligations of both parties were reinforced by the family bond. Such obligations were, it appears, intended to be hereditary, for the obligations of descendants are also mentioned in the bronze inscriptions. The ideas of righteousness sanctioned by Heaven, and the observance of proper relationships between men and men, expressed by gifts, were the principles which made possible the organisation of the state both for peace and for war.

An example of such organisation is seen in the creation of small states as buffers against hostile groups such as the northern nomadic tribes. The state of Yan, established near Peking, acted as such a buffer. It is clear that even these distant areas had ties with the Zhou capital. For in this area, as has been noted, hoards of bronze vessels have been found, many of which are cast in shapes and with decoration which belong to the metropolitan tradition. Far-flung the empire may have been, yet this was no provincial outpost but an important section of the state in close contact with the capital.

Warfare

Conquest and political control have been mentioned already as the subjects of some of the most important Western Zhou texts. In the poetry of the *Shi Jing* there is also a glimpse of the personal hardships imposed on men. In some instances war is portrayed as a matter of grief, endurance, exile, and death:

> Minister of War
> We are the king's claws and fangs.
> Why should you drive us on from misery to misery,
> Giving us no place to stop in or take rest.

> (*Shi Jing*, Mao 185, trans. Waley, p. 118).

The Zhou had taken the Shang state by war, but it still remained to gain full control over their kingdom.

First there were the prolonged campaigns to the south and east. Later the nomadic tribes to the west became an increasing threat, until finally they drove the Zhou eastwards from their western capital in 771 BC. The Zhou, therefore, had to maintain permanent armies of foot soldiers and chariots. The armoury of dagger-axes (72) the bows and arrows (35) show that the Zhou used weapons similar to those of the Shang.

Chariots were admired, no doubt, because they were associated with wealth and power:

> The war-chariots were well balanced
> As though held from below, hung from above.
> Our four steeds were unswerving
> Unswerving and obedient.

> (*Shi Jing*, Mao 177, trans. Waley, p. 127).

III *above* Bronze ritual vessel, the *Kang Hou gui*, early Western Zhou period. The vertical ribbing and the bands of roundels alternating with 'stars' are derived from Shang vessels. The majestic proportions and the flamboyant handles are Zhou innovations. The vessel was probably cast in the Henan region and lacks the eccentric details of bronzes from Shaanxi province. Height 21 cm, width 42 cm.

IV *below* Bronze ritual vessel, the *Xing Hou gui*, early Western Zhou period. The smooth, sagging outline should be contrasted with the upright profile of the *Kang Hou gui* (colour III). The body is decorated with two elephants with broad spirals on their bodies. Around the foot rim are reticulated dragons in thin ridged relief. A *gui* decorated with similar elephants has been excavated from a site near Peking. Height 19 cm.

72 Bronze dagger-axe, early Western Zhou. The decoration includes a small plastic animal head. Length 25.4 cm.

But chariots cannot have been very practical. It must have been impossible to take large numbers of them long distances to campaigns on the frontiers. Ruts in poor roads, bad terrain, the summer rains with floods, and broad rivers would have completely incapacitated them. None the less, as with the Shang, they were a symbol of the might of king or lords. Indeed, the burial of chariots with complete teams of horses and their drivers demonstrates as much. The wooden chariot, which in shape the Zhou took over from the Shang, would have glistened with bronze. Straight bands decorated the sides of the box, and bronze parts were used as components of the axle and the harness. In the early Western Zhou, the most important and decorative section of the axle was a round shaft-holder attached near the box of the chariot with its flat flange lying along the axle towards the wheels (73). On the other side of the wheel was the axle cap, kept in place by a linchpin. Such axle caps became shorter during the centuries of the Western Zhou. At the same time, the shaft fitting was replaced by a somewhat larger and completely circular set of bronze fittings.

The system of yoking the horses to a cross-shaft had always been important, and a bronze fitting in the shape of an inverted V was used for this purpose, reinforced at the top by a boss or tube. At a later date, the other two ends of this V-shaped yoke were decorated with two finials. A jingle was attached to this yoke and shaft complex. The actual harness of the horses was richly ornamented with a frontlet at the centre of the face (74), and bronze ornaments forming a mask on the eyes and nose. A further mask was often mounted above the ears. The thongs of the harness were decorated with beads, cowries,

v Bronze ritual vessel, *zhi*, middle Western Zhou period, tenth century BC. The plumed birds are particularly fine. Some excavated examples are decorated with a more staccato version, while later forms are shown in broader ribbons. Height 19.7 cm.

73 *above* Bronze fitting, early Western Zhou. Such fittings were used to decorate the shafts of chariots. The coiled dragons on this bronze are seen on some of the earliest Zhou bronzes, presumably cast in Shaanxi. They can be compared with dragons on bronzes from Gaojia-bao in Shaanxi. These dragons are shown with a ridge emphasising the coil. Length 20.2 cm.

74 *left* Bronze horse frontlet, early Western Zhou. A similar ornament, which lay along the nose of a horse, has been excavated near Peking. Height 20 cm.

75 *below* Bronze bit with two cheek-pieces, middle Western Zhou. Width 17 cm.

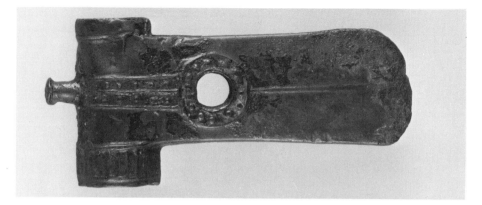

76 Bronze dagger-axe with tubular socket, Western Zhou period. Similar axes have been excavated near Peking and in Liaoning province. Length 15.6 cm.

or bronze plaques, and passed through decorated cross-tubes. A bit with rectangular cheek-pieces was used from the late Shang period. By the end of the Western Zhou this plain form had been elaborated, and a great variety of designs, particularly of coiled dragons, was in use (75). These copious and often hampering bronze ornaments underline the ceremonial nature of the chariot, which must have been an awesome sight. The charioteer was always armed, and in the burials is usually found with bow and arrows, dagger-axe, and short knife.

Such knives recall the earlier discussion (see p. 51) of the relationship of the peoples of the centre of China with those on the periphery. The contact and conflict continued throughout the Western Zhou. Weapons found in the northern and north-western areas of China, in Hebei province and Inner Mongolia, illustrate the results of this interaction. Small knives or daggers continued to be important, particularly as such weapons were to be useful to peoples who came to live a mobile nomadic life on horseback. Many of the types in use resemble those of the Karasuk culture of south Siberia. Daggers with hollow handles and animals on the pommel are characteristic of Hebei province. In place of the more usual Chinese halberd, the peoples of this peripheral area used an axe with tubular socket. The blade was either elongated and rounded, or almost circular (76).

Bronze vessels

The Western Zhou period as a whole saw the reversal of the two major stylistic developments of the bronze vessels of the Shang dynasty. While the forms of vessels became in general more complicated throughout the centuries of Shang rule, those of Zhou were initially very complex and were gradually simplified. A similar trend can be observed in the decoration. From the relatively abstract patterns of the bronzes of the Zhengzhou period developed the explicit designs, some apparently depicting specific animals, of the late Shang period. In the Western Zhou, on the other hand, the designs were first elaborated, then rendered in progressively more abstract and simplified forms. Those vessels which can be accurately dated by their inscriptions enable the pace of these changes to be documented with some precision. However, it is clear that the development was far from uniform. New styles were introduced and then, as in the Shang period, existed alongside older ones.

The bronzes of the Western Zhou are most conveniently discussed in three main groups or phases. These phases correspond to the early, middle, and late stages of the Western Zhou. The three stages will be outlined and then discussed in greater detail:

STAGE I   The early Western Zhou: the reigns of King Wu, King Cheng, King Kang and King Zhao. The bronzes are very varied in form and decoration. There are three main groups: a) bronzes in the late metropolitan Shang tradition; b) bronzes in a flamboyant Zhou style; c) bronzes that retain traces of their origin in earlier Shang traditions. All three groups show the exploitation of existing bronze styles.

STAGE II   The middle Western Zhou: the end of the reign of King Zhao, the reigns of King Mu and King Gong. The bronzes of this stage are best known for their smooth shapes and their decoration of birds. They represent the creation of a new style, with an emphasis on decoration executed in narrow modulated ribbons.

STAGE III   The late Western Zhou: from the reign of King Li to the reign of King You. Bronzes of this stage are decorated with bold abstract patterns. The source of these patterns is to be found both in designs already current in Stage I, and also in the methods of transforming decoration used in Stage II. The use of abstract patterns was part of a revival of earlier bronze traditions.

The great variety in the bronzes of Stage I was a consequence of the different and quite distinct origins of bronze styles of that time. Metropolitan Shang tradition was necessarily an important source. Once the Zhou had conquered Shang territory, they controlled their bronze casters and patronised their foundries. Some early Western Zhou bronzes are, as a result, almost indistinguishable from those of the late Shang. Others, while being cast in the Shang tradition, show small and sometimes important differences. A *fang ding* belongs to this latter category (77). It has a rectangular body set upon four slender legs with decoration in sunken line. This vessel shape evolved continuously throughout the period of the Shang and early Western Zhou, changing from a comparatively deep vessel on short and fairly thick legs to one with a much shallower body on high and slender legs. A *taotie* face at the centre of each panel is derived from Shang Style v decoration, seen for example on the *you* (48). The ears of

77 Bronze ritual vessel, *fang ding*, early Western Zhou. The exaggerated curling horns of the *taotie*, and the hooks that fringe them, are features that were popular in the latter part of the early Western Zhou. Height 21.9 cm.

the *taotie* are slightly incongruous as they are turned back-to-front. Even more unusual are the flamboyant S-shaped horns, fringed with small hooks. The form of these horns is taken from the small dragons sometimes used as horns of the *taotie* on Shang vessels, as on the *fang yi* (colour I). On the *ding*, all reference to the zoomorphic character of the dragons has been lost and the hooks added instead to enliven what might otherwise have seemed a dull detail. Small hooks are seen on some Anyang bronzes, but here they are used in greater profusion than was characteristic of Shang practice. In other respects the decoration conforms to Shang traditions, both in the details of the small dragons on either side of the *taotie*, and in the careful separation of the panels by ridges and flanges. Indeed, in vessels of this character the clearly articulated bronzes of the Shang survived the conquest.

However, the bold and almost eccentric horns on the *taotie* on the *ding* (77) are in keeping with the bronze-casting traditions that the Zhou preferred. Bronzes of the conquest period that can be associated with the Zhou have been found not only in Shaanxi, the ancestral homeland of the Zhou, but also in the provinces of Sichuan, Gansu, and Liaoning. This geographical area forms a broad arc to the west and north of the central area that was occupied by the Shang. A *gui* decorated with a bird characteristic of this provincial bronze-

78 Bronze ritual vessel, *fang ding*, early Western Zhou. The bird design is similar to, if less elaborate than, that on a *gui* excavated in Shaanxi province (69). A small head inserted in the main panel on the central axis is also a feature of Zhou design. The vessel may therefore be a product of the ancestral Zhou homeland in Shaanxi, which lay at the heart of the Zhou kingdom. Height 22.2 cm.

casting tradition has already been mentioned (69). This is not an isolated example of a bronze decorated with the Shaanxi bird. The same bird is seen on a *zun* found in the same area, and it is also known on a number of bronzes in museums, including a *fang ding* in the collection (78). Just as this bird can be differentiated from birds on bronzes of the Anyang tradition, so other Zhou motifs can be distinguished from their Shang counterparts. The most important of these designs is a dragon with a bold coiled body, seen on a chariot fitting (73). It appears on a number of vessels excavated in Shaanxi province, but is never seen on bronzes that belong to the Shang tradition. On the vessels, the dragon is paired with another, facing it, about a central axis. Both dragons have their gaping jaws facing forwards towards each other, rather than downwards, as in this example. This pair of dragons had its origin in the Shang *taotie* face executed in the relief form of Style v: each dragon is derived from half of the face. However, these dragons bear little or no resemblance to the two dragons in the Anyang tradition, formed from the two parts of the *taotie* face as seen earlier on a *li ding* (54, see p. 75). Indeed, at first it is difficult to establish a connection with the *taotie* face. Two features indicate that the origin of the motif can be found in the *taotie*: the teeth in the gaping jaws, and the pronounced eyebrow seen on most examples of the group. These two details are seen, of course, on the *taotie*, and are almost never found on the more usual kinds of Shang dragon. On the chariot fitting, the head of the dragon is turned down and the jaw lies in the place that would have been occupied by the jaw of the *taotie*. On the vessels, the position of the motif is slightly changed, and the head of the dragon is moved through ninety degrees so that the jaws open forwards towards the other dragon. With this change in direction, the eye and eyebrow (here indicated by no more than a slight moulding) were turned on their side. The conspicuous coiled body is possibly the outcome of the transformation of the large curved horn, in the form of a bird's tail, seen on some forms of the *taotie*. It often embraces a smaller coil derived from the body of the creature. All the examples of this motif are in relief, and many are enhanced by a narrow ridge or spine, a treatment that added considerable clarity to such designs and was very popular with the Zhou.

Neither the bird designs nor indeed the coiled dragons filled the available areas quite so completely as the *taotie* patterns would have done. The effect of these designs was simple and bold, but, because they were more specific, they were much less flexible than the *taotie*. The casters, therefore, recalling perhaps the complex Shang designs that must have been their model, inserted extra elements to add density to the decorative schemes. So it came about that small heads, which on Shang bronzes were traditionally placed in subordinate borders, were sometimes added to the main panels of design on Zhou bronzes (78). This practice contributed to the progressive breakdown of the architectonic schemes of bronze decoration favoured by the Shang. Despite this tendency to add a degree of confusion in the organisation of the decoration, bronzes from the Zhou area have a bold and indeed forceful character.

It is possible to go further and characterise the style associated with the Zhou as flamboyant. Many of the most famous bronzes in this style have large, projecting hooked flanges and beak-like extensions on the lids. A few remarkable vessels have large horizontal beams projecting from the sides. It is not certain, however, that all these vessels should be directly associated with the Zhou, either before or after the conquest. There may have been several centres producing rather flamboyant bronzes. On the other hand, even if some were made in other regions, such bronzes incorporated details that also became part of the Zhou bronze style. Prominent among such features are large animal heads with pronged horns used to decorate handles. After the Zhou conquest, bronzes of this character were influential in the former Shang area. The *Kang Hou gui*, found in Honan rather than Shaanxi, illustrates the impact of the flamboyant style on the bronze design of the ancient Shang centres (colour III). An unusually high foot with a vertical moulding was a new departure in keeping with Zhou preferences, and the treatment of the handles is equally bold. These are heavy and substantial, and are crowned by large projecting animal heads. In itself the decoration is not unusual, consisting of an area of narrow vertical ribbing below a border of alternating stars and roundels. These are carried out in clear relief with an assurance entirely typical of the Western Zhou.

Some of the bronzes made about the time of the conquest have a square stand or podium. Such stands were used especially for *gui* vessels. They are not characteristic of Shang bronzes and seem to have been a Zhou choice. The recently excavated *Li gui* is supported on such a podium. This *gui*, as already mentioned, is associated with the Zhou, not only because it was found in Shaanxi, but also because the inscription ·cast inside it mentions the Zhou conquest. The introduction of the square podium may be associated with the new popularity of certain vessel shapes, notably the *gui*, the *you*, and the cylindrical, or *gu*-shaped, *zun* (83). The pairing of the *you* and the *zun* was particularly favoured by the Zhou, and the importance of this combination is recorded by the survival of a bronze altar associated with a specific *zun* and a pair of *you*. A podium attached to a vessel may have been an alternative to such an altar. A discussion of the sources of this podium must also take account of a *zun* vessel, decorated in Style III, which stands on a square base of the same type. Although this bronze may belong to a fairly late stage in the Shang dynasty, its context is the provincial tradition of the south, which incorporated many middle Shang elements. There is, then, the suggestion that a possible source of this square podium is to be found in southern provincial bronze casting.

Indeed, several elements of the flamboyant Zhou bronze style appear to be derived from the south. However, as yet it is not possible to demonstrate with certainty the stages in the transmission of southern fashions to the north-west. Hooked and curly flanges are among the features which seem to indicate that some sort of contact between these two, rather distinct, bronze-casting traditions was important. Curly flanges are first seen on middle Shang bronzes found at Zhengzhou, and, as a consequence of the extensive influence of the Shang at this time, they are also found on southern bronzes. While straight flanges were used at Anyang in the later Shang, the hooked versions persisted in the south. Hooked flanges, on a modest scale, are also seen on a vessel of the Shang period found in Shaanxi. It seems probable that the hooked flanges of the middle Shang survived in provincial centres, and provided the model for the extraordinarily exaggerated flanges popular with the Zhou.

Other details, seen first on southern bronzes, and later on those of the Zhou, include the fully modelled dragon with a snake body, double-bodied animals, and some birds. Although these creatures are not unknown on bronzes from Anyang, they were certainly more prominent on southern bronzes. The flamboyant bronzes of the Zhou seem therefore to have important points in common with bronzes from other provincial centres as well as features derived from the metropolitan tradition. Although the precise locations of the provincial foundries is not known, bronzes related to the flamboyant Zhou tradition have been found in Shandong as well as in the south and in the north-west.

79 *left* Bronze ritual vessel *ding*, early Western Zhou. Not only is the hooked plumage on the birds unparalleled on bronzes known to be Shang, but details such as the wings, which are not correctly aligned with the head and body, demonstrate the provincial character of this bronze. Height 26.7 cm.

79a *right* Bronze ritual vessel, *gu*, late Shang dynasty. The Arthur M. Sackler Collections, New York. Around the foot of the vessel a *taotie* face is suggested by two confronted dragons: two prominent eyes are visible below S-shaped horns; the bodies are turned down unlike those of the more usual *taotie* (44). Below the eyes bold scrolls suggest the jaw of the *taotie*. Scrolls of this form were the source of the shape and position of the wings seen on the birds on the *ding* (79). Height 25.5 cm.

At a provincial centre, whose location is as yet unknown, were cast bronzes decorated with birds with plumage fringed with hooks. Such birds regularly appear in confronted pairs as on a *ding* (79), and are quite distinct from both the Shang bird and the Shaanxi bird discussed above. The most compelling feature of the motif is the row of insistent hooks along the flowing plume and tail; these add tension and interest to this strange and in some ways ungainly bird. Similar pattern-making effects are seen on the *fang ding* (77), and are a particular variant of the flamboyant style. This combination of a bold and identifiable motif with an elaboration of the outline by hooks was quite distinct from the earlier concern with pattern seen on Shang bronzes. On the bronzes of the Shang, decorated in Styles I, II, and III, the *taotie*, birds and dragons are seen to emerge from a complex of lines, but with this bird the bronze caster had started with a clearly defined motif that he had then worked back into a patterned surface by means of the hooks. This use of bold hooks can, however, be shown to be a reinterpretation of the cusped outlines of much earlier designs originating in Styles II and III that survived late into the Anyang period alongside Styles IV and V.

There are yet further relationships of this bird design to the main Shang tradition to be traced. An important feature is the position of the wing. This is strangely placed with the front of the wing pushed well forward so the tip arrives directly below the eye instead of in the natural position behind the head. Pairs of hooks at the breast and the claws draw the birds together so that the eyes, the wings and the claws form a unit and seem to refer to the eyes and jaw of a *taotie*. These birds are not, however, simply derived from a transformation of the *taotie*. Instead they appear to have been formed by analogy with dragon designs of the Shang. In the late Shang period not only had the *taotie* been divided into dragons (54), but new forms of the creature had been created by joining together confronted pairs of dragons. Such late variants of the *taotie* had down-turned tails rather than the more usual up-curved S-shaped body and tail (79a). On occasions the two dragons did not quite meet at the central line dividing them, but were drawn together by small projecting hooks. The birds on the *ding* seem to have been created by reference to earlier dragons: thus the hooks on the breasts of the birds are similar to those on the dragons, the wings so strangely aligned with the eyes are elaborated by analogy with scrolls shown beneath the eyes of the dragons, the down-turned tails of the birds follow the tails of the dragons, and their crests derive from the S-shaped horns of the dragons, having taken on the flowing line of the S-shaped plume of the Shaanxi bird. In this way the birds have replaced the dragons within the framework set by the original Shang motif. This bird design is known only from a few bronzes, but as one of these rare pieces is a *gui* on a square podium, a vessel shape associated with the Zhou, it may be presumed that the bird was in fact developed within the bronze tradition of the west and north.

The flamboyant style, which seems to have been prevalent at the time of the conquest and shortly afterwards, had been evolved in parallel with and as an alternative to the surviving architectonic relief style of the Shang. The Zhou had, however, broken with Shang traditions in the following ways: in the use of large hooked flanges and of square bases for some vessels, and in their preference for the motifs of birds and of dragons with coiled bodies. Yet more radical departures are seen in the use of the logic of a single head with two bodies, appropriate to the *taotie*, for other creatures, and in the disregard for the strict divisions of the horizontal registers by placing subordinate features within the main decorative register, thus crowding the main motif. These last two developments did most to erode the Shang traditions of bronze design.

While the bronzes of the flamboyant style can be seen as representing a significant break with Shang practice, an equally numerous group cast in the late Shang and early Western Zhou were more conservative, and indeed perpetuated features of middle Shang styles. The survival alongside each other of the five Shang styles was mentioned in the previous chapter. This has proved to be a very important phenomenon in the early Chinese bronze tradition. It appears that, as each style was invented, the increasingly elaborate designs developed in the new style were also carried out in the old one. For example, following the first primitive *taotie* designs in the thread relief of Style I, complicated spiral and hooked versions of the *taotie* face were developed and executed in the broad but modulated line of Style II. These more complex designs were at the same time rendered in the thread relief of Style I. Such elaborate versions of Style I were thus later in date than the simple Style I designs. Although, the bronze casters who continued to use Style I when Style II was in vogue were to some extent behind the times, they may have adhered to Style I because it was preferred in the region they inhabited. Certainly the centres of innovation in bronze design seem to have been situated in different regions at different times. Thus, complicated versions of Style I are found in Shaanxi, an area which seems to have been less advanced in its tastes than north-eastern China, where the Style II and III versions in generously modulated line were popular. When, at a later date, Anyang came to the fore in bronze casting, and Styles IV and V were developed, the earlier styles survived especially in provincial areas. Now not only thread-relief Style I was old-fashioned; so too were the modulated line designs of Styles II and III. This background is essential to the understanding of the so-called 'triple band' and related designs, an important group of decorative patterns of the late Shang and early Western Zhou.

The name 'triple band' is applied to registers of decoration, consisting of repeated elements each arranged in three narrow tiers. On a *gui* (80), each of these three tiers contains rows of spirals, with an eye in the central row at one end. At the other end the rows terminate in fins. The thin, wire-like thread relief is reminiscent of Style I, but the pattern is more complex than those of the true Style I, and is indeed an adaptation of the designs of Style II. Such spiral 'triple bands' were derived from the Style II designs, executed in thread relief, which were popular in Shaanxi. Another familiar form of the 'triple band' design includes rows of small upright quills, as on a *he* (81). Such quills could only have been derived from Style III, but are seen here again in thread relief. In this case it appears that the seemingly old-fashioned designs of the thread-relief versions of Style II were updated by a detail taken from a yet more advanced style. There are several other forms of the thread-relief 'triple band', including one in slightly broader line with an emphasis on hooks rather than spirals or quills. On *jue* vessels, the narrow bands

80 *above* Bronze ritual vessel *gui*, early Western Zhou. The lid of the basin is unusually tall. Fine scroll and quill designs, described as the 'triple band', are among the most common forms of decoration on early Western Zhou bronzes. Several vessels decorated in this way were excavated at one site near Peking, including a *gui* of similar shape missing its lid. Height 17 cm.

81 *right* Bronze ritual vessel *he*, early Western Zhou. The quill elaboration of the mask on this bronze is one of the most common versions of the 'triple band'. This type of lobed ewer is reminiscent of pottery vessels. Height 19.2 cm.

were sometimes butted up against one another to cover the whole vessel with decoration. The effect achieved was closely related to other forms of late versions of Style III and IV discussed below.

In addition to the thread-relief designs, there were important groups of patterns executed in the broader lines of Styles II and III. Although these patterns had originally been shown in a modulated line, the later patterns descended from them were generally executed in a more even, broad line. These designs could either be used to fill quite narrow bands, or to cover the larger areas of the side of a vessel. The broader versions were particularly popular on the *gui* and *zun* vessels. Although excavated evidence is not, as yet, very helpful, it seems probable that the designs were popular in both north-western and north-eastern China.

In turn, Style IV, with the main motifs shown against a *leiwen* background, produced its own late descendants. An important design consists of the *taotie* face, shown with long horizontal quills against a *leiwen* background. Although this design is popular on early Western Zhou bronzes, it was first seen on pieces cast at Anyang (44). Similarly confined to narrow bands are designs derived from patterns of dragons against a background of spirals. But more important were the *taotie* designs which in the late Style IV patterns could, like those descended from Style III, be used to cover the whole surface of a vessel. This form was particularly popular on the *he* vessels. In several examples the *taotie* face is outlined in smooth line among dense *leiwen*. This decoration refers back to the transitional forms bridging Styles III and IV as on the *jia* (53). At the time of the conquest there seems to have been an attempt to clarify some versions of these designs. As part of this effort, the outlined *taotie* was executed in spined relief, among the *leiwen*, and this in turn gave rise to a whole new group of decoration. Likewise the narrow bands of dragons, seen around the foot of a *zun* (83) were outlined, and rendered in spined relief so giving birth to the crested or reticulated dragon encircling the foot of the *Xing Hou gui* (colour IV).

One important outcome of this survival of the Shang styles was a range of patterns, based on a form of the *taotie*, in which all the elements were disjointed and separate. This variant of the *taotie* had first appeared in relief in a subgroup within Style V, as on the Shang *fang yi* (colour I). It was then adapted to late versions of Style IV, now appearing flush with the *leiwen* background, seen here on a Shang *jue* (82). This is an instance where developments made in a later style gave rise to new forms of design in one that already existed. This dismembered form of the *taotie* appears to have been adopted in both Shaanxi and Gansu, for *jue* vessels with baroque versions have been found in these two areas. A late Shang *zun* in the Art museum, Princeton University, is decorated with a comparable *taotie* face (83). The face has a broad cusped nose at

82 *left* Bronze ritual vessel, *jue*, late Shang dynasty. The decoration consists of the features of a *taotie* dissolved among *leiwen*. A *zun* with a similar design has been excavated in Shandong province. Height 19 cm.

83 *right* Bronze ritual vessel, *zun*, late Shang dynasty, in the Art Museum, Princeton University. The Arthur M. Sackler Collection. Around the centre is a design of a *taotie*; its dismembered features are shown against a *leiwen* background; around the foot are dragons with long beaks outlined in a smooth line among *leiwen*. Height 24.1 cm.

the centre, between slanting eyes with a somewhat lax outline. Above the eyes are eyebrows but no horns, and below are curved lines which remain from earlier representations of the jaw. The ears are likewise reduced to curved C-shapes. All these details are very flat, and flush with the *leiwen*, which fills the area between the different parts of the face. Behind the ear of the *taotie* is a further eye at the centre of a small motif consisting of projecting quills. This motif is derived from the small, somewhat abstract, dragon filler-designs seen on such Shang bronzes as the *yu* described in chapter three (45). The same motif, which had dropped out of use at Anyang, was found on Zhou bronzes, as on the *gui* from Wugong xian. On the *zun* it has been transformed into a bird with an S-shaped plume, a small beak, a large leg with a broad claw, and a quill apparently representing the tail. In this way a Shang motif was assimilated to the Zhou interest in bird patterns.

Around the foot of the *zun*, a border of dragons is treated somewhat differently. The creature shown is a dragon in profile, with a long curved beak or trunk, and an S-shaped plumed tail behind a narrow body enclosing an eye. A scalloped jaw, derived from the *taotie*, and a small claw are shown on the underside. This dragon is taken from Style III designs, such as those on the shoulder of the *pou* (47). Instead of being rendered in solid elements, as is the *taotie* around the centre of the *zun*, this dragon is outlined in a smooth line amidst the *leiwen*. In this it resembles the decoration of *he* vessels, mentioned above, derived from Style IV. The borders of small circles adopted from Style I are characteristic of many provincial vessels made in the Shang period. This tradition has been examined at some length, as it produced not only the 'triple band' and related designs, but also gave birth to new styles, particularly to new pattern-making styles, in the middle and late Western Zhou (see p. 119).

These later versions of the principal Shang styles, whether of late Shang or early Western Zhou date, are found on vessels with shapes derived from ceramics. Such bronzes were cast in smooth plain shapes and only rarely have flanges. Many of the forms that were popular, notably the tri-lobed vessels, the *li* and the *he*, had been important at a much earlier stage, in the middle Shang. It is tempting to associate the reappearance of these forms with the renewed popularity of the middle Shang decorative styles. Indeed the interest in middle Shang vessel shapes appears to be related to a concern with early forms of decoration. Moreover the *li* vessels, in particular, while not taken up at Anyang, seem to have remained popular in Shaanxi, as did the middle Shang decorative styles. The wide cylindrical *zun* also made its appearance following examples in ceramics (83). Again, inspiration from middle Shang vessels seems important. A short wide form of *gu* had been popular at Zhengzhou and Panlongcheng. Later Shang *gu* were slender and tall. At the very end of the Shang, wider versions of the *gu* were revived, now as a *zun* vessel, and appear to allude to the earlier shape.

This large group of bronzes in ceramic-related forms, decorated with the late versions of Shang Styles, can be contrasted with the more flamboyant bronzes described at the beginning of this chapter. However, like the other group, they contributed to the modification of the Anyang traditions of the Shang.

This transformation of Shang bronze traditions by the Zhou opened the way for the innovations of the second stage of the Western Zhou. Once again, the use of ceramic forms for bronze vessels was important. A goblet-shaped *zun* was prominent among the new forms introduced at this time (84). This wide vessel, with an S-shaped profile, on a short foot was ultimately derived from a pottery container of the late Shang period. The bronze form seems to have become important late in the reign of King Kang and to have become widespread during the reigns of King Zhao and King Mu. The earlier forms were comparatively tall and were followed by more compact versions. The form of *li* vessels was also altered by reference to ceramic examples, such as a *li* in the collection, excavated at Pudu cun (85). The striations on this *li* were quite easily produced in pottery and this sort of decoration was then imitated in bronze. The tomb at Pudu cun, which can be dated to the reign of King Mu, on the evidence of an inscription in a *he*, provides a useful reference point for this new concern with ceramic forms. Grooved pottery vessels have also been excavated from this tomb. Such pots were almost certainly decorated by turning the vessel, when nearly dry, on a wheel, while holding a sharp instrument against it. This would have cut narrow horizontal grooves, leaving wider, slightly convex areas between each groove. At first, bronze vessels were made in direct imitation of such ceramics, and had horizontal convex ribs between narrow grooves. However, it was natural to apply the technique used for decorating pottery to the pottery mould. Thus in the late Western Zhou the moulds came to have narrow grooves between shallow convex ribs, which, when used to cast the vessels, produced concave grooves on the bronzes (92).

These smooth bronzes of the middle Western Zhou were often attractively decorated with birds. Several different forms of bird were popular simultaneously, being derived from several separate sources. The Anyang and the Shaanxi traditions were both influential. From the Anyang bronzes were taken the neat compact birds with short tails turned down through a right angle, as on a *you* (86). Some birds resemble the dragon with a long sinuous

tail so closely that it seems evident that the dragon had been turned into a bird (84). Indeed, decoration of birds proliferated at this time, often taking the place of dragons. A particularly beautiful form of the bird had a long crest and tail that were elaborated to fill the whole area of a large panel of decoration, instead of just a narrow band (colour v). This bird, which generally has a reversed head, can be shown to be derived ultimately from the Shaanxi bird, and also appears to be related to a form of large S-shaped dragon popular at the beginning of the Western Zhou, best known from a basin excavated in Liaoning province. The exchange of one creature for another accounts for the disappearance of the dragon with the coiled body (73), and its replacement, during the reign of King Kang, by the elephant, as on the *Xing Hou gui* (colour iv). Just as the large plumed bird retained the general outline of the S-shaped dragon, so the elephant shows details that likewise recall the earlier motif. The spiral on the body of the elephant in spined relief is taken from the coil on the dragon.

The patterns of birds appear to have stimulated the creation of new forms of dragon design by analogy. Various dragon designs, confined to narrow bands, had always been known, including those executed in late forms of Style iv, as on the *zun*. The different forms of dragon were now rendered in narrow ribbon-like elements similar to those used for the bird with the dragon tail on the goblet-shaped *zun* (84). Indeed, this ribbon-like rendering may have been adopted to clarify designs that now seemed less clear and precise as the late versions of the Shang styles began to lose their appeal. This subjection of all available designs to the same ribbon treatment is a characteristic of the

84 *far left* Bronze ritual vessel, *zun*, middle Western Zhou, tenth century BC. This type of smoothly shaped wine vessel seems to have been derived from a ceramic vessel of the late Shang period. The birds seen here are derived from dragons with long sinuous bodies. Height 18.7 cm.

85 *left* Earthenware vessel, *li*, middle Western Zhou, tenth century BC, excavated at Shaanxi, Pudu cun. The form of this vessel proved very influential and many late Western Zhou *li* were cast in related shapes; compare (94). Height 14.6 cm.

86 *right* Bronze ritual vessel, *you*, early Western Zhou. The shape of this *you* recalls vessels of the Shang period (48), but the handle has been attached across the long rather than the short axis. In the next stage the height of the vessel was reduced in proportion to its width. Height 25 cm.

87 *above left* Bronze ritual vessel, *he*, middle Western Zhou. Several different types of Western Zhou *he* are known; this one is characterised by its three legs and pronounced lobes, and can be compared with a *he* excavated at Fufeng. Height 22.8 cm.

88 *above right* ritual vessel, *ding*, middle to late Western Zhou, tenth-ninth century BC. The S-shaped dragons, here shown without a *leiwen* background, are a simplified and later version of those on the *he* (87). Height 21 cm.

89 *below* bronze ritual vessel, *gui*, middle Western Zhou. A *gui* with similar profile and form of handles, dated to the twenty-seventh year of Mu Wang, corresponding to the mid-tenth century, has been excavated at Qishan in Shaanxi province. Height 15.7 cm, diameter 29.5 cm.

middle Western Zhou. No sooner had the S-shaped dragon been reformulated in narrow ribbons, with embellishment of fine quills or plumes, as in the upper border on the *zhi* (colour v), than the motif began to be simplified in several successive stages (87, 88).

It was during the middle Western Zhou that pattern making, the principal feature of the bronzes of the third stage, came to the fore. By contrast with much of the Shang period, there had, in the early Zhou, been significant attempts to clarify ornament rather than to exploit its ambiguity. None the less the potential for pattern making had always been there. It reappeared as a significant element in two forms in the middle Western Zhou. First, the newly developed motifs, the birds and the S-shaped dragons, immediately underwent changes that were directed towards increasing their ornamental qualities. A long-tailed bird on a *gui* illustrates this tendency (89). The tail of the bird is split off from the body, and the bird has begun to disintegrate into separate abstract elements. Second, the motifs of a much earlier period, primarily the *taotie*, became prominent, again in forms derived from the dismembered face seen on the *jue* and the *zun* (82, 83).

The *taotie* contributed to one of three major pattern groups, the other two consisting of S-shaped patterns taken from the dragon, the bird, and the eye and quills, and a series of wave patterns. Patterns derived from the *taotie* had the longest history. The dismembered form, popular in the north-west (83), was the source of the middle Western Zhou versions confined to narrow bands, seen, for example, on a *ding* excavated at Pudu cun (90). Here the separate, rather staccato, elements of the early form are drawn out in longer ribbons, and interlinked with one another. The connection of this new pattern with the early dismembered *taotie* is evident in that they both depend on an outline of the different features, rather than on an indication of a solid face. In versions of the late Western Zhou, the ribbons were further separated, and the references to the face became more obscure (91 bottom). Hooks on such late patterns recall the hooks and quills on the much earlier faces of the Shang period. At the same stage of the late Western Zhou, a different form of *taotie* pattern was also very popular (91 top). This difference is accounted for by the separate source from which it is descended. A continuous line around the eye remains from the combination of the two elements, the horn and the nose. This detail is seen on bronzes of the early Western Zhou in which completely recognisable forms of the *taotie* have been modified by reference to newly fashionable forms of plume, properly belonging to dragons rather than to the *taotie*. Indeed several vessels are known decorated with elaborate, but dismembered, *taotie* faces developed in parallel with the plumed dragon or bird designs. On the bronzes such patterns cover a large area instead of being confined to narrow bands.

The patterns formed from the bird and the S-shaped dragon were equally

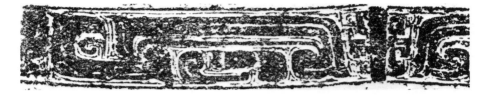

90 *above* Rubbing of the decoration on a *ding* excavated at Pudu cun, middle Western Zhou, tenth century BC. This pattern is based on the dismembered *taotie* face seen on earlier vessels; compare (83). Later versions of patterns derived from the *taotie* are shown below (91).

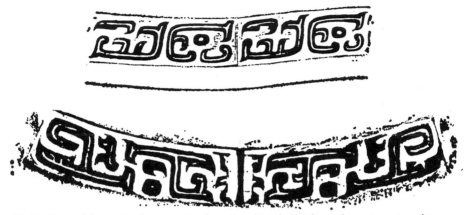

91 Rubbings of decoration from an *yi* and a *gui* excavated at Qishan, Shaanxi province, late Western Zhou. Both patterns are derived from the *taotie* face. *Above*, this example rearranges the *taotie* so that the two halves of the face, each identified by the eye, are turned in the same direction; the element of the pattern with no central eye derives from the extended body. *Below*, a more elaborate design shows the full face complete with two eyes and eyebrows, and with bodies on either side.

various. Several quite different designs were assimilated to each other complicating the story. For example the long-tailed bird with its head turned around became more closely identified with the S-shaped dragon. All these patterns were then rendered in simplified line with broader elements than before, and with less attention to narrow plumes (88). Related to this group were patterns derived from the eye and horizontal quills. It is not, however, always easy to decide what are the precise origins of a design. Interlocking g-shaped elements on a *gui* (92) may have been derived from the eye and quills, but it is also possible that they are a simplified form of the *taotie* seen on the *ding* from Pudu cun. The concern with patterns confined to narrow borders had led to an amalgamation of motifs from several sources into a reduced number of designs.

The third type of ribbon design is illustrated by the grand wave patterns on

92 Bronze ritual vessel, *gui*, late Western Zhou, ninth-eighth century BC. The concave grooves on this vessel imitate grooved pottery of the tenth century BC. Western Zhou bronze casters derived inspiration from ceramics both at this time and also at a very early stage in the dynasty. Height 23 cm.

93 Rubbing of the decoration on a *ding* excavated at Kezuo xian in Liaoning province, early Western Zhou. Below the band of *taotie* designs, a V-shaped pattern, possibly derived from cicadas, is given prominence by the use of a variety of spined relief. In other designs the same V-shaped scroll is transformed into a pair of confronted dragons.

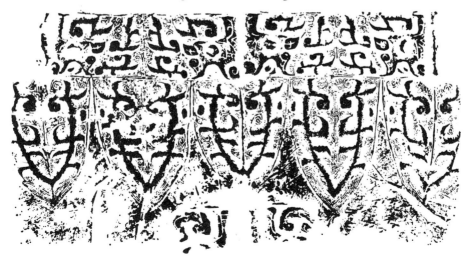

94 Bronze ritual vessel *li*, early Eastern
Zhou, eighth-seventh century BC. Vessels
in this shape, but with shorter legs, were
very popular in the late Western Zhou
period, and many examples have been
excavated in Shaanxi province. Dragon
designs on the Western Zhou pieces are
more rounded than the present example.
The angular version can be compared
with bronzes from the Eastern Zhou site
at Xinzheng. Height 13 cm.

the ninth century *hu* (colour VI). This design arose ultimately, and perhaps
rather unexpectedly, from the cicada and related decoration of the Shang
dynasty, (*yu* – see p. 65). On many Shang vessels the cicada is shown with
its tail pointing downwards. A typically early Western Zhou version of the
cicada design is seen on a *ding* excavated in Liaoning (93). Here the treatment
of the design has resulted in the emphasis on a linear pattern within each panel.
Such panels were also used to enclose pairs of confronted dragons. The full
sequence of progressively more abstract Zhou designs, to which these complex
motifs had given birth, can best be followed in the decoration on a group of
large basins which are not represented in the British Museum. On these basins
the V-shape of the panel was greatly enlarged to fill the whole height of the
vessel. The multiple changes in the design within each of these panels, resulting
in ever-increasing abstraction and simplification, were similar to other trans-
formations of designs in the tenth century. In addition to the use of the V-shaped
panel to contain a pair of confronted reticulated dragons, some panels enclosed
taotie designs. In the late tenth and ninth century, such designs within the
panels were rendered in ribbon patterns. The outline of the panels was joined
up to make the great waves, while the rest of the design was progressively
abstracted. The pair of confronted dragons is still, however, just visible within
some of the loops on the *hu*. A narrow border containing an undulating wave
pattern had already been known in the middle Western Zhou well before
the grand wave pattern was fully developed.

So far the three groups of design described have been confined to bands or
narrow registers. Sometimes they appear in a single band, at others in tiers
of registers. They had in this form an inherently dynamic progression around
the vessel. But all three groups, with their emphasis on ribbons and lines, had

the potential to be used in a different way. They could be developed to fill a broader area rather than a horizontal band. The panels of the *zhi* (colour v), which were completely filled by the plumed bird, show one way this was done. The main mechanism of change, however, was to concentrate on a section of a vessel and to alter the direction of the ribbons of decoration, turning them back on themselves and interweaving them. On a small lobed *li* (94) the shape of the vessel made it necessary to confine the design to a series of distinct areas, rather than arrange it in bands around the vessel as a whole. Some of the earliest excavated examples of such 'interlace' decoration have been found on this particular shape of vessel. Alternatively it is seen on small fittings in which the space to be filled is equally limited. This creation of the interlace was a momentous development with consequences that ramified throughout the Eastern Zhou period (see p. 149).

The changes that brought about the use of these abstract patterns on the bronzes of the late Western Zhou appear simple and logical. However, the success of these designs entailed the abandonment of the more specific bird or dragon motifs. This use of abstract patterns appears, therefore, to have been the result of deliberate choice rather than chance evolution. The reason for suggesting that this was indeed the case is the simultaneous appearance of certain vessel shapes with the use of the abstract patterns. Significant among these shapes were a *hu* or wine vessel of oval cross-section and the *gui* on the square podium, both vessel forms characteristic of the late Shang or early Western Zhou rather than the beginning of the late Western Zhou when, together with the new patterns, they gained in popularity. The *hu* was made for only a short period, but the *gui* on a podium remained in use into the Eastern Zhou. It would appear that emphasis was deliberately being given to earlier vessel shapes. At the same time, the vertical ribbing, seen on such early vessels as the *Kang Hou gui*, was given new prominence. In this context, the preference for abstract patterns, and especially those patterns derived from the *taotie*, can be seen as part of a concern with, and even a revival of, early bronze styles in which pattern making had been important.

Two approaches thus alternate in the creation of the bronze designs of the Western Zhou. Invention of new motifs and vessel shapes was important at the time of the conquest, and then again during the middle Western Zhou. Alongside, there was a persistent interest in the bronze decoration of the past, seen both in the 'triple band' decoration, and then later in the bold abstract designs on the bronzes of the late Western Zhou. Such preservation of ancient styles, and their recreation in new forms with a new life, was to remain an enduring feature of Chinese art. In this instance the return to abstract patterning made possible the inventions and discoveries of the Eastern Zhou bronze designs.

Bells

In the discussion of the decoration of ritual vessels, the southern industries, mentioned in the previous chapter, have not been considered in any detail. Bronze vessels must have been manufactured in the south into the Western Zhou period. As before, they followed the shapes of those made in north China. The decoration showed, however, idiosyncratic southern versions of designs originating in the north (119).

The south played a particularly important part in the manufacture of bells. Indeed, the southern industry provides the bridge or transition between the ceremonial bells used in the Shang period (95), and the development of graduated sets on which ceremonial music was played in the Eastern Zhou period (see p. 155). The shapes of these important musical instruments of this latter period are quite distinct from those of the Shang. As Virginia Kane has shown, two kinds of southern bell formed the link in the sequence of development between the Shang type and the bells of the Eastern Zhou.

The ancestors of the two southern types of bell were first, the Shang ceremonial bell, and second, the small harness bell. The Shang ceremonial bell had been mounted mouth upwards, and usually belonged to a graduated set of three, all struck by a hammer rather than by clappers. This ceremonial form was imitated in the south, where it is found decorated with designs that are related to the *taotie* on the double-ram *zun* (colour II). This survival in the south of a bronze bell, originating with the Shang, gave rise to later forms. The new versions retained the solid handle and the cup shape, but were hung the other way up. To enable them to be hung, when in this reversed position, a small loop was attached to the solid handle and the bells then hung obliquely. They were cast in graduated series. The bosses that are a constant feature on bells of this form also derive from the designs worked out on the southern examples. Such bells are found in northern tombs from the tenth century, when they seem to have been imported from the south. In the eighth and seventh centuries they came to be widely manufactured in the north.

In the early stages the other bell, the harness bell, was much smaller than the type just discussed. But subsequently, in the southern regions, large and very baroque examples hanging from a loop were cast, and they, like the other group, were struck from the outside. Some had large flanges incorporating birds in openwork. Only a few of this short-lived tradition of very large bells are known. Before the end of the Western Zhou, smaller bells without projecting flanges were evolved. In these, the shape taken from the harness bell was combined with decoration derived from that seen on the large bells with solid handles. An example from the second half of the Western Zhou period is in the collection (96 left). The meanders in sunken lines, decorating the two

95 *left* Bronze bell, late Shang dynasty, Anyang period, twelfth-eleventh century BC. Bells in graduated sizes were made in sets. Undecorated bells in this shape have been excavated from the tomb of Fu Hao at Anyang. Height 19 cm.

96 *right* Bronze bells, late Western Zhou. *Left*, from southern central China. *Right*, from north China. Height 14 cm, 17 cm.

S-shaped dragons and the central axis, are similar in style to those seen on many of the earlier southern bells, and indeed to that on the *taotie* face of the double-ram *zun* from Hunan. The S-shaped dragons on this small bell can be related to the abstract patterns on another bell of almost identical shape and size, and appear to be the prototype for this simple design (96 right). The second bell is similar to many excavated in northern China. The close relationship between these small southern and northern bells suggests that both the practice of casting bells, and the initial designs, were introduced into the north from southern China. This bell shape survived into the Eastern Zhou period (122).

Jades

Some Western Zhou jade carving can be compared with bronze decoration. A small pendant (97) has a pattern of S-shaped dragons similar to that on the bronzes of the second stage. An elaborate handle with birds and dragons, can also be related to middle Western Zhou bronzes (98). The plumed bird on the handle resembles the luxuriant birds on the *zhi* (colour v). Both jades demonstrate that skilled carving of the material not only survived the conquest but was further advanced under the Zhou. On the elaborate handle (98) and the *huang* pendant (97) pronounced bevelling of incised lines is used to enliven the designs. This was an innovation of the early Zhou period. The complex design of entwined creatures on the handle underlines the mastery with which the jade carvers of this period handled the material and the motifs.

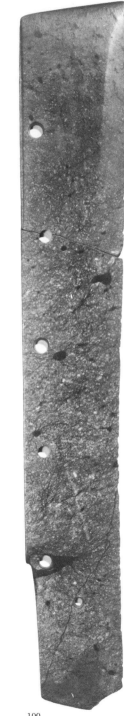

97 Jade pendant, *huang*, middle Western Zhou, tenth century BC, decorated with a neatly worked variation on the S-shaped dragon design (87). Confined to restricted areas on jades, such dragons were often shown with their bodies interlinked. Length 8.9 cm.

98 Jade handle with an incised design of a bird with two dragons, middle Western Zhou, tenth century BC. Ingenuity was needed to arrange three creatures in a small area. A subordinate dragon is placed behind the claw of the bird which stands on the head of the main dragon. Such designs contributed to the development of the interlace (117). Length 26 cm.

99 Jade bird, early Western Zhou. Length 6.5 cm.

100 Jade knife, Western Zhou. This elegant sceptre is descended from Shang and neolithic predecessors. On the neolithic pieces the holes served to attach a wooded grip, but here have no function. Length 37.6 cm.

98

100

Animal pendants or amulets likewise show a new liveliness that was an advance on the rather more stiffly formal qualities of the animals and birds of the Shang period. Stags, hares, and birds are shown in more varied and natural poses in which the movement and motion of the particular animal is captured (colour VII). Jade birds, in parallel with those in bronze decoration, became as widespread as jade fishes had been in the Shang dynasty. The close relationship of such birds (99) to the earlier fishes is seen in their long tails, bifurcated at the end like those of fishes, and in the unlikely addition of fins. These animal amulets were particularly popular shortly after the conquest, and had almost disappeared, with the exception of the still ubiquitous fish, by the time of the fall of the Western Zhou capital in the eighth century BC.

In other respects the jade-carving tradition remained conservative. The simple ceremonial implements still contained allusions to their Neolithic prototypes. Despite the cut-away portion making the handle or grip of a vertical blade (100), the general shape of a sceptre, and holes along one edge, are the direct descendants of the same features of the horizontal Neolithic knife with its holes along the upper edge (see p. 59). Jade discs likewise continued to be important both in the ritual of daily life and in burial.

Conclusion

The Zhou people had taken over the traditions of a strong and highly advanced state. Some, or even a large degree of, continuity was inescapable, as the Zhou had probably borrowed much of their culture before the conquest from the Shang. At the same time, the culture of the late Shang period, particularly in bronze casting, showed signs of new and rapid change. This process was accelerated by the Zhou conquest. The Zhou seem to have given preferences to certain practices − for example, the use of long inscriptions cast in bronze vessels − and abandoned others, principally the use of inscriptions on oracle bones. A similar choice or discrimination is seen in bronze decoration. Birds already existed as a motif available for decorating bronzes, but the Zhou paid especial attention to them, elaborating them in a wide variety of ways. Although continuity with the Shang period was pronounced, the Zhou state adopted new practices and new artistic styles very rapidly.

While the literary texts present a picture of unified and strong control of the Zhou empire, the excavated evidence suggests that the consolidation of their rule was slow. In addition, the southern areas maintained their own traditions, as they had under the late Shang, indicating that China was as yet far from unified. Indeed, such independence seems to have increased rather than decreased in the Western Zhou period. The flowering of this development of regional independence will be the main theme of the next chapter.

4 The Eastern Zhou

In 771 BC, the Western Zhou, whose capital lay in an exposed position in the west of China at Changan, present-day Xian, were forced by pressure from the nomadic tribes to move eastwards to Luoyang. From that date until the fall of the dynasty in 256 BC, the period is known as the Eastern Zhou. The new importance of Luoyang is illustrated by the very large number of archaeological sites found there dating from the mid-eighth century and later. There is a corresponding decline in the material of this period excavated in the western area near Xian.

The Eastern Zhou period is, in its turn, subdivided again into the Spring and Autumn period, and the period of the Warring States. The point of division is usually taken at 481 BC. This is the last year for which there is an entry in the annals of the State of Lu. These annals are known as the *Spring and Autumn Annals*, and it is from the title of this text that the whole period up to 481 BC takes its name. The bare historical outline given in the annals is elaborated by another text, the *Zuo Zhuan*, and the two texts are sometimes referred to collectively by the latter title. All but the first few decades following the year 481 BC are covered by the rather less factual historical text, the *Zhanguo Ce*, or *Discourses of the Warring States*. A historical sub-division is thus traditionally established, almost fortuitously, by the survival of two documents. Capricious as such a division may at first sight seem, the nature of these two texts inevitably affects the understanding of, and indeed the whole approach to the Eastern Zhou period.

The historical evidence

The two main texts are in themselves entirely dissimilar works. The first is a laconic day-by-day chronicle. This is expanded with factual information and some dramatic narrative passages in the *Zuo Zhuan*. By contrast, the second text is an exercise in argument and exposition defending a thesis about the nature of the alliances and warfare needed to keep in balance the two large states of Qin and Chu, whose power threatened all the lesser states.

101 Bronze bell, Eastern Zhou, sixth-fifth century BC. This one of a set of twelve or thirteen bells. The inscription relates events of the period shortly after 600 BC concerning the state of Lü, situated in present day Houzhou in central southern Shanxi. Height 33 cm.

These two documents, various in themselves, make a striking contrast with those of the Western Zhou period which have already been discussed; namely the *Shu Jing* and the inscriptions on the bronze vessels (see p. 94 above). The Western Zhou documents imply the existence of a unified state giving allegiance to a single ruling house. The texts of the Eastern Zhou period, on the other hand, set out a complicated historical record in which many states or centres of power are seen to compete, and in which alliances and battles alternate in an unrelenting struggle for power. The contrast is the result of progressive changes occupying the latter part of the Western Zhou period, when the growth in the power of minor princes led to the breakdown of centralised political authority. This process culminated in the collapse of Zhou power under an immediate external threat in 771 BC. The Zhou court established at Luoyang no longer commanded any but nominal allegiance from regions formerly under the sway of the Western Zhou.

The Spring and Autumn Annals are a direct product of this political situation, for they are the official record of events kept by the semi-autonomous state of Lu for its own administrative purposes. The *Discourses* in turn are the outcome of the ever-increasing warfare between such autonomous states, for the purpose of much of the discussion in this document is to give a prescriptive formula for a stable balance of power.

Inscribed bronzes of Eastern Zhou date are comparatively rare, but a few can be persuasively connected with the historical record set out in the texts. For example, two bronzes in the collection are associated with particular states or with particular events: a bell (101) can be ascribed to the state of Lü in

Houzhou, in southern central Shanxi; and the pair of *hu* (colour VIII) commemorate an important inter-state conference. But, unlike inscriptions of the
Western Zhou, their information adds little to what we already know from the
transmitted texts. Instead, the knowledge derived from the texts, when related
to the inscriptions, enables the bronzes to be dated and in some cases assigned
to particular areas of China.

Other important historical evidence is to be found in poetry and in the great
philosophical writings of this period. The most important surviving poetry is
collected together in the *Chu Ci*, or the *Songs of Chu*. These poems are the product of the imagination and beliefs of the peoples living in areas near the
Yangtze (see p. 164). The philosophical texts, on the other hand, were in the
main written in the north during the struggles for power between the independent states.

Excavations

Matching this abundance of written material, there is a similar wealth of
excavated evidence. Known Eastern Zhou sites far outnumber those of the
Western Zhou. Although this may be partly a matter of chance, the situation
must also reflect the increased density of population, and the spread of authority
away from the original centres of power into a much wider area of China.
Several major cities have been excavated, among which the most important
are Yanxiadu, the capital of the northern state of Yan in present-day Hebei
province, and Houma, the capital of the state of Jin, in Shanxi province. It is
helpful to consider the excavated material in relation to the particular states
with which it can be associated. As it happens, much of the archaeological work
has taken place near the Yellow River. This area formed part of the state of Jin
before 450 BC, and was then divided among the three states of Zhao, Wei, and
Han. To Zhao, in northern Shanxi, belong the sites of Liyu and Handan, and to
Wei, Houma, Fenshuiling, Shanbiaozhen in Ji xian, and Liulige and Kuwei cun
in Hui xian. One of the most important excavations belonging to the early
Eastern Zhou is of a site at Shangcunling, which lay within the area of the
state of Guo until it was annexed by Jin in 655 BC. In the north-east, as well as
Yanxiadu, is the site of Tangshan; and in Shandong province, the important
sites of Linzi and Sufutun have been excavated. Further south, in Hubei and
southern Henan, a number of sites have been excavated which were formerly
part of the state of Zeng.

In place of the hoards of bronze vessels that are so important in Western
Zhou archaeology, complete tombs of the Eastern Zhou period have been
found in respectable numbers. These tombs belong to the shaft type already
discussed (102). In form, a tomb consisted of a neat rectangular pit in which

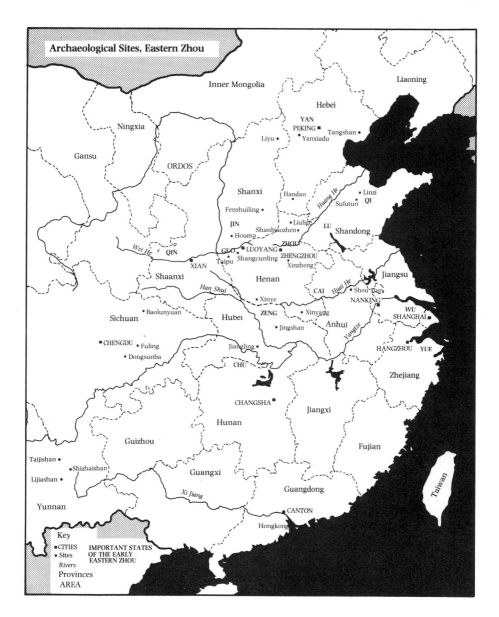

Archaeological Sites, Eastern Zhou

Inner Mongolia

Liaoning

Hebei

YAN
PEKING ■
Liyu •   • Yanxiadu   • Tangshan •

Ningxia

Gansu

ORDOS

Shanxi
Fenshuiling •   † Handan   • Linzi
Sufutun •   QI

JIN   • Liuli
Shanbiaozhen •   LU
• Houma   Shandong
GUO ■ LUOYANG ■   ZHOU
Wei He   QIN   Taipu • Shangcunling   ZHENGZHOU
XIAN   • Xinzheng
Shaanxi   Henan
Han Shui   CAI   Huai He   • Shou an
• Xinye   NANKING
ZENG   • Xinyang   WU
Sichuan   • Baolunyuan   Hubei   • Jingshan   Anhui   SHANGHAI ■
Yangtze
■ CHENGDU   • Fuling   Jiangling •   HANGZHOU   YUE
• Dongsunba
CHU   Zhejiang

CHANGSHA ■
Hunan   Jiangxi

Guizhou   Fujian

Taijishan •
• Shizhaishan   Guangxi
Lijiashan •   Guangdong
Xi Jiang

Yunnan   • CANTON
Hongkong

Key
■ CITIES   IMPORTANT STATES
• Sites   OF THE EARLY
Rivers   EASTERN ZHOU
Provinces
AREA

Jiangsu

a coffin was placed to one side; sometimes the bottom of the shaft was lined by planks forming an outer coffin. Various types of sand and gravel were used as fill, and towards the end of the period a mound was placed over the tomb. Grave goods surrounded the coffin, with personal items, particularly weapons and jades, placed inside the coffin with the body. Such grave goods, as in all the previous periods described, were articles of daily or ceremonial use, of

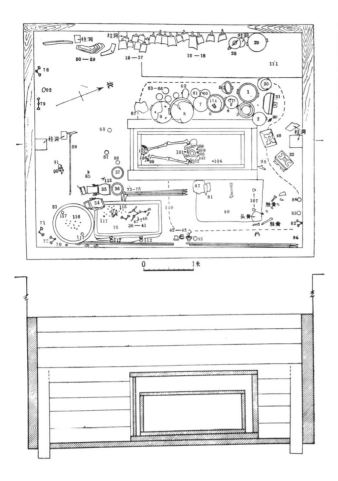

103 *above* Earthenware vessel, Eastern Zhou, fifth century BC. The handles are copied from metalwork, e.g. the handles of the *hu* (colour VIII). Height 30.2 cm.

102 *left* Plan of an Eastern Zhou shaft tomb at Changzhi Fenshuiling in Shanxi province, sixth-fifth century BC. In addition to bronze vessels and weapons the tomb contained sets of bells and musical chimes.

high quality, and included items made of precious materials. With the exception of some pottery vessels used in place of bronze (103), they were not substitutes made primarily for burial.

For the Western Zhou period, long circumstantial inscriptions provide the best evidence for dating bronze artefacts, and hence the decorative styles they carry. The evidence for dating objects made in the Eastern Zhou rests instead on typology developed for the whole complex of tomb finds. Accurately datable individual objects are extremely rare, so too much often depends on those which exist; more must therefore be made of the burial complex as a whole.

During the period of the Eastern Zhou the contacts and discontinuities between different areas that have been remarked upon occasionally in earlier chapters became a general rule. Much of this chapter will be devoted to pointing out and examining regional differences. As this will be one of the major themes of the chapter, it is here that the areas which lie outside the mainstream of Chinese history and art will be discussed. Contrasts between the different regions can be seen most clearly in this period; at the same time most of the states were gradually drawn together by combat and exchange, culminating in the unification of the empire at the hand of the state of Qin (221–207 BC). In these centuries the casting of bronze became much more widely distributed, and developed in the most distant regions of the lands we now call China, assuming an indigenous character in many areas. In this way these more peripheral regions of China acquired the technologies and characteristics of the culture of central China. The complete development of each area cannot be outlined, and this chapter will concentrate on the time that saw the beginning of an interaction between these outlying areas and the main centres. The discussion will none the less cover a period longer than the exact duration of the Eastern Zhou. Some localities were of importance from the Neolithic period onwards and were gradually assimilated during the Zhou period, while others remained relatively independent until at least the middle of the Han dynasty (206 BC–AD 220). But this seems the most appropriate section in which to include them all. The chapter will therefore range much more widely than the previous ones, to take in places and events as diverse as the bronzes cast near the shores of Lake Dian in Yunnan province in the south-west, and the Tagar culture in the Yenisei valley in southern Siberia.

Historical outline

By the time the *Zuo Zhuan* commentary opens in 722 BC, the Zhou king was no longer supreme ruler. The gradual failure of the delegated authority, with its tendency to become hereditary and independent, had led to the formation of independent states. The ties of dependence to the Zhou kings were of no practical significance to the nominal vassal princes. The rulers of the individual states, large and small, were effectively sovereign. In the Spring and Autumn period there were more than a hundred of them. During the earlier part of the period there were three major northern states: Qin, in Shaanxi province; Jin, further east, mainly in Shanxi province; and Qi, in the extreme east in Shandong. To the south lay the vast state of Chu on the Yangtze River. The royal domain of Zhou was situated on the Yellow River together with a number of small, powerless statelets. Among these, only two, Zeng and Guo, are of some significance by virtue of their weakness. Bronzes associated by their inscriptions with these states can be dated with some degree of accuracy, as it is known when the states were absorbed by greater powers.

Wars were continuous throughout the Spring and Autumn period, but their scale was relatively small. Diplomacy played a large part. At the beginning of the period many of the rulers were related by blood, and warfare was a family matter. The largest force involved was that in a battle between Jin and Qi in 589 BC, in which eight hundred chariots and twelve thousand men took part. More often the fighting forces were much smaller. Wars were protracted and their effects gradual rather than sudden and dramatic. One hundred and ten states were gradually extinguished or annexed, leaving twenty-two by the end of the Spring and Autumn period.

The pattern of political relationships and warfare was dramatically different in the Warring States period. Although fewer states were swallowed up, the size of armies was vast, numbered now not in thousands but in tens of thousands. Chu was no longer the only menace. In the mid-sixth century the western state of Qin had entered the competition for the central plain. This made for a more complex balance of power and of alliances. The *Discourses of the Warring States* is taken up with arguments for and against alliances with the two major powers, Qin and Chu. The south-eastern states of Wu and Yue, formerly as much on the periphery as Chu, also became involved. Yue was subjugated by Chu in 333 BC.

Despite an interminable series of wars and conquests, a measure of order was maintained. A widespread desire for political unity was manifested in the idea of hegemon or *ba*. The most notable example of the selection of such a hegemon took place in the 680s. As a result of the northward expansion of Chu towards the small states in the central plain, the latter turned for protection to Qi, and to its ruler Duke Huan (685–643 BC). In 681 BC Duke Huan convened a meeting at which a mutual defence treaty, sanctified by oaths, was signed. A second conference was held in 680, and in 678 Duke Huan was designated hegemon. In 656 BC Chu signed a peace treaty and for the first time agreed to send tribute to the Zhou king. Although in a sense this was a submission, it was at the same time a triumph for the Chu state: Chu was at last explicitly accepted into the Chinese world. After this date the hegemon was never again so important, although the office continued in existence for another two hundred years, and conferences were held from time to time. The title of hegemon passed to the Dukes of Jin after Duke Wen of Jin won a decisive battle against Chu at Chengpu in Shandong province in 632. It remained with Jin until that state disintegrated in the second half of the fifth century.

The inscription on a pair of *hu* (colour VIII) in the collection, datable to the early fifth century, is thought to commemorate an inter-state conference held at Huangchi, near Kaifeng. The Huangchi conference was summoned in 482 BC by Fu Chai, king of the south-eastern state of Wu, who assembled the other princes and demanded to be made hegemon.

The same period of political near-chaos saw the growth of philosophical thought in a wide range of schools. At a time when political survival and military success was all, what is known ordinarily as philosophy is better described as political thought. The writings of the Confucians, Confucius (*c.* 475 BC) and Mencius, who lived during the fourth century BC, and those of the Legalists, Shang Yang and Shen Buhai, also active in the fourth century, and Han Feizi (*c.* 280–233 BC), were attempts to provide a theoretical solution to the political problem. Broadly speaking, Confucianism was concerned with the correct behaviour appropriate to each person's position and status in society. From a proper observance of such ordering a peaceful society would result. While the Confucians believed that the hierarchy necessary for the stability of society could be maintained by virtuous example and moral exhortation, the Legalists thought that it had to be imposed and enforced by a system of rewards and punishments.

This flowering of philosophy had two important aspects. In the first place it could not have taken place without patronage. The increase in the number of states, each with a ruler needing advice, was an important factor in the growth of a number of different schools, and accordingly several of the great philosophers of the period served as ministers of state. Secondly, the rise and support of the philosophers was part of a large and complex sequence of social changes in these states. Previously a royal family, surrounded by its immediate relatives, had conducted state business, diplomacy, and warfare with methods appropriate to a family; but gradually a much wider social group became concerned in government. The transfer of power was not simple or abrupt, not had it fully taken place by the end of the period. A significant step was an increase in the power wielded by important ministers, or even the seizure of effective power by the ministers. The great ministers subsequently brought about their own downfall by adding inter-family jealousies to state rivalries, and thereby compounding the warfare. By the Warring States period, such families had by and large obliterated themselves, leaving their functions to be taken on by the *shi*, or knights and stewards. This happened at a time when the states had grown greatly in size and had had to acquire a more systematic administrative organisation. It is here that there was a place for advisors. As the bonds of tradition had been broken, new systems and, above all, new sanctions were required. These gave rise to the idealised descriptions of the state propounded by Mencius and Han Feizi.

But a more practical solution to the breakdown of centralised authority and of the family system of government was the growth of the first stages of a bureaucracy. The states of Chu and Qin played an important role in this development. The following features can be traced in their state organisations: ministers or officials were regularly changed; hereditary posts declined in numbers and promotion was made on a personal basis; the unit of territory controlled by each official was limited.

These political developments took place at a time when major social changes were also at work. It is possible to infer from changes in agricultural practice and the growth of towns that there was a substantial increase in the size of the population. New areas were opened up for farming, and iron casting was developed to provide agricultural implements. This second phenomenon is of particular interest. Iron is a relatively cheap material, as it is one of the most abundant metals in the earth, while bronze is expensive. The use of cast-iron tools suggests that there was a need for more tools, stone proving an inferior material and bronze too costly.

Cast iron is not a particularly suitable material for agricultural implements, being brittle and liable to fracture with shock. Its widespread use was probably the outcome of the relative cheapness of iron, and the efficiency with which the Chinese could cast it. Casting is a sophisticated if inappropriate method for working iron. In China, as elsewhere, the earliest method used involved smelting the ore at relatively low temperatures. The result was a mass of iron and impurities, called a bloom, that had to be reheated and hammered to consolidate the iron and eliminate the impurities. Further heating, hammering, and quenching were required to improve the properties, especially the carbon content of the resulting wrought iron, which was very pure and consequently very soft. Steel of ideal constituents can be obtained by a judicious use of this method.

However, in the Eastern Zhou period, the Chinese did not develop the later stages of wrought iron and steel manufacture; instead, they turned to casting iron, a technique not exploited in the West until the late Middle Ages. To make cast iron, a very high temperature (c. 1200 °C) is required so that iron can be extracted from the ore in liquid form and poured into a mould. The technical skill needed to attain high temperatures was already available to the Chinese in their development of kilns, and in their elaborate foundries with methods for handling large quantities of molten metal. They therefore adapted their existing technology for a new material and did not exploit this material in the most suitable way. Not until the Qin and Han periods were wrought iron and steel fully developed.

It seems likely that iron casting began in the sixth century BC. Tools of certain fifth-century date have been excavated and such tools have recently been analysed in China. From the analysis it has been shown that, after casting, the tools were heated again and worked to reduce the carbon content; for cast iron has a carbon content of about 5%, and it is this which makes it brittle. A reduction of the carbon content by reheating and working gives it greater toughness, although the hardness is reduced; and this type of iron, with a carbon content of 3%, is known as malleable iron. This development was an important step towards the manufacture of steel.

Alongside the use of iron tools and the expansion of agriculture came an increase in trade. This major economic change has to be inferred from a great deal of scattered evidence. Once established as a fundamental principal the increased pace of the economy explains a whole group of observations which can be made about the period. Most of these are difficult to illustrate in a museum, though archaeological excavation brings them to light. The most conspicuous change was the great increase in the number of cities built during the period: seventy-eight are now known, constructed during the Spring and Autumn period. All the cities had several features in common. They were built on level plains near waterways, laid out on a north-south axis, and enclosed by *hang tu* walls, oblong or square in shape. Earthen platforms served as foundations for the buildings of political or ceremonial importance. There were specialised sections for different industries or crafts. These cities were much more compact than the web-like federations of settlements which made up the earlier towns.

This pattern was not static, and important developments took place during the period. As with Shang cities, only the aristocratic section was walled in the cities of the early Eastern Zhou. But in later cities of the Warring States such as Linzi, a Qi city in Shandong, a second enclosure was built around residential and commercial streets. This underlines the growing importance of the non-aristocratic element. Streets became markets. At the same time roads were constructed to take the trade in luxury goods such as jewellery, curios, feathers and leathers. One item which must have been part of this trade was the glass bead. Glass was not a substance much prized in China. Few items were ever made in glass, and those few were usually looked on as a poor substitute for jade. Beads, especially those with multi-coloured inlays, known as eye-beads, were an exception (104). They were extraordinarily close imitations of Middle Eastern and Egyptian articles which must have found their way to China and then been copied locally. The Chinese versions can be distinguished chemically from the Middle Eastern prototypes because they contain barium and the originals do not. Other valuable items were later described in poetry, as in the *Zhao Hun*, *c*. 240 BC, from the *Chu Ci*: 'Qin basketwork, silk robes of Qi and silken banners of Zheng'.

104 One pottery and five glass beads, Eastern Zhou. These beads are remarkably similar to beads from the ancient Near East. The pottery example, second from the left, appears to be a copy of a glass type. Average width 2.5 cm.

Although much trade was carried on by barter, the development of coinage reflects the growth of trade. The appearance of coinage indicates that trade involved more than the simple exchange of one item for another. Exchanges were carried out over some distance and required middlemen. Coins made such exchanges easier. But, more importantly, the introduction of coinage on a large scale suggests that both entrepreneurs and rulers were using this growth in trade to increase their revenues. Indeed, from about the fifth century BC each state had its own coins. Such diversity of coinage would clearly be more useful for fiscal purposes than merely to facilitate trade between different states. At a very early stage, cowrie shells and jade had been exchanged as a form of currency. The earliest true coins were cast in bronze in the form of spades and knives. Most carried inscriptions identifying the individuals, cities, and later the states that issued them. These were produced in various denominations, sizes, and weights. The round coin with a square hole suitable for stringing on cords was introduced by the state of Qin and was made standard throughout China after the Qin unification in 221 BC.

Warfare

The numerous inter-state battles of the time are described in the texts. The statistics of the casualties established from these accounts show that the scale of warfare increased during the Eastern Zhou. The weapons of the time corroborate these changes. It is useful, however, to describe first those elements which remained the same.

One weapon which persisted in use was the dagger-axe, carried by infantry and charioteers. Its typological evolution is clear, and well documented by excavation. As the blade was made narrower and more elegant, an extension at right-angles along the staff became necessary to buttress it. This is already seen in a weapon of the Spring and Autumn period, which has a sharp point on an otherwise clumsy blade (105 top left). After this stage the blades became increasingly narrow, often with curved or scalloped edges. Two particularly attractive versions are clearly ceremonial weapons; one is in openwork (105 middle), while the other has a fine inlaid design (105 bottom). A straightforward version of the main Warring States type is accompanied by a bird ornament for the top, and a finial which went at the other end of the staff (105 right). This type of finial is generally associated with the Changsha region of Chu. It is descended from the shorter finial ornaments, with birds and snakes, that come from the northern area of China and date from the sixth century (106 left).

The spear, like the dagger-axe, is a weapon that continued in use without interruption from the Shang period. During the Eastern Zhou there was a

105 Four halberd blades
and a finial, Eastern Zhou:
a, seventh-sixth century
BC, width 17.5 cm; *b*, fifth
century BC, width 16.1
cm; *c*, third century BC,
inlaid with gold, width
30 cm; *d and e*, halberd
and finial from the same
weapon, fifth-fourth
century BC. Width 24.3
cm, length 15.3 cm.

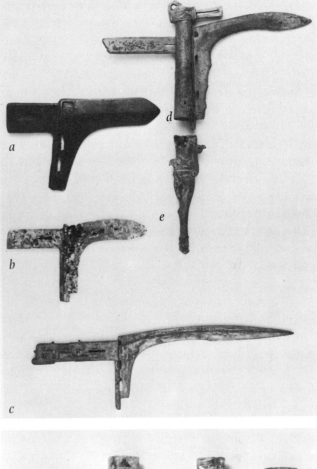

106 Four bronzes used
to decorate the ends of
the wooden shafts of
halberds. Eastern Zhou.
The decoration of three of
the finials includes a bird
with the head and beak
pointing away on one side
and the tail projecting on
the other; *a*, sixth-fifth
century BC, length 12.6
cm; *b*, from Changsha,
fourth-third century BC,
length 17 cm; *c*, inlaid with
silver, fourth-third
century BC, length 17.5
cm; *d*, fifth-fourth century
BC, length 14.8 cm.

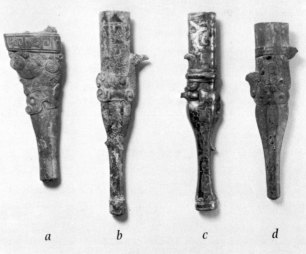

general change from broad to rather narrow spearheads (107, 142, left). The finest example in the collection is one of the earlier broad pieces. It is elaborately decorated and must have been a ceremonial weapon. An inscription on it is inlaid in the ornamental characters known as 'bird' script. Weapons thus inscribed are usually associated with the Kings of Yue, who ruled a small state in south-east China until its conquest by Chu in the fourth century BC. Paradoxically, weapons with inscriptions mentioning the Yue kings are not usually excavated in the territory of Yue. They are more often found in tombs belonging to the Chu state. On the spearhead is a pattern in the surface of the metal composed of a repetitive motif of three triangles. When examined under a microscope, the metal shows changes in layer and surface which suggests that the pattern may have been etched. The weapon would first have been waxed, the pattern then incised in the wax, and the whole then dipped in some acid. Other designs produced by the same technique are represented in the collection by two swords. All the weapons decorated in this way seem to be associated with the south.

These weapons represent an element of continuity in warfare. With a consideration of the chariot, one of the major changes in the fighting force becomes apparent. From descriptions in texts and from excavated finds it is clear that chariots were still of some significance in the Spring and Autumn period. There have been some remarkable excavations of groups of chariots of this date, notably at Shangcunling and Hui xian. At these sites the shape of the chariots have been reconstructed from the ghosts left in the soil by the decayed wood. Surviving hubcaps testify to use of chariots in the sixth and fifth centuries. Other chariot fittings include bits and small harness ornaments. The introduction of a parasol with small hook-like fittings on the end of the spokes may be a sign that the chariots were used less in warfare and more in civil life. Bronze

107 *above* Bronze spearhead, Eastern Zhou, fifth-fourth century BC; inlaid in gold with an inscription in 'bird-script', and decorated with turquoise inlay and a geometric pattern. Length 28.6 cm.

VI Bronze ritual vessel, *hu*, late Western Zhou period, ninth century BC. A number of similar *hu* have been excavated from Shaanxi province. The wave pattern is particularly effective on bronzes of this shape and on deep basins. Height 45.5 cm.

VII *above* Four jade pendants in the shape of animals, Western Zhou period: stag, height 5.5 cm; rabbit, length 4.5 cm; tiger, length 5.8 cm; fish, length 6 cm. A rich group of similar animals was found in a group of tombs at Baoji, Shaanxi province.

VIII *below* A pair of bronze ritual vessels, *hu*, Eastern Zhou period, fifth century BC. An important inscription is cast around the necks. The decoration is very similar to that on a basin in the Freer Gallery, Washington, which can, on the basis of its inscription, be dated to the early fifth century. Height 48.3 cm.

108 Four swords, Eastern Zhou, illustrating the development from a short blade, with a tang for insertion into a separate handle, to a longer and more elaborate weapon cast together with its hilt and guard: *a*, from southwest China, late Eastern Zhou, but reflecting the earlier form of the sword used in metropolitan China during Western Zhou. Length 33 cm; *b*, Eastern Zhou, sixth-fifth century BC. Length 35.5 cm; *c*, fifth-fourth century BC. Length 47.5 cm. Swords of this type with a hollow hilt were an intermediate form, preceding the development of the solid hilt with two rings. They survived for a longer period in southern China. *d*, the fully developed Eastern Zhou sword, fourth-third century BC. Length 58.2 cm.

a   *b*   *c*   *d*

fittings of this date, both those recently excavated and those preserved in museums, are much less abundant than in the Western Zhou.

Chariots may never have been very effective in combat but they had certainly been important as part of a display of power. However, by the second part of the Eastern Zhou they were declining in importance as an item of prestige. Their role as a symbol of wealth or status was being taken by very beautiful individual weapons, such as the inlaid spearheads and swords. This change reflects an important change in warfare. As the scale of fighting increased, chariots ceased to play a significant role. Both the very large size of the armies, and the extremely varied terrain over which battles were fought, made them less valuable. It was probably battles with the states of Chu and Yue which spelled the end of the chariot. These southern areas were either mountainous or flooded, hardly suitable for wheeled vehicles. On the other hand their great fertility made it possible to support large armies of foot soldiers.

At the same time the infantry was joined by mounted soldiers as a significant section of the army. This was part of the general spread of the use of the horse for riding in Central Asia from the eighth century BC. Skirmishes with mounted nomadic tribes of the Ordos regions (see p. 177) made it necessary for the Chinese to ride. With cavalry came the use of the short sword. Rather surprisingly, and at complete variance with the practice in western Asia, the sword was not widely current in China before the Eastern Zhou. A few earlier swords, of Western Zhou date have been excavated at Zhangjiapo. At this time the sword, as yet without an integral hilt, was of little importance. This sword remained in fashion in western China but in the main centres had, by the seventh century, been superseded by a sword with a narrow hilt and guard. Although simple hollow-hilt swords continued to be made, usually in the south (108 left), the main type of Chinese sword was cast with a solid hilt with rings around which a binding of woven silk could be held (108 right). Such swords often had a decorated pommel and guard, inlaid with gold as in one fine example. In later centuries the pommel and guard were sometimes made of jade. The full range of jade fittings for a sword consisted of the following: a pommel ornament; a guard; a chape at the end of the scabbard that prevented the tip of the sword from piercing the scabbard, which was often made of lacquered bamboo or leather; and a slide fixed to the scabbard, from which it could be suspended from the waist.

Not only the use of the sword but also ornaments for belts were adopted by the Chinese from nomadic practice. A belt hook was the first ornament. The earliest belt hooks of the late fifth or early fourth century were of elaborate but delicate casting, decorated with scrolls or granulation (colour x, left). They rapidly became a vehicle for elaborate ornament, being inlaid with geometric designs, both on a shield shape and later on a simple bar shape (colour x, centre). A whole group resembles carved wood and is consequently known as 'chip-carved' (colour x, right). Such brilliantly decorative belt hooks are a late phenomenon, and were fully developed in the Western Han period. Together with the interest in individual beautiful weapons they illustrate the emphasis on personal decorative items seen in bronze production in this period.

The large-scale use of short daggers and belt hooks was a nomad choice. In return the Chinese gave to the ancient world one of its most powerful weapons, the cross-bow. The composite bow had been known since the Shang period. It continued in use throughout the periods of the Spring and Autumn and the Warring States. The arrowheads in the collection reflect the continued use of this weapon (35). But the Chinese were the inventors of the trigger

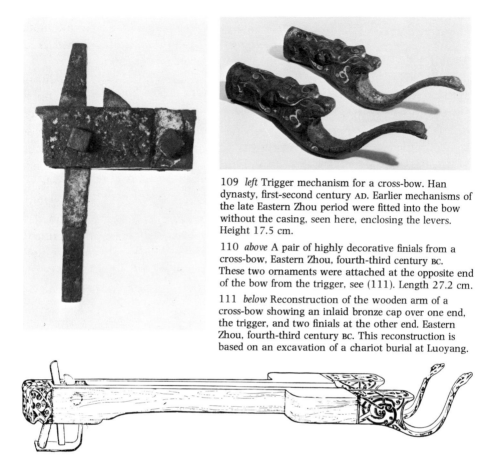

109 *left* Trigger mechanism for a cross-bow. Han dynasty, first-second century AD. Earlier mechanisms of the late Eastern Zhou period were fitted into the bow without the casing, seen here, enclosing the levers. Height 17.5 cm.

110 *above* A pair of highly decorative finials from a cross-bow, Eastern Zhou, fourth-third century BC. These two ornaments were attached at the opposite end of the bow from the trigger, see (111). Length 27.2 cm.

111 *below* Reconstruction of the wooden arm of a cross-bow showing an inlaid bronze cap over one end, the trigger, and two finials at the other end. Eastern Zhou, fourth-third century BC. This reconstruction is based on an excavation of a chariot burial at Luoyang.

mechanism which made the cross-bow possible (109). The essential condition for the manufacture of the trigger was precision of casting, so that the different parts could be correctly assembled and work properly together. Several beautiful fittings were used to adorn this weapon. Among them were ornaments on which there was apparently some rubbing strain (110) since they were reinforced by leather or cloth stitched along the S-shaped bend. Until recently the purpose of this particular ornament has baffled art historians and archaeologists. But now an excavation (111) has demonstrated that these fittings may belong to a cross-bow. The weapon was clearly very efficient, and was used not by mounted cavalry, but by foot soldiers defending the walls of the many new cities of the period. Later it came into use on the stretches of frontier wall which the states constructed as protection against the nomads, and which were to form part of the Great Wall of China. In succeeding centuries the cross-bow was carried far to the west with the soldiers who moved the borders of the Han empire into Central Asia (see p. 185).

Sacrifices and religious beliefs

Most of the bronze vessels and jades which have survived were used in sacrifices and ceremonies. In so far as the purposes of these rituals can be reconstructed from texts and excavations, they appear generally to have been concerned with matters of state. The *Zuo Zhuan* records sacrifices being made in the following circumstances: at the death and burial of the lord; with the offerings of spoils from conquests; at times when rain was sought; at eclipses; at the making of covenants; and for the walling of cities. In the thirteenth year of Duke Zhuang it is recorded (663 BC): 'In the ninth month, or *gengwu*, the first day of the moon, the sun was eclipsed, then we beat drums and offered victims to the land.' (James Legge, *The Chinese Classics*, vol. 5, p. 117). The practice of offering sacrifices at times of burial may have led to the burial of the vessels in tombs. It is certainly in tombs, rather than in hoards or sacrifice areas, that the majority of vessels have been found both in this period and earlier.

In the first part of the Eastern Zhou, as indeed in the Shang and Western Zhou periods, bronze vessels had been intended first and foremost for use in sacrifices, and had only secondarily been buried in tombs. It is not particularly easy to reconstruct such groups from the vessels found in these earlier burials as they are often mixed in dates and types. However, in the later Eastern Zhou particular vessels shapes appear regularly and consistently in tombs. Thus, although these later vessels may have first been used for a sacrifice, they were clearly made with the purpose of burial in mind.

At this time, the emphasis on the vessel as a burial item is underlined by the growth in the use of alternatives for bronze, for example the pottery containers from the north (103). The vessels buried in tombs in the later Eastern Zhou were no longer so often associated with sacrifices carried out in connection with the important functions of the state; they were instead primarily intended to embody the wealth of a powerful man and to ensure his well-being in an afterlife. At the same time there was a growth of an interest in magic and in a range of spirits other than those of the ancestors.

This change, from the use of ceremonial items in rituals connected with the state to their adoption for purposes of securing the safety of an individual after death, can be documented in connection with another important material, namely jade. The use of jades in the early Eastern Zhou, particularly as jade sceptres and discs, in matters of state, is mentioned in the *Zuo Zhuan*. Officials and rulers are described as carrying sceptres and as offering tracts of land and villages in exchange for jade discs. The offering of the sacrifice to a river in the form of a jade disc is also noted. Even more concrete evidence has been produced by the excavation of a site at Houma, in Shanxi province, where repeated

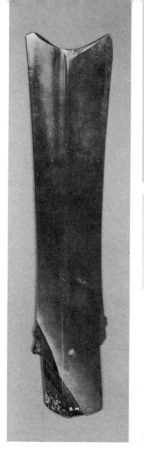

113 Jade plaques from veil coverings in burials, Eastern Zhou, seventh-fifth century BC. The veils, which are the precursors of jade suits, have been found in tombs at Luoyang. Early plaques were decorated with interlinked C-scrolls (*below left and right*); later ones had incised dragon heads (*top*). Average length 3.5 cm.

112 *left* Jade sceptre, Eastern Zhou, sixth-fifth century BC. This type of ceremonial sceptre was first used in the late neolithic and early Shang period. A bronze weapon was also made in this shape in the early Shang period, one example having been found at Erlitou. The bronze weapon had a short life, but the jade form continued to be made, and has been found in the Eastern Zhou sacrificial burials at Houma, Shanxi. Length 35.8 cm.

sacrifices were made. The sacrifice pits, generally rectangular in shape, are aligned north-south with a small pit on one side. Buried in these pits were horses, oxen, sheep, and even one duck. In the small side-pits were the jades, and most of the pits contained more than one, usually between three and five. Among these were sceptres similar in shape to some in the collection (112). In shape these blades have evolved from jades made in the Shang period in imitation of bronze weapons then current. They were undoubtedly concerned with political matters rather than with any question of personal existence in an afterlife. These tablets are buried in association with various treaties signed or meetings convened, and they record 'oaths' or 'promises' made during these meetings. The events described on the tablets concern the political rivalries in the state of Jin in the late fifth century BC.

But a change in the use of such jades was taking place. The burial of jade discs on the corpses of the dead suggests that they were intended to aid the soul of the dead man. The introduction of jade plaques sewn on the veils or head coverings of the dead was the first step towards a jade suit (113). Jade suits in turn were introduced to preserve the body as an abode for the soul. The whole preoccupation with mortuary jades is a very important sign of change to a concern for the individual and his fate after death, with the magical properties of jade, and with the journey of spirits.

114   Three bronze mirrors, Eastern Zhou, fifth-fourth century BC. *Left*, decorated with two *taotie* faces back to back, each one made up of curls. The other two are slightly later and their curl patterns are derived from the *taotie*. *Right*, mirrors of this type are found in the area of the Chu state. Diameter 9 cm, 8.8 cm, 10 cm.

Mirrors

At the same period, mirrors were cast in bronze, polished on one side and decorated on the other. Inscriptions, sometimes incorporated in the design on the back of later mirrors, illustrate another aspect of the preoccupation with cosmology and with the spiritual world. They suggest that the mirrors and their decoration had the property of eliminating or guarding against attack by evil spirits.

Most of the mirrors which have been excavated belong to the second half of the Eastern Zhou, or were indeed made in the last century or so of that period. A few much earlier mirrors are known, including a small group from Fu Hao's tomb at Anyang. The majority of early mirrors belong to the fifth century and follow the bronze designs of that date. Two types are represented in the Museum. On one the decoration consists of two *taotie* faces (114, left). The thick broad rim is a characteristically early feature. A piece with a similar rim has a design of curls enhanced with spirals (114, centre). The curls are so organised that they can be read as an abstraction from the *taotie* face. This method of creating an abstract pattern from a representational design is also seen in jade carving of this date. On jade, similar curl patterns were abstracted from designs of dragon-heads in profile. The mirrors discussed above precede the standard type of the fourth and third centuries, decorated with backgrounds of curl designs, and particularly associated with the state of Chu (114, right).

The second variety of early mirror consists of two separate pieces with a design in openwork in the upper layer. Excavated examples are known from Sichuan and Changsha, and it is likely that this is a southern type of mirror. The designs often consist of confronted dragons or birds. A later group of mirrors

is likewise decorated with finely drawn dragons and birds, which can be compared with similar decoration in other materials notably lacquer and inlaid
metal (115).

This group, which appears to be descended from the layered type of mirror,
is known as the Luoyang group. The term 'Luoyang' is a misnomer, as most
of the known examples, and the textiles, lacquers, and inlaid bronzes to be
compared with them, have been found at southern sites in Sichuan, Hunan,
and Hubei provinces. It is with these areas that this group of mirrors is best
associated. The third type of later mirror is the so-called dragon-scroll group
(116). These, like the curl group, can be associated with the region of the state
of Chu. It is noticeable that, although a few mirrors of early date have been
excavated from northern states, the bulk came from southern sites. Thus an
artefact originating in metropolitan China was taken over with enthusiasm
in an area where it fitted attitudes and beliefs particularly well.

Bronze, jade, and lacquer decoration: families of ornament

The section which now follows sets out the sequence of bronze decorative
styles of the period, and the related designs on other materials. This was, by
any standards, a very fertile period for decoration of all types: the inventiveness

115 *left* Bronze mirror, Eastern Zhou, fourth-third century BC. The background of interlinked Ts
closely resembles textile patterns. Mirrors of this type have been excavated in Hubei and Sichuan
provinces. Diameter 14 cm.

116 *right* Bronze mirror with dragon decoration, Eastern Zhou, fourth-third century BC. This
thin and fragile mirror has a fine background pattern of scrolls and triangles. Most mirrors of
this type have been excavated from sites in the Chu area. Diameter 19 cm.

of the ornament is fascinating, and the changes that can be documented make it possible to understand the artistic concerns of the time more completely.

However, the distinctions between the different styles used to ornament artefacts in the Eastern Zhou, and also the absolute chronology of the styles or stages, are both still very uncertain. The dependence of outlying regions on the central areas during the Shang period led to a close inter-relationship of bronze styles. This has made it possible for scholars to present a detailed analysis of the decoration of bronzes of that dynasty. Inscribed vessels of the Western Zhou period have permitted the evolution of bronze designs in that period to be reconstructed with some accuracy. As yet the same degree of understanding has not been achieved for the bronze designs of the Eastern Zhou. A broad progression is evident, but there are many difficulties in setting out a detailed and accurately dated sequence of evolution of bronze decoration. One obvious difficulty is created by the regional differences that intrude on the sequence. This makes any attempt to present one single line of development a fairly meaningless exercise. Another reason why it may be wrong to seek a simple sequence is that the diversity of ideas was now so great that even in one bronze-casting centre several groups of contrasting types of bronze were cast at any one time.

There are few bronzes which can be accurately dated by their inscription. Several attempts have been made to use these, and some dated tombs, to provide reference points for a sequence of bronze styles. None has as yet been completely successful. The bronzes of the Eastern Zhou will be considered in five main phases. Within these phases, the bronzes can be arranged in family groups. It is the internal sequence within each of these groups that has yet to be worked out. Decoration in lacquer and jade will be included in this section, as designs in these materials influenced bronze decoration. In return, lacquer and particularly jades were greatly influenced by bronze casting. This sort of comparison between designs on different materials proves important in confirming the broad outlines of the developments in bronze.

The table below summarises the main features of the five phases to be discussed:

	BRONZE	JADE
First phase: eighth–early seventh century BC	Large-scale patterns (117)	Isolated examples reproducing elements of bronze patterns
Second phase: seventh century	Small scale repetitive interlace (120)	Small scale repetitive S-scrolls and dragon heads executed in incised lines (113 left)

	BRONZE	JADE
Third phase: seventh–sixth century BC	Variations in forms of interlace, some very small, some larger, with a variety of textures (122, 101)	Dragon-head designs in bevelled lines; introduction of striation (113 right)
Fourth phase: sixth–fifth century BC	a) Northern and central dragon interlace, including Liyu type (123) b) Southern, Huai type, raised hooks and scrolls derived from the northern interlace (114 bottom) c) Representational designs, beginning of inlay	a) Dragon heads in relief proceeding from rather rough to very smooth examples (135) b) Spirals arising out of the dragon heads, first irregular, then more regular (136) c) Occasional figures; openwork designs of interlinked creatures
Later developments of this phase took place during fourth–third centuries BC	Regular cast versions of the above types particularly on mirrors; inferior cast designs on vessels (126)	Regular versions of (a) and (b) above and also incised spirals (137)
Fifth phase: fourth-third century BC	Mainly inlaid patterns with some cast designs (132)	Fluid birds and animals, incised hatching and striations as surface decoration (139), some types developing from (a) above

First phase: eighth–early seventh century BC

The bronze decoration of the Eastern Zhou period as a whole has a distinctive character. It is made up of abstract designs based on interlace and the repetition of motifs. In this context the bronzes of the first phase are best seen as a prelude to the main developments of the Eastern Zhou, for they are transitional in character. Bronzes of this first phase, of the late eighth and early seventh centuries, retain many late Western Zhou features. A *hu* (117) is an example of such a transitional piece. The two main features of the *hu* that belong to traditions of the Western Zhou are the smooth, almost slack, shape and the broad bands of the designs. The triangle pattern around the neck is bold and repetitive, and is not found on later Eastern Zhou bronzes. On the *hu*, the bodies of the two main dragons are intertwined, taking the interlace, first seen in the

117 Bronze *hu*, transitional Western to Eastern Zhou, eighth century BC. An almost identical vessel has been excavated at Shan xian Taipu in Henan province. The interlaced dragons are earlier seen in designs on jades of the middle Western Zhou, and occasionally on bronzes of the same date (119). The combination of dragon and bird is likewise a device taken from jade designs. Height 25 cm.

Western Zhou (see p. 123), a stage further. More interesting at this stage are the elements of the design which overlap. An ear of a dragon lies over part of the body. This method of obscuring one part of a creature by another part was an important step in the development of the more complex interlace designs of the succeeding centuries. Bronzes decorated with similar broad, if rather flat, versions of Western Zhou designs have been excavated from a cemetery of the Guo state at Shangcunling in Henan province, and from various sites of the Zeng state in Hubei province. Many Western Zhou forms and decorative styles persisted among these bronzes. Other bronzes that also retained Western Zhou designs on the more advanced forms developed in the Eastern Zhou have been excavated at Shan xian Taipu in Henan province.

Excavation at such sites shows that the interlace was also well developed in this first prelude period. At this stage, interlace was used concurrently with the bland large-scale geometric designs and represents the new style which was to oust the older tradition (118). The most important Eastern Zhou contributions to be recorded are the reduction in size of each unit of interlace, and the repetition of units to build up a textured pattern. Reduced scale and repetition is here taken to be the main characteristic of the second phase.

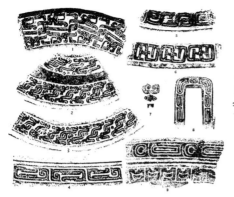

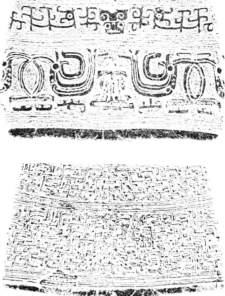

118 *above left* Rubbings of the decoration on
bronzes excavated at Xinye, Henan, late
Western to early Eastern Zhou. The large
scale patterns belong to the Western Zhou
tradition while a new trend is seen in the
smaller interlaced designs.

119 *right, above and below* Rubbings of the
decoration on bronzes of the middle Western
Zhou, from Tunxi in Anhui province. *Above
right*, birds similar to those on the *zhi* (colour
v), are shown in an unusual form with their
plumes linked together. The detail also seen on
jade carving of the tenth century BC was
exploited in the development of the interlace in
the Eastern Zhou (117); *below right*, a pattern
of hooks, symmetrically divided at the centre,
in which the original dragons and *taotie* faces
have been submerged beneath repetitive
patterns.

Second phase: seventh century BC

This transformation may have been brought about as a result of influence
from the repetitive designs on the pottery of south-eastern China. Pottery
styles inevitably had an effect on bronze design as bronzes were cast in pottery
moulds. Techniques for decorating ceramics were thus naturally transferred
to the moulds. The impact of such pottery designs is seen on bronzes of Western
Zhou date that have been excavated in the south-east at Tunxi in Anhui province (119). The decoration of these bronzes is so unusual, and at times so
obviously based on earlier local pottery with geometric patterns, that it must
be presumed that they were made in the area. On them the typical Western
Zhou designs have been transformed in ways relevant to the discussion of the
Eastern Zhou interlace. Patterns of interlocking parts, rather than emphasis
on clear definition of motifs, is a salient characteristic. All the elements are
reduced and repeated. This same repetition and reduction of decorative
elements could have been adopted in the north by imitating either such
southern bronzes or the southern ceramics. Bronzes from the Zeng state,
already mentioned, are later in date than the Western Zhou bronzes from
Tunxi. They show repeated interlocking S-shaped patterns which appear

to be derived from the southern bronzes (118). As a result of changes of this sort, the designs of the first phase were reduced in scale, repeated, and cast with a very little relief. These three features of the second phase are seen in the design on a *fu* (120, 121). In summary, the first two phases represent the first stages in the transition from Western Zhou to Eastern Zhou, with the disappearance of the broad-banded large-scale design and its replacement by the small-scale interlace.

Third phase: late seventh–early sixth century BC

The designs of this phase consist of a group of intermediate styles that together form a bridge between the flat interlace of the early Eastern Zhou and the full-scale use of three-dimensional detail. Use of three-dimensional detail was to be the main feature of the fourth phase. The intermediate group includes a variety of bronzes that are very different in detail, but share some similar decorative principles: they all retain a type of interlace confined within rectangular units;

120 *opposite above* Bronze ritual vessel, *fu*, Eastern Zhou, sixth century BC. At this stage the potential of the interlace, seen in the interlinked dragons, was not carried very far, and the pattern is made up of separate repeated units which are not joined to each other. Height 32 cm, length 32 cm.

121 *opposite below* Detail from the base of the *fu* shown in (120).

122 *right* Bronze bell, Eastern Zhou, sixth century BC. Bronze decoration at this time was enriched with a variety of decorative textures, as on the bodies of tigers forming the handles of this bell, and also in the interlaced dragons with bodies made of fine strands in the surface decoration. Lacquer fragments painted with similar dragons have been excavated at Changzhi Fenshuiling in Shanxi province. Height 14.8 cm.

they all show some three-dimensional studding, or sunken detail such as striations, giving a textured effect. The use of studding or textured detail was the first step towards a three-dimensional character. These effects are like those of impressed pottery. One of the best examples of such interlace is seen on a bell (122). The interwoven strands of the design are punctuated as if held in place by studs. The strands of interlace resemble some recently excavated examples of lacquer of the same date. It is as though the lacquer painters adopted the motifs which were then available to them, among them interlace, but added to them the fluidity and fine line that were more easily achieved on lacquer. This new treatment was then readopted into bronze casting.

Another example of the designs of this intermediate group is seen on a second bell (101) whose decoration points towards the next phase. On the upper surface is a competent example of the early flat type of interlace. But the lower panel includes a bold and rather open scheme of snake-like dragons. This freedom and three-dimensional detail was to recur.

Fourth phase: sixth–fifth century BC

This phase is one of the best known and most studied. Although the main characteristics of the decoration of this phase appeared in the sixth and fifth centuries, its principle features persisted in modified forms well into the period of the Warring States. This phase embraces two major, related categories of bronze, known respectively as the bronzes of the Huai and the Liyu styles. Because many bronzes of this period are misleadingly attributed to the Huai style, it will be considered first. The Huai style is not well represented in the collection. The name is taken from the Huai River in Anhui province, where so many of the bronzes of this group have been excavated. Actually such bronzes have been found over most of the area of the south, including the state of Chu in Hubei and Hunan provinces. They make up the largest group among those excavated from the tomb of the Marquis of Cai. This tomb can be dated to a time before the mid-fifth century, and thus supplies a terminal date for the early Huai vessels. The most conspicuous feature of the Huai bronzes is their knobbly textured decoration. This feature came about with the emphasis of repeated elements of the dragon interlace as raised knobs and scrolls, until these took over the design and covered the whole vessel. Finally the original interlace disappeared.

In the Warring States period of the fourth to third centuries BC, such designs appeared in a more regular form, and were often flattened without the substructure of the interlace. Many of the mirrors, popular in the Chu area, are examples of this flatter type (114 bottom). The Huai style was thus the culmination of the interest in studding and textured effect on an interlace of dragons, first seen in the third phase. By and large, most Huai bronzes belong to the second half of the fourth phase, and such later examples can be seen as a southern alternative to the Liyu style.

123 *left* Bronze ritual vessel, *ding*, Liyu type, Eastern Zhou, sixth-fifth century BC. Decorated with fully developed flat interlace of the Liyu type, seen on the moulds from Houma, this *ding* has unusual legs, drawn smoothly out of the body, to be contrasted with those on another *ding* (125). Height 16 cm.

124 *opposite* Bronze bell, Eastern Zhou, fifth century BC. This large bell is one of a set of twelve or thirteen of which a number still survive. Moulds for the many different types of decoration seen on this bell have been found at Houma. Height 54 cm.

125 *above* Bronze ritual vessel, *ding*, Eastern Zhou, sixth-fifth century BC. The rectangular interlace is less well developed than the full Liyu version with dragon heads and curling bodies. Height 15.3 cm.

126 *right* Bronze ritual vessel *hu*, Eastern Zhou, fourth century BC, inlaid with triangles in silver around the neck. The interlace is highly stylised and is composed of pairs of intertwined dragons alternating in direction. Height 31.7 cm.

The Liyu style, contemporary with the early Huai style of the Cai tomb, is a northern or central, rather than a southern, type of bronze decoration. By tradition it is given the name of 'the Liyu style' after a group of bronzes excavated at Liyu in northern Shanxi in 1932. This site, however, lies much further north than the area where bronzes of this type are usually found, in central and southern Shanxi and Henan. A *ding* (123) best represents what is usually described as the Liyu style. The layers of dragon interlace, enlivened with detailed geometric textured designs, are typical. But this family must be seen as encompassing a much wider range of bronzes. A large group of bronze casting moulds and models, excavated at Houma, the Jin capital of Xintian, has shown that what is called the Liyu style is only one among a much larger group of bronze patterns. Such a range of designs must have developed over several centuries. The main features of this group are the use of interlace designs based on dragons, and their arrangement in horizontal registers. Unlike the Huai group, the decoration does not show a tendency to spread into an all-over textured decoration. With the use of separate registers, a number of different designs might appear on any one piece (124).

Among the moulds found at Houma is one which corresponds to the patterns seen on a small *ding* (125). From the shape of the vessel itself, it can be deduced

127 Bronze axe, Eastern
Zhou, fifth century BC.
Liyu type with a fantasy
of intertwined dragons
and birds. Length 13.4
cm.

that this piece belongs to an early stage in the sequence of bronzes within the
Liyu group. The rectilinear arrangement of the interlace and the flatness of
the execution are also early features. A number of similar designs have been
designated proto-Liyu by scholars. Though they are rightly regarded as earlier
than the typical Liyu bronzes, it is more appropriate to regard the whole range
of northern bronzes with interlace as comprising a group in which the Liyu
bronzes are only one type, and therefore to avoid the term 'proto-Liyu'. The
main reason for subordinating rather than emphasising the Liyu bronzes is
that a straightforward progression of the Liyu bronzes does not provide a
sequence of styles which can encompass all the related designs that are known,
or even all the types found at Houma.

Liyu and associated bronzes are quite well represented in the collection.
It is generally argued that those with lower relief are earlier than those with
layers of interlace, and raised elements such as ears and snouts. The *ding* (123)
has low relief or flat decoration and the incribed *hu* with leaf crowns around
the lid, already mentioned, have layered relief designs (colour VIII). The *hu*
are dated to the early fifth century on the basis of their inscription, and also that
of a basin in the Freer Gallery of Art, which has a very similar type of decoration. Bronzes with flat design are thought to belong to the decades prior to that
time. However, as with bronze decoration of other periods, it is likely that the
earlier style survived alongside the introduction of the relief designs. They are
both clearly earlier than a flat baroque version of this sort of design seen on
a *hu* (126). Both the shape of this vessel and the inlaid triangles around its
neck date this piece to the Warring States. It is therefore an example of the
survival or perpetuation of the styles of the fourth phase into the period of
phase five. In place of the lively relief of the earlier pieces, the flat symmetry
shows a decline in invention and casting skills.

One of the most attractive features of northern bronzes with the interlace of
phase four is the great variety of detail and texture included with the interlace.
In many instances this decoration is worked out in three dimensions. Such

128 *left* Bronze *hu*, Eastern Zhou, fifth-fourth century BC, possibly originally inlaid with lacquer. A *lian* or toilet box with an exquisite design inlaid in silver, related to this bronze, has been excavated at Hubei Jiangling. Height 26.5 cm.

129 *above* Detail of (128).

detail may include three-dimensional animals seated on a lid (123), or intertwined dragons on an axe (127). The intricacy of individual pieces is remarkable, with several animals combined in even the smallest examples. Surface texture is enhanced in a variety of ways, the most obvious being the use of three-dimensional hooks or curls as on the bell (124) or the *hu* (colour VIII). Even more intriguing are the small filler-designs applied to the elements of the decoration. These derive from the geometric patterns of the Western Zhou. They include, on a miniature scale, the spiral and triangle design, and scale patterns. The ubiquity of these particular filler-designs underlines the fact that, once a pattern was taken into a decorative repertory, it could then reappear in a wide variety of forms at any time. In this context it can be noted that the *taotie* reappears widely in this period mainly as an ornament securing a ring-handle.

There is another family of bronzes within the fourth phase, unfortunately not well represented in the collection. It is the family, or rather families, of bronzes on which animals, birds, and men are depicted. They may be cast or incised, and even inlaid with copper. The designs include both elaborate scenes of men hunting, and ornaments consisting of paired or balanced figures. A late example, a lidded *hu* (128), can be related to this group by the birds around the neck. This is a motif found on many of the bronzes of this type.

130 *above* Half of a ritual vessel, *dui*, Eastern Zhou, fifth-fourth
century BC. The vessel consisted of two identical parts making a
spherical container when together; separately, each half could be
used as an offering dish standing on three feet. A bronze with similar
decoration has been found at Changsha. Height 12.8 cm, diameter
25 cm.

131 *right* Wooden platter on a stand, *dou*, Eastern Zhou, fifth-fourth
century BC. Photographed from below to show the lacquered design
of dragons in red and black. Height 26 cm.

Fifth phase: fourth–third century BC

The same *hu* can also be related to the main family of the last or fifth phase, the
inlaid designs. Here the most important design, seen in all three bands around
the body is an exotic form of the *taotie* face. The face is to be found in the sunken
elements rather than in the cast relief which forms the ground (129). Because
the spectator's attention is drawn more naturally to the relief area, the actual
face is, at first, rather difficult to see. Originally, however, it was probably
inlaid, perhaps with lacquer, and would in that condition have been easier to
distinguish. The pair of triangles in the upper border are a characteristic of a
whole group of inlaid bronzes to which the lower half of a *dui* (130) also belongs.
The most important feature of these inlaid bronzes is the fluid shape of the
taotie on the *hu*, and the dragons on the *dui*. This is undoubtedly an influence
from lacquer painting. The relationship is clear when the decoration of the
dui and a lacquer *dou* (131) are compared. Wooden vessels painted in red and
black lacquer were widely used during the second part of the Eastern Zhou,
and were particularly popular in the Chu state (see p. 165). The close association between inlay and lacquer painting is seen in the fine examples of inlay
which have been excavated from the provinces in which lacquer was also a
primary product, namely Hubei, Hunan, and Sichuan.

But although this interaction between lacquer painting and bronze designs

133 *above* Bronze ornament from the
shaft of a chariot, Eastern Zhou, fourth-
third century BC, inlaid with gold and
silver. A similar fitting was found at
Henan Hui xian. Length 16.5 cm.

132 *above left* Bronze ritual vessel *hu*,
Eastern Zhou fifth-fourth century BC,
inlaid with copper and turquoise. Height
25 cm.

134 *below left* Bronze ritual vessel *hu*,
Eastern Zhou, fourth-third century BC.
An almost identical bronze has been
excavated at Changsha. Height 31.2 cm.

IX *above* Silver belt buckle, Ordos region,
fourth-third century BC. An impression of
a textile on the reverse shows that this
buckle was cast in the same way as some
of the plaques from the Siberian Treasure
of Peter the Great. The Xiongnu, living on
the borders of China, copied from peoples
living further west this method of
reinforcing the casting mould with cloth.
Length 13.5 cm.

X *below* Four bronze belt hooks, Eastern
Zhou period, fifth-third century BC. *Left to
right*: a mask supported on a large round
stud, length 5.1 cm; shield-shaped, inlaid
with gold and silver, length 10 cm;
bar-shaped, inlaid with silver, length
15 cm; in the shape of a mask with the
bar attached to the top of the head, gilded,
in 'chip-carved' style, length 10.6 cm.

is the key to understanding the inlay group, to start at this point is to start in the middle of the story. The earliest bronzes with inlaid designs were probably made in the sixth–fifth centuries, and include such well-dated items as the inscribed spearhead (107). Even more characteristic of the early forms of inlay is the geometric decoration of triangles inlaid with copper and semiprecious stones on a *hu* (132). This use of copper rather than the more precious metals, gold and silver, is also an early trait. The design based on triangular elements is a fundamental scheme that is seen at a much earlier date, for instance in the border on the *fu* (120), an early Eastern Zhou piece.

The purpose of inlay was generally very different from that of cast designs. The glowing effect of the different metals and precious stones was new and seductive (133). Casting was probably used to produce the initial pattern, which was refined and inlaid by further working of the metals when cold. In general there was an over-all decline of invention in decoration that relied exclusively on casting. This has been noted in connection with the rather bland design on the *hu* (126), which perpetuated into the fifth phase a style of cast decoration originating in the fourth.

Bronzes of the Warring States period from the Chu area illustrate the same decline. The influence of the inlaid designs is obvious in the triangle pattern around the neck of the *hu* (134), with swirling lines confined within the geometric scheme. But without the liveliness of the inlay the piece is rather staid.

A similar progression can be documented by examining a group of finials. The two earlier ones (106 left) are particularly bold and lively. But by the fourth to third century, there had evolved a type which should be associated with the *hu* from Chu, on which the decoration has lost all vitality (106 second from the left). The intermediate step, as with the vessels, is supplied by an elegant inlaid example (106 middle right). The exceptions to this general decline of casting were belt-hooks, which developed their own special qualities (colour x), and the mirrors already mentioned.

Jade decoration

The changes in bronze decoration traced through the five phases described above can be paralleled by similar developments in the decoration of jades. The fact that so many of the general features of the decoration of bronzes can be matched on jades confirms the validity of the proposed scheme by permitting a comparison of the sequences established in the two media.

XI *above* Lacquered toilet box, Han dynasty. Monsters and animals are hidden among the cloud scroll. Diameter 21 cm.

XII *below* Bronze pole ornaments inlaid with silver, Han dynasty, second-first century BC. Height 23.1 cm, 24.5 cm, 10.4 cm.

135 *above* Long jade bead, Eastern Zhou, fifth century BC, with a close-fitting pattern of dragon heads. The striated areas seen in (113 right) are here greatly reduced in size. Length 14.5 cm.

136 *below* Jade belt ornament, Eastern Zhou, fifth century BC. The four linked rings are all carved from a single small pebble of jade, a considerable technical feat. Length 21 cm.

The parallels between jades and bronzes will be set out here in the form of a summary of the five phases already described. A general correspondence between jade and bronze decoration has been touched upon in connection with the earlier periods: the relationship between designs on jade and those on bronze became especially important in the Eastern Zhou. The geometric or semi-geometric patterns of Eastern Zhou bronzes seem to have appealed particularly to the jade carvers.

The first preliminary phase of Eastern Zhou bronze decoration represented here by the *hu* (117) with decoration in Western Zhou style, has few parallels in jade. Coiled dragons are the only pieces in the collection which can be associated with bronzes of this date on the basis of excavated evidence. The production of jades at this time, and even in the subsequent or second period, is very slight. Jades of the second period are characterised by decoration in small-scale repetitive interlocking designs. Representing this type are the linked S-scrolls on the two veil plaques (113 left), which correspond to the rectilinear S-shaped dragons on the *fu* (120).

In the foregoing discussion of the bronzes, the next group, belonging to phase three, was regarded as transitional. This term was chosen because the variety of bronze designs of this stage form bridges of different types between the very distinct families which make up both phase two and phase four. In the same way, in the sixth century, there was a corresponding variety of bridging designs between the compact repetitive designs on jades of phase two and the families of phase four. Here the transition is marked by the growth in importance of designs based on a dragon face in profile, and the use of concave or bevelled lines and striations (113 top). This increasing interest in texture

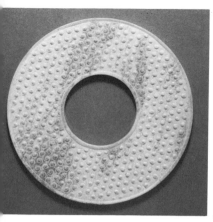

137 *above left* A jade disc or *bi*, Eastern Zhou, fourth-third century BC, with widely spaced raised spirals. Diameter 14.4 cm.

138 *above right* Pair of green jade pendants in the shape of dragons, from the area of the Chu state, Eastern Zhou, fourth-third century BC. Length 11 cm.

139 *right* Jade pendant, Eastern Zhou, fourth-third century BC. Length 9 cm.

parallels the accents and emphasis produced by the knobs and studs on the bronzes of phase three.

As in bronze, two families dominate the fourth phase. Of these two, a family of jades decorated with spirals corresponds to the Huai style, while those with dragon heads are the equivalent of the northern group, including the Liyu bronzes. From an examination of the jades it is clear that the northern group is the dominant one. In the first place it is this variety which shows continuity with the designs dating from the seventh century. Dragon heads in simple incised lines appear on jades at least as early as the second phase. The spirals are a secondary motif, for these evolved from the dragon-head designs in the late sixth century. The jade dragon-head designs came to be executed in three dimensions (135) in the late sixth to early fifth century. From a disintegrated form of this head emerged the irregular spirals (136). Thereafter both designs continued side by side. In the same way, it can be argued that the Huai style in bronzes should be seen as emerging as the specific regional development from the general, predominantly northern, bronze interlace of dragons.

In the late fifth and early fourth centuries both these styles were executed with greater regularity and smoothness. The detail of the dragon heads and the spirals, and their arrangement across the jade surface, was carefully planned and executed. On a *bi* (137) the raised spirals are well spaced and completely uniform against a very flat background. At the end of this sequence incised spirals, seen on dragon pendants (138), parallel the rather repetitive and inferior cast designs on bronzes, for example the S-shaped spirals in sunken line on a finial (106). The similarity in the development of the designs on jades and bronzes is confirmed by these last examples, as both the jade dragons and the bronze finial were made in the state of Chu.

At the same time, that is, during the fourth phase, openwork jades had been carved that reproduced complete sections of interlaced dragons. These were further developed in the fifth phase when the fluid lines of inlaid bronze provided a new model. The same sweep of line, found in silver or gold, is seen in birds or mythical creatures carved in jade (139). Another feature of this type of jade is the use of a great variety of textures. These too are often found on bronze with inlaid granules, parallel lines or striations, and criss-cross, all of which have their counterparts in jade.

One of the conclusions to be drawn from the comparison of bronzes with jades is that the concept of families, rather than the idea of a simple developmental sequence, is the most suitable. As the development is less complex in the jade medium, it is possible to see more clearly than in the bronzes that a given family, such as the dragon heads, continued for some time beside other groups arising along the way. The other important result of this discussion of the jades is that it throws additional light on the way in which the bronze designs evolved, suggesting in particular that all the styles of phase four, both in bronze and in jade, arose out of an interlace of dragons. Thus the Huai style, like the Liyu and the northern styles, is such a group descended from dragon interlace.

The state of Chu

The previous section of this chapter set out an argument taking account of, but not underlining the regional differences of China. The rest of the chapter will be devoted to a review of the different areas, stressing their individual character. Most important of all was the central southern region under the control of the state of Chu. The Chinese living in the north regarded the peoples of Chu and of other southern states as non-Chinese. This may have reflected certain racial differences that were in fact about to disappear. But the power and prestige of Chu were far greater than this grudging view of its position on the periphery of the Chinese world would seem to allow.

The archaeological and textual evidence for the origins of this state, and for its geographical boundaries, are by no means unambiguous. Extensive finds of the fourth and third centuries in the provinces of Hunan, Hubei, and Anhui are attributable to Chu. Before that, Chu seems to have been concentrated in the southern and western portion of this area. At the beginning of the Eastern Zhou, Hubei was occupied by small states, among them the state of Zeng already mentioned. Chu gradually absorbed these states, and in the same way annexed Wu and Yue in Jiangsu and Zhejiang provinces. Throughout the Eastern Zhou period, Chu was a major threat to the northern states. Even after its defeat by a coalition in 632 BC, the northern states still did not feel strong enough to invade Chu itself.

Though almost despised as non-Chinese, and having to struggle even to be admitted into the system of treaties, Chu evidently admired and assimilated Chinese culture. In its initial stages the state was probably contemporary with the end of the Western Zhou period, and emulated their methods of government. Thereafter, government organisation seems to have been more efficient in Chu than in other states, with the exception, towards the latter part of Eastern Zhou, of Qin. In contrast with the political confusion in the north, the Chu state enjoyed the benefits of continuous government under a single ruling house. It seems likely that important steps towards a bureaucratic organisation, rather than one based on family ties, developed here.

It is not so much the ways in which Chu emulated or influenced the north which have intrigued art historians, but rather the profound contrast between its culture and that of the north. Different crafts predominated in the south, among which the casting of mirrors, fine inlay work, lacquer, and textiles have been mentioned. Even the jades made in this area differed in colour and execution from the jades of the north. These were the materials in which the ideas and visions of Chu were given form. Both the fascination of these ideas, and the inventiveness of design and craftsmanship, led to their wholesale assimilation into the art of the Han dynasty.

The *Songs of Chu*, some of which date from the end of the Eastern Zhou period, are the best source for Chu beliefs. They also provide the earliest instance of the later quite conventional lamentations of a minister or official dismissed by his ruler. The most famous poem is the *Li Sao*, or 'Departing from Sorrow', by Qu Yuan, a minister who suffered this fate:

> How well I know that loyalty brings disaster;
> Yet I will endure: I cannot give up.
>
> (*Li Sao*, lines 21 and 22, translated by David Hawkes,
> *Ch'u Tz'u, the Songs of the South*).

This became an increasingly familiar plaint in the Han period. Its first appearance here in Chu reinforces the notion of the rotation of ministers, which must have brought with it the disappointment of men like Qu Yuan. Bureaucracy does not, however, appear as the main subject of this poem. Instead, images

140 Carved wooded figure of a man with antlered head and a long tongue. Eastern Zhou, fourth-third century BC, probably from Hunan province. Apart from the antlers, the figure is carved in Litsea wood. Similar figures have been found at a number of sites in the Chu state, and antlered figures are also painted on one of the coffins found at Mawangdui (181). Height 44 cm.

of the strange spirits of heaven and earth abound; the poet travels on the clouds looking down at the world like an immortal.

In this southern region a large number of spirits were venerated and feared, and shamans were used to intercede and communicate with them. Some of the poems in the *Songs of Chu* are the incantations recited by shamans:

> Open wide the door of heaven!
> On a black cloud I ride in splendour,
> Bidding the whirlwind drive before me,
> Causing the rainstorm to lay the dust.
> In sweeping circles my lord descending.
>
> (*Chiu Ko Ta Ssu Ming*, lines 1–5, trans. Hawkes).

The wearing of antlers seems to have been significant in these shamanistic rituals. It seems probable that carved wooden figures with such antlers represent the shamans or their powers (140). These figures, often painted in lacquer, have been excavated from a number of tombs in the area. Late examples of the motif are seen on the painted lacquer coffins of the Han dynasty.

Of the spirits inhabiting the world of the Chu songs, some were beautiful and benign, others ferocious. It was a world haunted in all quarters. Most frightening of all were the fearful monsters of the south, and of other parts of the world, who would beset the wandering soul. In a poem recited to summon back the soul of a dying man, fierce monsters are portrayed:

There are coiling snakes there and the great
    fox that can run a hundred leagues,
And the great Nine-headed Serpent who darts
    swiftly this way and that, and swallows man as sweet relish.
O Soul, come back! in the south you may not linger.

(*Chao Hun*, lines 16–18, trans. Hawkes).

An intriguing jade pendant shows a creature very like this monster (141). In
the jaws of a coiled, tiger-headed snake a man is held spread-eagled. On either
side are two further spirits in the shape of human-headed birds. This kind of
hybrid creature is characteristic of southern mythology, and some of the most
vivid depictions appear on a unique silk painting from the Sackler Collection
in New York. The jade may, however, have been carved in central or even
northern China as the rest of China adopted these hybrid spirits from Chu.
A text describing the different parts of the world and their inhabitants, the
Shan Hai Jing, or 'Classic of the Mountains and Seas', describes many strange
creatures. This text seems, if not to have originated in the south, to have been
heavily influenced by southern ideas.

Sichuan

The western province of Sichuan was always an important staging post in the
transmission of northern Chinese culture to the south. Links with Chu are
seen in the inlaid bronzes, lacquer, and silk textiles found in Sichuan, all popular
materials in Chu. Sichuan is named in the texts as one of the principal places
in which lacquered objects were manufactured. Excavations have shown that
Sichuan also communicated with the northern states, by two quite separate
routes.

    Dramatic earthenware urns (12, centre) from Li fan in the west of the pro-
vince, near the Tibetan foothills, illustrate the first area of contact with the

141 Green jade carving, Eastern
Zhou, fourth-third century BC.
A coiled monster holds a man
spread-eagled in its jaw, while on
either side two man-headed
winged spirits stand on snakes.
An almost identical carving is in
the Gugong in Peking. Width
5.7 cm.

north. The boldness of the form, and the modelled spirals on the body, indicate a general connection of such pieces with the much earlier painted pottery of the Xindian culture in Gansu already discussed (see p. 26). On the other hand, the Lifan urns are roughly contemporary with a group of small bronzes in the shape of animals, and these can be related to bronze items made by people in the Ordos area (see p. 177) at the same period. So in a single area of Sichuan are found the influences of two quite separate traditions, both of which emanate from the same north-western area of China.

The other, eastern, half of Sichuan was divided into two parts, the kingdoms of Ba, represented by sites near Jialingjiang, and Shu, in the plain of Chengdu. The area of Ba is particularly noted for a type of burial in which a dug-out canoe was placed in a shaft-grave. In Shu, shaft-graves of more ordinary northern styles were found. An important feature common to both kingdoms is the survival, into the Eastern Zhou period, of weapons that can be related to northern Chinese types of earlier date. Here the rather conservative spirit of Sichuan responsible for the Lifan urns is seen in a different aspect. In three weapon-forms this same perpetuation of early types is observed. Dagger-axes, for example, follow the Western Zhou variety (see p. 101) of some centuries earlier, and emphasise the relief tiger's head seen on the Western Zhou examples. Spearheads (142 right) do not use the frontal loop characteristic of the northern Eastern Zhou spearhead (142 left) but have instead small loops on either side used for securing the weapon to the shaft, a feature taken over from earlier spearheads of Shang date. Likewise swords from Sichuan and areas further to the south-west (108 left) follow the shape of rare early types excavated in Western Zhou contexts in Shaanxi province at Zhangjiapo, rather than the contemporary early Eastern Zhou type with a cast-on hilt (108 right). But the story of the sword is more complicated than this. Knives and swords, including swords without hilts, were always popular in the nomadic north-west. The peoples of Sichuan not only adopted the primitive sword from the northern areas, but also took over the small knife used in metropolitan China and more especially in the nomadic areas. These knives were enlarged in size to become the forerunners of the long single-edged sword with ring-handle of the Qin and the Han. Thus one of the important types of sword which conquered China for the Qin was developed in the west, where the Qin had their stronghold.

The axes from Sichuan area are of a very special type (143). Their derivation from the shouldered stone axes of the Neolithic remains evident. Indeed, the stone shouldered axe that was found over much of southern China and south-east Asia in the Neolithic period was imitated in bronze in several areas, including Guangdong and Yunnan. This axe type is shared by the cultures of the southern region well into the Bronze Age.

143 *left* Bronze axe, Eastern Zhou, fifth-third century BC, from Sichuan province. The slight shoulders on this axe are derived from earlier shouldered stone axes. Length 15.7 cm.

142 *above left* Two bronze spearheads, Eastern Zhou, fourth-third century BC. *Left*, a metropolitan type; *right*, a spearhead from Sichuan. Length 26.7 cm, 21.7 cm.

144 *right* Bronze drum, Eastern Zhou, fifth-third century BC, from Sichuan province. Height 42.5 cm.

In other respects Sichuan made its own contribution. The etched animals seen on the sword already mentioned (108 left) are a feature peculiar to the south-west of China. Other artefacts were typical of the area: a gong or drum (144) is an elongated form of the southern drum, although its animal handle is taken from the north-west. On the other hand, a simplified form of Eastern Zhou bell found in Sichuan is a type shared with the southern area around Canton.

Yunnan

It was by way of Sichuan that some elements of the extraordinary bronze culture of Yunnan were transmitted from the north. The Museum is fortunate in possessing a group of bronzes which illustrate the contrast between the bronzes of this southern area and those made in the main metropolitan centres. Although most of the bronzes from Yunnan are considerably later in date than the rest of the material discussed in this chapter, they are a notable instance of the regional diversity already mentioned. Moreover, they predate the spread of metropolitan Han bronze styles into the area. This latter development was the outcome of the establishment of centralised organisation over the whole country by the Han dynasty, bringing with it the cultural ideas and aims of the north.

Unlike other peripheral areas, for example the state of Chu, the peoples of Yunnan were not much affected by the wars of the Eastern Zhou period. However, by the Han dynasty, the central power came closer and Yunnan was of sufficient interest to be described in the official history. The most important site to have been excavated in this area is the necropolis at Shizhaishan on the south-east shore of Lake Dian. Other sites are known, namely Taijishan on the opposite side of the lake, Lijiashan well to the south-east, and Liangwangshan, which is said to be the provenance of the bronzes in the British Museum. Activity was centered on the lake, which played an important part in the livelihood of the people. Shizhaishan seems to have been the principal cemetery, for the golden seal of a king of Dian has been excavated there. This seal is believed to have been awarded by the Chinese to Dian after their submission in 109 BC. Most of the bronzes belong to the century or less before this date, but some, it is now agreed by the Chinese excavators, may be as early as the Warring States.

The clearest and also the most dramatic picture of the society of this area is to be found in the very lively and finely modelled scenes cast in the round and arranged on lids of drums. The Shizhaishan drums were used as cowrie containers. Drums of this general shape are widely distributed artefacts and are found as far north as Guangxi and Sichuan. Similar scenes are cast into the

146 *right* Bronze musical instrument, Eastern Zhou or Han period, third-second century BC. From Liangwangshan, Yunnan province. Height 31.8 cm.

145 *below* Part of a decorated drum, Eastern Zhou or Han period, third-first century BC. From Liangwangshan, Yunnan province. This section came from the upper part of the side of the drum, where it curved out from below the flat top.

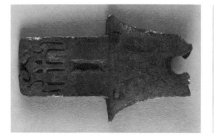

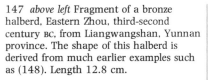

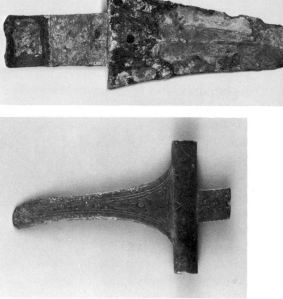

147 *above left* Fragment of a bronze halberd, Eastern Zhou, third-second century BC, from Liangwangshan, Yunnan province. The shape of this halberd is derived from much earlier examples such as (148). Length 12.8 cm.

148 *above right* Bronze halberd, late Shang or early Western Zhou, eleventh-tenth century BC. Length 32 cm.

149 *right below* Bronze halberd, Eastern Zhou, third-second century BC. From Liangwangshan, Yunnan province. Length 25.5 cm.

sides of the drum (145), illustrating a way of life dependent on boats and the lake. The liveliness of such scenes is quite unlike the stylised geometric or abstracted designs found on bronzes further north. The three-dimensional modelling of an ox on a gourd-shaped musical instrument (146) displays the remarkably realistic representation achieved by craftsmen in this area.

The connection between this area and Sichuan, and through Sichuan with the traditions of a much earlier period in the north, can be seen in the weapons. Several types of dagger-axe found in Yunnan are derived from Shang and Western Zhou types rather than from later Eastern Zhou pieces. An example with a triangular blade and a square tang (147) follows closely the form of metropolitan dagger-axes made more than a thousand years earlier (148). The cast figures on this piece show a remarkable resemblance to an excavated halberd from Hubei province of the Eastern Zhou period. This comparison reinforces the suggestion of an important route of contact linking the areas of Hubei and Hunan, Sichuan and Yunnan. A more common dagger-axe form is decorated with fine spirals and geometric designs, often interwoven with snakes (149). Two observations of general significance can be made about this piece. In the first place, the very fine geometric designs are arguably a reinterpretation of the fine spirals on the early halberd (148). On the other hand, the shape of the weapon, with its tubular socket, is derived from a north-western weapon form of the Western Zhou period (see p. 103).

South-east China

To complete the survey of southern China it remains to describe a different group of cultures, those of the south-east. This area too was regarded as non-Chinese by the northern authors of the surviving texts. For this reason, and because it lacked a continuous bronze-producing culture, it is difficult to relate it chronologically to events in the north.

As described in the chapter on the Neolithic, south-east China from Shanghai to Canton formed a distinct area. Here early developments were succeeded by a southern variant of Longshan types. From this developed the pottery with impressed geometric designs by which the area is best known. The geometric pottery constituted an indigenous tradition contemporary with the Shang and Western Zhou periods. At the same time, some pottery with impressed designs has been found in the north. The sherd excavated from Zhengzhou with impressed S-shaped designs is a northern example. Since geometric patterns occur on sherds found on the east coast that predate Shang, it seems likely that this use of impressed repetitive geometric patterns was introduced into the northern metropolitan area from the east-coast cultures. The influence of the local geometric designs in late Western and early Eastern Zhou bronzes by way of the intermediate stage of local provincial bronzes has already been discussed.

On the south-east coast, the earliest pottery with impressed geometric designs was relatively soft (150). Associated with it were a few bronze weapons and implements, divination by scapulimancy, and a life with some settled agriculture. At the same time hunting and gathering, represented by large shell-mounds, was important. Stone implements, both edge-ground adzes and pointed blades similar to those of the Longshan stage, remained in use (see p. 31).

By the second half of the Zhou period, pottery made in the south-east was very sophisticated, often fired to a high temperature. The pottery of two sub-regions within this area as represented in the collection. Several pieces belong to the Jiangsu-Zhejiang region: a heavy jar with a neatly worked-out diamond or diaper pattern (151); and a jar with a feldspathic glaze (152). High-fired ceramics with feldspathic glaze, that is a glaze made with feldspar, were widely manufactured in this area in the Western Zhou period. They varied in importance until, from the Han period, their manufacture was of continuous significance.

A wide variety of impressed designs is also illustrated by ceramics from much further south, from the area near Canton. The Museum has a large group of material excavated from the islands at Hong Kong. Stamped designs used in the area of Guangdong are extremely elaborate. Diaper pattern of the Zhejiang type is found in more complicated forms, both large and small (153).

150 *above left* Sherd of soft
earthenware with impressed
geometric design, *c.* 1000 BC,
from Lamma Island, Hong
Kong.

151 *above right* Heavy earthenware jar, Eastern Zhou. Similar
pots have been excavated in
Jiangsu province. Height 11.2
cm.

152 *right* Earthenware jar,
Han Dynasty. The jar has a
feldspathic glaze around the
shoulders. Height 15.3 cm.

153 Fragment of hard earthenware with an impressed
diamond design, Eastern Zhou,
from Lamma Island, Hong
Kong.

One of the most pervasive designs is the so-called 'double-*f* (154). This particular design is a useful case in which to examine the relationship between the designs of northern bronze casting and those on the pottery of this semi-independent south-east region. As already mentioned, some patterns on the bronzes were derived from geometric patterns on Neolithic pottery from eastern China; subsequently bronzes in turn exerted an influence in later types of geometric pottery. The double-*f* design has been interpreted as arising out of the transfer to pottery of bronze and jade designs executed in double or parallel lines, seen for instance on a Shang jade bird (60). However, the origins of the double-*f* design can be traced with yet greater precision to its source in an earlier form seen on a sherd found at Hong Kong (155). The design on the sherd is derived from a star-shaped motif known from Shang and early Western Zhou bronzes, seen on the *Kang Hou gui* (colour III). But on the sherd the design of the roundel is sunk, instead of being in relief as it is on bronzes. As a result, attention is drawn, not to the sunken main motif, but to the raised outline of the motif; and the points and indentations of this outline are rendered by *ff*s.

This emphasis on the *f*s of the outline, rather than the star-shaped centre, may have come about for technical reasons. The geometric designs on the pottery were produced by stamps; if the star-shaped motif of the bronzes was

154 Fragment of hard eathenware with an impressed double-*f* design, Eastern Zhou, from Lamma Island, Hong Kong.

155 Soft earthenware sherd with impressed designs in alternating bands of a rolling spiral and sunken whorl outlined by *f*s. From Starling Inlet, Hong Kong; *c.* 1000 BC. The soft earthenware of this sherd indicates that it precedes in date the more highly developed sherd in (154).

156 Bronze weapons from sites near Hong Kong, a sword, an axe, and a halberd, Eastern Zhou. The dragon and *taotie* face designs of Western Zhou bronzes (87) are here transformed into abstract patterns. Length 32.3 cm.

copied in its original relief form on to the stamp, then the design impressed into the pot would have been reversed, and shown sunken, so emphasising the outline, as in the sherd (155), now brought into relief. Such concentration on the outline gave rise to the *f*-pattern. Once the double-*f* gained independent status as a motif in its own right, it could be produced in relief on the stamp, generating the standard form of the double-*f*.

Prominent among the many vessels made in the south are the cups on stands known as *dou*, which were often glazed. This vessel shape may have survived from the offering stands of the Longshan tradition, where it was a ubiquitous form. However, as the same cup on a stand is found among Western Zhou vessels as a ceremonial ceramic form, with only occasional bronze counterparts, it seems likely that it was reintroduced into the south from a Western Zhou context. Again the period of transfer or influence appears to be the early Western Zhou.

Artefacts in other materials further demonstrate contacts between the north and this southern region, illustrating again the transfer of Shang and Western Zhou motifs. The designs on bronze weapons, notably a sword (156), are derived from the S-shaped dragons of the Western Zhou period. The interest in S-shapes at the expense of the actual dragon, is in keeping with the southern tendency to transform northern representational designs into abstract patterns. These weapons show a distinctly conservative tradition, for they include a short sword derived from Western Zhou prototypes and a type of halberd taken from early Eastern Zhou examples. The eclectic nature of the combinations suggests that the objects are all of the Eastern Zhou and not earlier.

The north-east and the north-west

While the areas of central and southern China were soon to become completely assimilated under the Han dynasty, the areas of the north resisted this process for much longer. The north-eastern cultures are poorly represented in the Museum. A sword with a C-shaped handle, known as an antennae sword, is an isolated example of metalwork from the north-east. Its flared edge associates the sword with a type of bronze spearhead found still further to the east, in Japan. The handle, however, can be specifically linked to daggers of the north-west and even to the distant European West.

When it comes to the north-west the Museum collections are very rich. There are large groups of knives from China proper, from the Ordos region to the north-west, and from southern Siberia. With these is a comprehensive range of belt-plaques and harness ornaments. The relationship between the curved knives of Shang and Western Zhou, and those of the Karasuk culture of south Siberia, has already been mentioned (see p. 103).

A similar comparison can be made between the straight and the curved knives of north-west China and those of the Siberian Tagar culture. The curved knives are the descendants of the animal-headed knives from Anyang. The straight knives originated in the hollow-handled knives of Western Zhou (see p. 103). Exact parallels for both types and several intermediate variations have been found in China. The comparison between the Chinese and the Siberian examples demonstrates that the linear bird pattern on the hilt of the Chinese knife was derived from the modelled bird on the knife from Siberia. The handle likewise illustrates the assimilation of a Siberian bird motif to the more characteristically Chinese design of a tiger face. Here the confronted birds make up the ears and eyes of the face (157).

This connection between the Ordos region and Siberia is the outcome of the identity and mobility of the populations involved. From about the eighth century, the inhabitants of Central Asia took to a way of life which was nomadic rather than settled. The new way of life was heavily dependent on horses. A preoccupation with horses and hunting is vividly illustrated in the decorative belt plaques and harness ornaments. In general terms they show fairly realistic animals in profile, with little attention to detail. The style originated in south

157 *right* Two bronze knives with bronze
birds on their hilts. *Right*, from south Siberia,
Tagar culture, sixth-fifth century BC; *left*, from
the borders of north-west China, Eastern Zhou.
These small daggers were not used in China
proper. Length 27.8 cm, 27.6 cm.

158 *below* Rectangular bronze belt plaque,
from the Ordos area, fourth-third century BC.
Two horses rearing back to back are attacked
by wolves. The striations on the animals are
copied from wood carving of the Altai region.
Width 8.9 cm.

Russia, incorporating motifs from several areas including the Iranian plateau. The most celebrated of all examples are the gold plaques made in eastern Siberia that were collected by Peter the Great and are now in the Hermitage in Leningrad. Tigers attacking stags and goats were a favourite theme – one transmitted to the Far East by way of the Altai. As yet, little attempt has been made to separate chronologically or stylistically the various types of plaque. There are several variants. Some plaques were made as solid rectangles on which the details of the bodies of the animals were cast in such a way as to imitate carved wood (158). Rare examples of a different style, with carefully modelled animals, were made in silver, and can be compared with the fine gold plaques in the treasure of Peter the Great (colour ix). In addition there are numerous small ornaments, the counterpart of decorative fittings found as far west as Roumania and Bulgaria. The repetition of a limited number of motifs contributed to the abstraction of the designs which progressed from representational to geometric ornament. Both the original themes of this ornament and the methods used to develop the abstractions were quite distinct from those used in the main centres of China. Excavated evidence is slight, but clearly the greatest number of items belong to the period of the peoples known to the Chinese as the Xiongnu (third–second century BC). The repeated attacks on the Han empire from this area suggests that the nomadic peoples were vigorous and well organised. The bronzes seem to have been made at a time when the nomads were at the height of their power and posed a considerable threat to the Chinese.

Conclusion

This chapter has described China in the period prior to unification under the Qin and Han empires. The origins of forms of warfare and political organisation, the use of large armies and the growth of a bureaucracy, all of which were to be significant under the Han, have been examined. This period saw the beginnings of the flourishing trade of the next period, and with it the development of coinage and the expansion of roads and cities. Gradually the peripheral areas of China came into increasing contact with the metropolitan region. Under the Han many of these regions were to be assimilated into the empire, but they retained some regional qualities in spite of the centralised control and the diffusion of culture. This strong, centrally organised political system, tolerating and indeed dependent upon some degree of regional difference, was to become the main characteristic of the Han empire. There was a parallel in art and manufacture. The immensely varied productivity of the different regions in bronze casting, lacquer, and textiles, for example, laid the foundation for the more unified but eclectic style of the Han period.

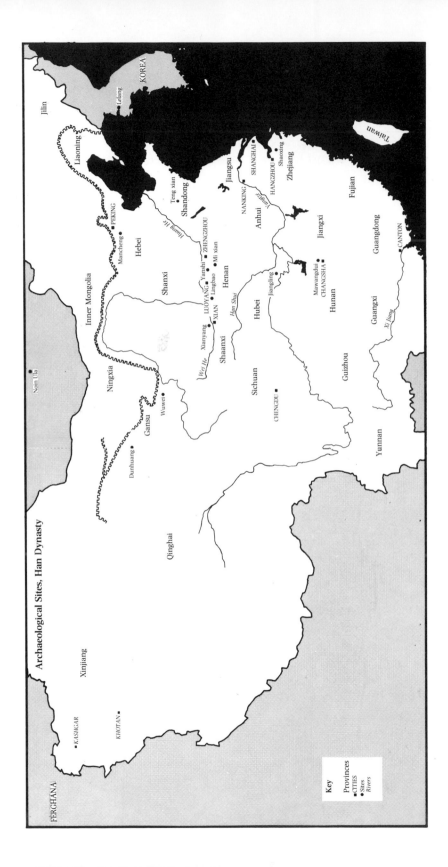

Archaeological Sites, Han Dynasty

KOREA

Lelang

Jilin

Liaoning

Taiwan

PEKING
Mancheng

Teng xian
Shandong
Huang He

Hebei

Shanxi

Inner Mongolia

ZHENGZHOU
LUOYANG Yanshi Mi xian
Lingbao
Henan

Jiangsu

SHANGHAI
Shaoxing
HANGZHOU
Zhejiang
Yangzi

NANKING

Anhui

Jiangxi

Fujian

CANTON
Guangdong

XIAN
Xianyang
Shaanxi

Wei He

Han Shui

Hubei

Jiangling

Mawangdui
CHANGSHA
Hunan

Guangxi

Xi Jiang

Ningxia

Sichuan

Guizhou

Noin Ula

Wuwei

Gansu

Dunhuang

CHENGDU

Yunnan

Qinghai

Xinjiang

KASHGAR

KHOTAN

FERGHANA

Key

Provinces
■ CITIES
● Sites
Rivers

5 The Han Dynasty

The unified state ascribed to the Zhou and even the Shang was achieved by the Qin (221–207 BC), and their successors, the Han (206 BC–AD 220). Contemporary with the Roman empire in the West, the Han dynasty was hardly aware of the great state at the other end of the Eurasian landmass. While Rome fell, the Chinese empire survived. The continuity of the Chinese empire is one of its most remarkable characteristics. Centuries of Han rule, adapting the Shang and Zhou precepts, established many practices and attitudes which remained with the Chinese until 1911.

The literature of the period is very large. For this discussion the important works are the historical texts. The history, the *Shi Ji*, compiled by Sima Qian (d. *c.* 85 BC), was the pioneering work in this field. It was followed in the later part of the dynasty by the *Han Shu* by Ban Gu (d. AD 92). These texts contain both extensive factual detail and exposition of the political controversies of the day. They are indispensable tools for the archaeologist as much as for the historian. The poetry of the time was also important, even if its relevance is less direct than that of the purely historical works.

Not only is textual evidence much more abundant than for the earlier periods, but the excavated material is more extensive than ever before. As was the case for the early dynasties already discussed, most of the sites excavated have been tombs. The contents of these tombs are very varied. The many precious items in jade, bronze, and lacquer are undoubtedly significant, but most important of all for our understanding of the life of that period are the earthenware models of buildings, figures, and scenes of farm life. For the first time, some tombs were decorated with stone slabs engraved with scenes showing every day existence alongside the others taken from history and mythology. Stamped earthenware bricks, which were more common, likewise include valuable detail of this type (159). With material of such diverse character, it is possible to write a more general description of the way of life in the Han period than could be done for the earlier dynasties.

Even with the wealth of evidence for the Han period, it is necessary to be cautious. Men of the day sought, after centuries of political strife, for stability

and order. Bureaucratic organisation and the systematic application of rules
were the practical means they used. Because they hoped for unity this is what
they described. One important aspect of this attitude, systematisation, is seen
in the re-examination of surviving ancient texts. This was stimulated by the
rivalry between two groups of scholars: the Modernists and the Reformists.
The Modernists worked from newly discovered copies of the ancient texts
written out in contemporary script (*jin wen*). The Reformists, on the other
hand, favoured those versions of the texts written in obsolete seal script (*gu
wen*). Two different policies of state emerged from these respective schools.
The Modernists had an expansionist programme when facing the problems of
the world around them: they sought unrestricted ownership of land; govern-

159 Rubbing of a brick from a tomb, Sichuan province. Han dynasty (first-second century AD).
In this kitchen scene, preparations for a meal are afoot: on one side a stove is being tended, on
the other a mixture is kneaded in a bowl; toward the rear, a fish is being prepared and an
animal dragged in behind a man. Height 42 cm, width 43 cm.

ment control of the iron and salt industries by monopoly; expansion into new territory. By contrast the Reformists looked back to ancient examples and sought to remove the political and social abuses of their time by the return to a 'Golden Age'. They advocated the control of land-holding and of retrenchment in foreign policy. Therefore the allegiance of the writer must be recognised before the evidence of any text of the Han period is considered.

The four centuries are all known as the Han dynasty; however, they encompass three or even four different periods, two long and two short. In the first place, although the Han dynasty was the most important ruling house in this period, the contribution of the Qin must not be overlooked. The state of Qin has already appeared as one of the participants in the diplomatic struggles and battles of the Warring States. Established in the west of China, in an area which from as early as the Neolithic period had provided a fertile stronghold, this highly organised and powerful state finally annihilated the others. There are few surviving remains of this short-lived dynasty, which failed soon after the death of its founder, the first emperor, Qin Shi Huangdi. Apart from the emperor's tomb, as yet unexcavated, and a number of small tombs, which have been examined, significant finds have included the site of the imperial palace and such remains as the standard coinage. The great tomb was legendary in its magnificence. A map of the world with rivers of mercury was said to have covered the floor. Life-size pottery figures of soldiers and horses forming a veritable army have been excavated from a nearby pit (160, 161). The expenditure on this task must have been enormous. Sustained effort was also required for the organisation of the state. Of this effort the coinage and the standard weights and measures are symbols. They are all that remains today of the systematisation and unification of the means of trade, of the army, and of the script, under the direction of a single ruler.

The Han dynasty was founded by the commoner Liu Bang, who became its first emperor, Gao Zu. He came to power in the conflicts that the oppression of Qin rule generated. Part of the policy of the Han was to mitigate some of this oppression. Despite this, bureaucratic organisation and territorial expansion, examples of Modernist policies, were the legacies of the first part of the Han dynasty, known as the Western Han (206 BC–AD 8). The strains inherent in an expansionist government produced a reaction starting in 70 BC, and seen in a marked way in the interregnum of Wang Mang, who set up the brief Xin dynasty (AD 8–23). Wang Mang, a Reformist by inclination, sought to re-establish what were believed to be the ideals of the Zhou kings, particularly in matters of the economic organisation of the state, namely, land distribution and taxation. His endeavours failed, and the Han dynasty was restored as the Eastern Han (AD 25–220). The capital was now established at Luoyang rather than, as earlier, at Changan near Xian. Great military expeditions continued to be

160 *above* Excavation of the
lifesize pottery figures of soldiers
and horses found near the tomb
of Qin Shi Huangdi.

161 *left* Pottery figure of a
soldier found near the tomb of
Qin Shi Huangdi. See (160).

launched; the economic conditions continued to worsen. As the great estates accumulated land and gained exemption from taxation, the ability of the government to organise the country internally and externally deteriorated. In the early third century the dynasty collapsed from the combined disasters of flood, and famine, the rebellions of the peasantry in the bands of Yellow Turbans and Red Eyebrows, and from the independent military might of the great generals.

Warfare and the silk route

Warfare was endemic throughout the Han period. Yet in the scenes of daily life, on tomb slabs or in tomb models, soldiers and arms play a relatively small part. The role of military authority was tacitly obscured. This omission should not be allowed to hide the essential role the army was to play. The poets were in no doubt about the realities of war:

> They fought south of the ramparts,
> They died north of the wall.
> They died on the moors and were not buried.
> Their flesh was food of crows.
>
> (From 'Fighting South of the Ramparts', translated by Arthur Waley,
> *Chinese Poems*, p. 52).

Long steel swords, which were far more impressive and effective than the short Bronze Age swords (162, 163) remain as a reminder of these battles.

During the first part of the dynasty, military campaigns were needed for several different reasons. Firstly, the internal conflicts gave rise to the long campaigns which culminated in the unification of the country. Only fifty years later, in 154 BC, the rebellions of the minor princedoms, set up at the Han conquest, led to further campaigns to restore order. Other wars were fought on foreign fronts, and through these the Chinese consolidated their hold over areas previously peripheral to their control. They moved out into Central Asia. This aggressive policy was in the main the work of Wu Di, the Martial Emperor (141–87 BC). It was he who subdued the south, including the tribes of the Nan Yue in 111 BC, establishing Chinese rule as far as the area we now know as North Vietnam. Similarly, with campaigns in the extreme north-east, he set up a Chinese colony in Lelang, in Korea, in 108 BC. This was the political background to the growing homogeneity of material culture throughout the Chinese continent and beyond. For in the wake of military conquest came the civil organisation to control the different areas staffed by Chinese from the metropolis. To the far south and the extreme north, the generals and the officials

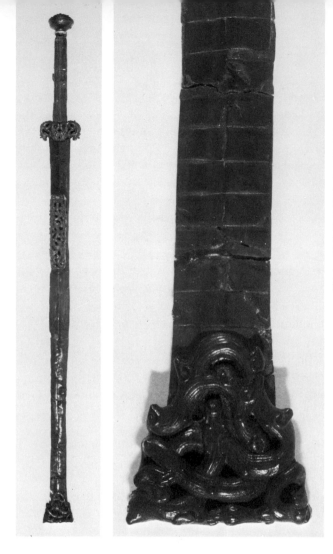

162 *far left* Iron sword in a bamboo scabbard, lacquered, with wooden fittings, Han dynasty, third-second century BC. Intricately carved wood-work painted with lacquer was a speciality of the part of central China formerly included in the Chu state. On this sword scabbard the wood decoration is a substitute for jade fittings. Length 85 cm.

163 *left* Detail of scabbard in (162).

took their prized possessions, their language, and their literature. Those in the north, at Lelang, homesick no doubt for the luxuries of their own country, imported lacquer, bronzes, and ceramics. Among them were bronzes with chased decoration which had been made in the south, in Hunan or Guangdong provinces (164). These particular bronzes, and the ceramic imitations of them (165), both well represented in the Museum's collection, illustrate the spread of a related material culture over the newly conquered areas. Although the bronzes and ceramics were first made in areas which were under strong northern control, they were then imported into and imitated in areas much less firmly integrated with China: Guizhou, Yunnan, and northern Vietnam, as well as Lelang (p. 206). The Han people could call on the products of all these areas to supply their soldiers in the north and south. Such were the practical results in day-to-day terms of the consolidation of Han power within China.

More famous, and with more spectacular consequences, were the wars that brought Chinese soldiers, diplomats, colonists, and merchants into Central Asia. The Xiongnu and other nomad tribes on the north-west border of China promoted, by their constant invasions, various defensive measures. The unification and combination of portions of the defensive wall into the Great Wall of China had been Qin Shi Huangdi's solution to the problem. Instead of trying to keep the nomads out, Wu Di resolved to take them from behind, by making diplomatic alliances with people to the west of these particular tribes. He put immense armies into the field, numbering in the region of 50,000 to 100,000 cavalry, supported by infantry and supply troops. At the same time, he sought a source of fine horses with which to match the mounted nomads on their own terms. For in the Far East the only known horse was the small, stubbly Przewalski horse. To achieve this double end, Wu Di sent Zhang Qian as ambassador to seek an alliance with the Yuezhi, a tribe that had been driven westwards by the Xiongnu. As far as alliances were concerned, the embassy came to nothing. During his long years away, part of which were spent as a captive, Zhang Qian reported the existence of fabulous horses in Ferghana, a province under the rule of the Central Asian kingdom of Sogdia. Several em-

164 *left* Bronze basin and cover, Han dynasty, second-first century BC. The decoration is incised rather than cast. Bronzes with similar decoration have been found in Han tombs in several areas of southern China. The delicate detail recalls lacquer ware with incised designs. Height 17 cm, diameter 20 cm.

165 *right* Earthenware tripod, Han dynasty, second-first century BC. This is one of a range of high-fired earthenware vessels with feldspathic glaze, made in imitation of bronzes with incised decoration from southern China (164). They are rarely carefully decorated and often left plain. Height 19.6 cm.

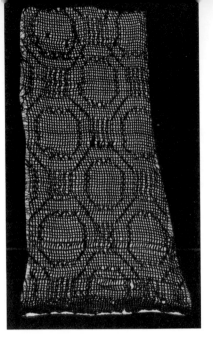

166 Fragment of woven gauze from the Caves of the Thousand Buddhas, Dunhuang, Gansu province. Han dynasty, length 8.5 cm.

bassies and many military campaigns later, the Chinese army achieved the submission of the Xiongnu, in 52 BC, and of Ferghana, in 42 BC. The supply of horses was theirs, and they are immortalised in the fine bronze castings buried in late Han tombs.

Horses were not the only item in the trade established along the routes through Central Asia made safe by the Chinese armies. Silk is the product which gave its name to this trade route. Small fragments of the brilliantly coloured and exotically woven fabrics have been found at oasis sites along these desert tracks. The silks in the Museum's collections were found at these sites early this century by Sir Aurel Stein (166). The cultivation of the silkworm and the weaving of silk had originated in China. Once the fine and brilliant material was known outside her borders, it was eagerly sought. The Romans, and later the Byzantines, imported it. Having acquired a taste for such dress, they sought the secret so that they could manufacture their own. Silk was coveted not only in the far west but also much nearer at hand. Chinese silks have been excavated from graves in Korea and from the graves of the Xiongnu chiefs at Noin Ula in Mongolia. For the first time in Chinese history a pattern of extensive trade can be documented. This trade was organised, not by private merchants, but by the officials in the form of government-sponsored caravans.

Bureaucracy and the economy

The feature that really distinguishes the Han dynasty from the dynasties that went before was not the extensive conquests but their institutions of government – in other words, the development of the bureaucracy. The main elements of bureaucratic government, short-term appointments, rotation of office, promotion by merit, the application of centrally ordered regulations, have already been mentioned. They were transmitted to the Han by way of the states of Chu and Qin. As the area now under a single authority was so extensive, such methods were developed to an unprecedented level. The system of examination of candidates for official posts saw its first beginnings with an edict in 196 BC that ordered officials in the commanderies to send able men to the capital city where their talents could be considered. The seal of office gave the official the authority which in earlier days had been asserted by military might, and of which the ceremonial weapon had been the symbol. The tally (167) was widely used to authorise instructions. In the Han dynasty, the chariot was seen exclusively as the conveyance of the official. These chariots are portrayed on the bricks from tombs. The role of such officials was speedily reinforced as the growing empire gave rise to the need for men and grain to staff and feed the army. With this growth the methods of taxation, grain storage, and transport were extended.

Management of the economy and the raising of revenue were all important in a large centralised state with extensive foreign territories. Statesmen were well aware of the economic problems of the day, and their views are best illustrated in a document known as the 'Debate on Salt and Iron', an account of discussions in 81 BC. This sets out the two conflicting arguments on the management of government and the economy, with particular emphasis on the imperial control of the monopolies: those of salt and iron. From a superficial reading of this text it would appear that imperial interest in the monopolies arose from a genuine concern for the balance of the economy as a whole. But the debate was really concerned with the purpose of government, and with claims and counter-claims that the extended foreign wars were draining China.

The importance of salt and iron are illustrated in a different way by scenes on the bricks from tombs. The complicated and sophisticated drilling for salt is the subject of one of the most famous bricks from Sichuan (168). The brick shows men with winding gear raising the salt, probably as brine, from a deep

167 Bronze tally, Han dynasty. The tally divides into two parts. It is inscribed with eight characters which can be translated 'tiger tally for the governor of Dong Jun'. In the Han period counties (*xian*) were divided into commanderies (*jun*). The *dong* (eastern) commandery comprised territory in southern Hebei and northern Henan. Length 7.5 cm.

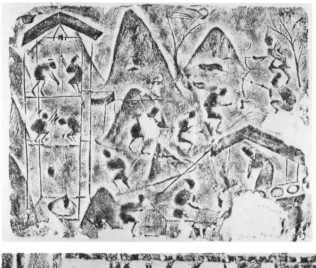

168 *left* Rubbing of a brick from Sichuan, Han dynasty, first-second century AD. Men are shown drilling for salt in a hilly landscape. On the left is a tall drilling rig. The salt is brought up as brine and flows along bamboo pipes to evaporating pans on the right. Height 37 cm, width 47.5 cm.

169 *below* Detail of a rubbing from a relief showing, in the bottom left, a round bellows, and to the right, iron forging. Han dynasty, excavated from a tomb at Hongdaoyuan, Teng xian, Shandong.

shaft. The brine was carried in bamboo pipes to pans above a furnace where the liquid was evaporated. Similarly, on a stone from a tomb, the use of a bellows associated with iron smelting is shown (169). Iron and steel were finally coming to supersede the use of bronze in China, not only for tools and farming implements, but also for weapons, ornaments, and even mirrors. Extreme inflation in the second half of the dynasty probably accounts for the scarcity of surviving bronze artefacts of the period, many having no doubt been turned into coinage. But a much greater use of iron, and therefore a much reduced use of bronze, was also a contributing factor.

Architecture

Chinese architecture and methods of construction were unique. From China the use of wooden structures of a particular type spread to a large part of the Far East, Korea, Japan, south-east Asia, and the Himalayan region. This wooden architecture is not always regarded as one of the Chinese major contributions, as wood perishes easily, and those civilisations whose peoples built in stone are better remembered for their architecture.

170 *above* Earthenware model of a house, Han
dynasty. A similar model is exhibited in the Shaanxi
Provincial Museum. The outward curving walls can
be contrasted with the vertical construction of
buildings from Henan (171). Height 44.5 cm.

171 *right* Earthenware model of a watch-tower, Han
dynasty, first-second century AD. The model shows a
building with wooden supporting members and a tiled
roof. Towers like this were built inside the defensive
wall of a compound of a large homestead. Height
86.5 cm.

But neither the large scale nor the accomplishment of Chinese architecture
must be overlooked. The buildings of the early periods are known to have been
substantial from their massive platforms. Their imposing qualities probably
derived from the repetition of halls and courtyards, rather than from great
height. For the Han period there are a significant number of tomb models and
representations on tomb bricks which provide important evidence on the appearance of the buildings. Thus, apart from a few earlier designs on bronze, the
Han is the first period for which it is possible to illustrate a pattern of regional
differences. A small squat house is typical of Shaanxi province (170), while a
tall multi-storeyed building is characteristic of Henan (171).

The lack of stone and the relative shortage of wood in the western areas of
China had determined the first important feature of Chinese buildings, foundations on solid platform constructions of *hang tu*, or stamped earth. The platforms can be seen in two forms in Han dynasty architecture: as the relatively
low, stepped foundations on which halls and towers were constructed; or as
massive, high fortifications for the bases of towers. In both types, the super-
structure, as had always been the case, was made with wooden columns

172 Stamped decoration in a brick showing a multi-storeyed building, Han dynasty, first century BC. This stamp is one of several different types seen on hollow bricks from Western Han tombs. A tomb constructed of large hollow bricks is seen in (183). Height of the detail 6 cm.

supporting the roofs. Initially simple single-storey galleries had been built around stepped terraces or platforms with another building on the top. By the Han dynasty the storeyed building, with one storey standing directly on another, had been developed.

This wooden structure was the most characteristic feature of Chinese architecture. In both low and many-storeyed buildings, the columns supported heavy tiled roofs. These in turn protected the columns and the relatively insubstantial material used for the walls. This type of building was extended, not so much by increasing its depth, but by adding units along the front length. Another unit could be added by increasing the columns by one. The storeyed building, shown stamped in a brick, consists of several units in width, each column representing an additional bay (172).

A row of columns supported a beam or purlin across the front of the building. To take the weight from a larger section of each purlin down into the column, the bracket was developed. At first such brackets were U-shaped, the centre point of the U standing on the column. In time this system of brackets was elaborated so that each bracket group over each column became very complicated. They could then take the weight from a large number of points along the purlin and cross or tie-beams down into the column. However, in the Han period, only relatively simple brackets were used.

The main structural element of each building was therefore a purlin supported on columns. These purlins in rows, one behind the other, lying along the width of the building, supported the roof. They were sometimes tied by a cross-beam from front to back of the building to prevent the pressure of the weight of the roof pushing them inwards or outwards. However, as each purlin had its own row of columns, they did not have to lie in a straight line in section. Instead, they could be arranged to form an arc and so support a curved roof. This method of holding up the roof was completely at variance with the system developed in the West. The typical western wooden roof structure is dependent on a system of roof trusses. A roof truss is a stable structural element, made of a braced triangle, and it supports the roof rigidly from front to back, rather than along its front length. The angles of the triangle determine the angle of the roof, and within this scheme a curved roof cannot be developed. Nor can a truss be used to support a large overhang on the roof, as the lower corners of the truss must lie over the main walls. On the other hand, the truss does not require the use of columns across the depth of a room, and makes possible the construction of large clear interior spaces. Chinese halls have, by contrast, columns throughout, at regular intervals, supporting the purlins.

Landscape

To the Han, buildings were part of daily life in towns or villages. True landscape was in some sense apart, a refuge physically and spiritually from everyday life. Even the wild mountains and fabulous palaces are widely separated in the long descriptions in the *fu*, or prose poems:

> The steep summits of the Nine Pikes,
> The towering heights of the Southern Mountains
> Soar dizzily like stacks of cooking pots,
> Precipitous and sheer.
> Their sides are furrowed with ravines and valleys,
> Narrow-mounted clefts and open glens,
> Through which rivulets dart and wind.
> (Burton Watson, *Early Chinese Literature*, p. 275).

To this, the gorgeous palaces form a counterpoint:

> Here the country palaces and imperial retreats
> Cover hills and span the valleys,
> Verandahs surrounding them on four sides;
> With storied chambers and winding porticos,
> Painted rafters and jade studded corbels,
> Interlacing paths for the royal palanquins,
> And arcaded walks stretching such distances
> That their length cannot be traced in a single day.
> (Watson, p. 277).

This long poem by the court poet Sima Xiangru (179–c. 118 BC) celebrates the royal hunting parks. There had been earlier hunting parks and one of their uses was for military training. The later Han parks were used also for an assertion of imperial authority on occasions of ritual and ceremony. At the autumn festival, deer were ritually hunted by the emperor. This was a formal display of might and inaccessibility.

What was new was an interest in landscape for its own sake and for its mystery. This was to become a recurrent feature of Chinese art. Such landscapes appear on ceramics and bronzes, particularly incense burners. The lead-glazed pottery hill jar (173) is a later version, for burial only, of the earlier bronze incense burners (174). Mystics who sought immortality would retreat into the isolation of beautiful landscape (see p. 196). The incense, rising as smoke out of the incense burner in the shape of a towering peak, represented the clouds hovering over the real mountains. On these clouds the adept hoped to rise and wander as an immortal.

In poetry, landscape is described for verbal and visual delight, and without such semi-religious connotations. In the same way, hills were part of the scenery on a brick illustrating saltmining (168). Other trees and plants appear

173 *far left* Earthenware model of an incense burner with green lead-glaze, Han dynasty, first-second century AD. The top is in the shape of a mountain, and around the sides animals prowl through a hilly landscape. Height 24.5 cm.

174 *left* Bronze incense burner, Han dynasty, first century BC–first century AD. The incense would have risen through the holes in the lid like mist over mountains. The bronze has chiselled decorations similar to that on the covered basin in (164). Height 21.5 cm.

175 *right* Detail of a rubbing showing the attempt by the Qin emperor to recover the ritual vessels of the Zhou dynasty. Men in a boat are hauling up a *ding* tripod, but at the last moment the head of a dragon emerges and bites through the rope. Han dynasty, from the offering shrines of the Wu family in Shandong, AD 147–168.

as narrative detail in larger scenes. The complexity achieved in the poetry is rarely attained in the visual arts. A certain routine formula recurs, with rounded hills rising one behind each other and animals shown confined within the frame of each hill.

Magic and beliefs

Two major schools of political thought, Legalism and Confucianism, have been mentioned in an earlier chapter. During the Han period, although these remained two separate and distinct philosophical schools, both embraced a wider range of concepts and became more eclectic. In some areas of thought they came close to the more religious beliefs of their day. Religion and ceremony have in most societies been adapted to buttress and reinforce the political system. The close relationship between the two in Han China is illustrated by the reinstitution of sacrifice by the emperor at Mount Tai in 115 BC. This sacrifice, which has been discussed by Michael Loewe, was regarded by the Han as a Zhou practice, and in ceremonies initiated in AD 56 they sought to recreate the ancient forms. The emperor was thereby taking to himself the political and ceremonial authority of the past dynasty. In the same search for authentic

Zhou practice, the books on ritual, principally the *Zhou Li*, were put together from more ancient sources by the Han. The attempted rescue of the ancient bronze *ding* vessels, shown in a rubbing from a shrine (175), illustrated the veneration for past practice and for what was believed to have been the 'Golden Age'. This act was part of the sequence of efforts that, as has been noted, is generally associated with the group of thinkers known as the Reformists.

The beliefs of the opposing school, the Modernists, were equally remarkable, and include, together with the mystical notions known as Daoism, ideas which today would be described as magic or as cosmological and numerological superstition. Daoism itself had by this time acquired an extraordinary dual character. The two different components of Daoism were the ideas set out in the late Zhou philosophical texts attributed to Laozi and Zhuangzi, and secondly, the cult of immortality by dietary regime and other semi-magical pursuits. The two streams of thought were originally quite independent, but at the beginning of the Han period they came together to form a complex of beliefs now all sub- sumed under the single term 'Daoism'. At first sight they seem completely at variance with one another. The message of the philosophical texts was quietist and escapist. One of the most famous stories in the Zhuangzi describes the philosopher's response to an approach from an emissary of the king of Chu, asking him to accept the post of prime minister. His reply went as follows:

'I have heard that there is in Chu a sacred tortoise that has been dead these three thousand years. The king stores it in a chest within a shrine. Do you think that this tortoise would have chosen to leave his bones as relics to be treasured by men, or do you think he would rather have been alive dragging his tail in the mud?'. The messenger replied, 'He would rather have been alive and dragging his tail in the mud.' So Zhuangzi said, 'Please go, I am going to drag my tail in the mud.'

This escape from the implied burden of office would appear to be a reaction to the development of the work of the bureaucracy. Escape often literally meant retreat to the rural life amid beautiful landscape. In this way it was consonant with the growing appreciation of landscape shown in poetry and in the decora- tive arts. It is here that the relationship between philosophical Daoism and the cults of immortality can most easily be illustrated. In the imagination it is only a small step from the retreat to high places in order to contemplate beauti- ful landscape, to the wish to ride through the heavens as an immortal surveying the landscape below. The idea of wandering among the heavens inspired decoration of fluid cloud scrolls painted on lacquerware (colour XI) which swirl with movement, suggesting the flight of the immortals.

The consequences of this complex of beliefs extended far beyond such fine painted and inlaid design. Active attempts were made to achieve immortality. Led by no less persons than Qin Shi Huangdi and the Han emperor, Wu Di,

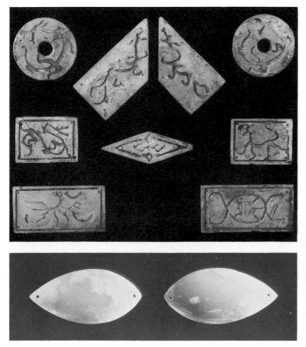

176 *left* Glass plaques, possibly from a pall, Han dynasty. These examples show the animals of the four directions: the Green Dragon of the east, the White Tiger of the west, the Red Bird of the south, and the Black Warrior (the tortoise and snake) of the north. The majority of the plaques are plain and rectangular, and all must have been part of a covering rather than a burial suit, which would have required carefully fitted plaques of graduated sizes.

177 *above and right* Jade eye-covers and a jade cicada placed on the tongue of the corpse, Han dynasty. Length 5 cm, 6.2 cm.

magicians were employed to seek and brew potions of eternal life. One of the strangest methods adopted, by those rich enough, was to have suits of jade plaques, joined with metal fastenings, made to encase their bodies after death. Jade, it was believed, without any grounds whatsoever, would preserve the body from corruption. This inhibition of bodily decay was to enable the attainment of immortality. While the jade preserved the whole body intact, it could house the earthly soul, leaving the spiritual soul to achieve immortality. Although the Museum has no example of a jade suit, a set of glass plaques, now much calcified, make up a pall or coffin covering (176). This was probably a substitute for a jade suit made for a man of lower rank. Even if not in the form of a complete suit, jade was thought to be powerful if used as plugs for the body and as eye covers, and carved as a cicada for the tongue (177).

In parallel with this preoccupation with the soul, there was an interest in the whole universe of spirits. As important as achieving immortality was the control of these spirits. Jade discs and sceptres were proper instruments for this purpose. In some representations, spirits are shown riding on jade discs. Jade discs were also moulded on tomb bricks to signify their function to assist

178 *above* Decorated hollow brick from a tomb, Han dynasty. Below two friezes of dragons, there appear a *taotie* face, a pair of warriors in front of fortified towers, and a pair of jade discs tied with silken cords. Jade discs are frequently shown in tombs, presumably as auspicious symbols to help the soul of the dead, or to ward off evil spirits. Length 55.8 cm.

179 *below left* Bronze mirror with a TLV design in the central area, Han dynasty, first century AD. The animals of the four directions, and the sun and the moon, are shown in fine raised line. They are encircled by an inscription that consists of a six-line poem describing the blissful life of the immortals. Diameter 16 cm.

180 *below right* Bronze mirror from Shaoxing, Zhejiang province, late Han dynasty, third century AD. There are four scenes on the mirror: at the bottom is Xiwang Mu, the Queen Mother of the West; at the top, Dong Fang Gong, the lord of the East. The battle of horsemen on the left is unusual and very lively. Diameter 21 cm.

the dead (178). Bronze mirrors, which are found in many tombs, played a similar part (179). The astrological and cosmological purposes are plain from the designs on them. The most complicated type is decorated with the so-called 'TLV design'. They have been given this name from the geometrical shapes invariably found on them, which resemble the TLV of our Latin alphabet. This combination of symbols may be related to a system of divination that was the ancestor of the modern practice of geomancy. These symbols are seen on boards that were in use from at least as early as the Warring States.

Among the animals shown in conjunction with the TLV symbols are the animals of the four directions. These are the Green Dragon of the east, the White Tiger of the west, the Red Bird of the south, and the Black Warrior, or tortoise and snake, of the north. In this scheme the fifth direction was the centre, represented by yellow. The scheme incorporated the five elements: fire, water, metal, wood, and earth. This system has been attributed to the philosopher Zou Yan (350–270 BC). Perhaps wrongly, the associated concepts of the complementary forces of *Yin* and *Yang* are also attributed to him. *Yin* and *Yang* represent the opposing qualities of dark and light, female and male, moon and sun, and so on. They are the formal expression of ideas of dualism long inherent in Chinese thought.

The Han period was a particularly fertile time for the formal articulation of ideas which had been prevalent for some centuries. It is probably from the south, from the area of Chu, that veneration of most of the strange immortals originated. Many are described in the pseudo-geographical text the *Shan Hai Jing*, which, it has been suggested, included elements derived from Chu mythology. Prominent among the spirits of the Han universe was the Queen Mother of the West, Xiwang Mu. In the *Shan Hai Jing* she is described as a fierce creature. But in Han representations in tombs or on mirrors she had become the beneficent goddess who presided over the western Daoist paradise (180).

Tombs

The visions of immortality meet with the scenes of daily life in the tombs of the Han dynasty. The number of excavated tombs of this period is large, and the tombs illustrate important changes that took place in burial practices. Most important was the change from shaft tombs to chambered tombs. The shaft tomb was used well into the Western Han period, especially in southern China. The tomb of the wife of the Marquis of Dai (*c.* 150 BC) [181] at Mawangdui shows the complex detail of such southern shaft tombs. An elaborate wooden structure forming an outer coffin, with compartments for burial goods, was placed at the bottom of a vertical shaft with stepped sides. The body, in one or more inner coffins, was installed in the centre.

Within less than a hundred years a completely different type of tomb, the chambered tomb, had begun to spread across China. There were two stages in this development: the construction of tombs with several rooms rather than a single pit, and the use of slabs or bricks to line these rooms. The north of China was the area in which the innovations in tomb design and tomb decoration seem to have been made. The most famous examples of early

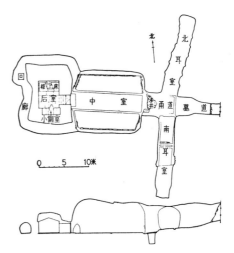

181 *left* Plan of the tomb of the wife of the Marquis of Dai (died *c.* 150 BC) excavated at Mawangdui. The massive framework was constructed of wood and set at the bottom of a shaft tomb. The three nested coffins in the centre are surrounded by compartments for burial goods, which included many of the personal possessions of the dead woman.

182 *right* Plan of the tomb of Liu Sheng, Prince of Zhongshan, late second century BC, at Mancheng, Hebei province. A rear chamber contained the body, while most of the burial goods were placed in the central room. There were also two side rooms stacked with less sumptuous offerings.

chambered tombs are the two tombs in the limestone cliffs at Mancheng in Hebei province, in which Liu Sheng and his wife Dou Wan were buried in jade suits (182). Rock has several advantages over earth for the construction of tombs. In it tunnels can be dug horizontally, as can a series of small, linked rooms. These small rooms could then be used for burial goods, which in a shaft tomb, had had by and large to be arranged in the pit with the body. A tomb hollowed out of a cliff also allowed a more varied layout to be used than had been possible in the shaft tomb.

When such chambered tombs were to be built underground, instead of in a cliff, some method of lining the chambers became necessary. The chambered tombs of the Western Han period were lined with large slab bricks made of clay. These large flat bricks resemble the flat stone slabs which lined the single-chambered cist tombs of the north, and this similarity suggests that the cist tombs may have been one of the models for the construction of the early brick tombs.

The tombs of the late Western Han period at Luoyang illustrate the combination of the use of multiple chambers with slabs. These tombs consisted of linked chambers on the Mancheng pattern, and were lined with large, hollow, slab-like clay bricks (183). Such early brick tombs were not constructed of small bricks. At intervals the roofing slabs were supported by vertical triangular slabs held on a central pillar. They also had a complicated and convincing representation of doors. On these and other prominent bricks in the tomb were modelled lifelike animal heads. Instead of the incised designs appropriate to a stone slab, these bricks were impressed with small repetitive stamps. These are either small and bold, biting deeply into the clay, or in larger scale producing thin raised lines making up a more elaborate composition.

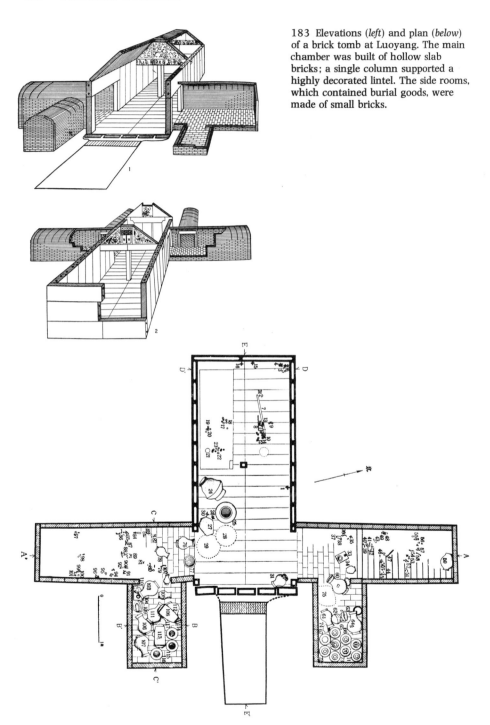

183 Elevations (*left*) and plan (*below*) of a brick tomb at Luoyang. The main chamber was built of hollow slab bricks; a single column supported a highly decorated lintel. The side rooms, which contained burial goods, were made of small bricks.

The next stage in the development took place in the area of Luoyang, where this type of brick tomb was popular. This was the construction of the tombs in small solid bricks. In other words, the brick in the shape of a stone slab was abandoned in favour of the true solid brick, used so that one of the narrow faces lined the tomb. Inevitably, the much smaller size demanded a new design, especially for the roof which was given a beehive form. This type of brick tomb was widely adopted in China, and is found as far south as Guizhou province and at Canton, particularly as tombs for northern Han officials. The scheme of designs on such bricks was necessarily smaller than on the large slabs. Only later were ingenious large-scale decorative schemes evolved to cross a whole sequence of such bricks.

Although the chambered tomb is found in most parts of China in the Han dynasty, there were many different regional variants. In Sichuan, idiosyncratic and particularly attractive brick panels (159) were used to line the tombs. In this same region stone slabs were used, and some hollowed rock tombs similar to those of Hebei were also made. Such rock-chambered tombs are in the main confined to the north-east and east of China, including Shandong province. In central and south-western Henan, a special form of square tomb constructed of decorated stone slabs has been found.

By the end of the Han period, extremely elaborate multi-chambered tombs are found in many parts of China. Throughout the Eastern Han period, tombs became more complicated and highly decorated. A tomb at Mi xian illustrates the continued emphasis on features that recalled a dwelling (184). This character of a house for the dead was already noticeable in the Western Han. By the

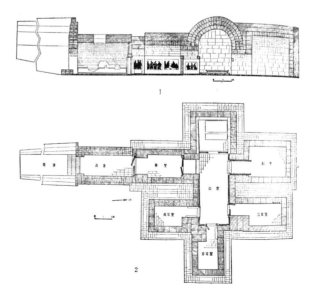

184 Plan and elevation of a magnificent tomb built for Zhang Boya (c. third century AD) at Mi xian, Henan province. The tomb was built of stone slabs decorated with scenes of daily life; all the doors and portions of the roof were also highly decorated.

185 *left* Two earthenware tomb-figures illustrating different regional styles, Han dynasty, first-second century AD. The smaller of the two is glazed and comes from a group shown playing a game. An almost identical piece was excavated at Lingbao, Henan province. The larger and coarser figure, which could have had hands inserted in the holes in the sleeves, is from Sichuan. Height 20 cm, 32.5 cm.

186 *right* Stoneware jar with feldspathic glaze, Han dynasty, first-second century AD, from south-east China. The provinces of Jiangsu and Zhejiang were the main areas where high-fired ceramics were made in the Han period. A similar piece has been excavated at Hangzhou. Height 33.8 cm.

late Eastern Han, the doors and rooms were even more elaborate. The functions of the different chambers of the Mi xian tomb are shown by the scenes depicted on the incised stone slabs. The first, inner, room has pictures of horses and chariots resting on the ground. This was the area where the guest would leave his chariot. Next to this room was one in which food was prepared for the banquet – in other words, the kitchen – and in a third room the feast was held. The host was presumably the dead man. The cost of the construction of such tombs must have been immense. The tomb at Mi xian is vast, and beautifully made, with closely fitting stone slabs. Above the tomb is a mound, and during the Han period the approach road to such tombs came to be lined or guarded by stone animals and buildings. Such figures were to guard the tomb against evil spirits. These chambered tombs must have been as expensive, especially in labour, as the large shaft tombs. This is a surprising observation, as they became fashionable at a time of great economic difficulties.

Indeed, this economic situation is reflected in the change from the burial of precious items belonging to the dead man to their replacement by substitutes in lesser materials. The burial of precious materials was forbidden. Objects of intrinsic value, bronze, gold, silver, or jade were no longer buried, and in their place earthenware models were used. This development, together with the evolution of the chambered tomb, transformed the character of the burial from that of a treasure chest to that of a model dwelling.

The changes in the contents of the tombs were various. The inlaid bronze fittings and the few surviving bronze vessels date from early Han. By the Eastern Han, even the vessels were made in earthenware. Models which came to be included in such late tombs are generally very informative. The area which produced the greatest numbers of figures and models was the region immediately around the capital of Luoyang. Important and interesting variants

were produced in many other provinces, particularly Sichuan (185). The buildings of the south are immortalised in models from tombs near Canton, and different buildings from Shaanxi and Henan have already been mentioned.

The provinces of the south, now under the control of the central authority of the north, had a flourishing ceramic tradition which was later to spread northwards. This included the large-scale production of stonewares with feldspathic glazes. Such pots with greenish glaze were made in profusion in an attempt to provide substitutes for the bronze vessels (186). While the northern lead-glazed pots seem a temporary expedient, appropriate only as tomb furniture, these southern pots were not only a superior form of substitute, but also represented an important advance in the development of Chinese ceramics. They mark an essential stage in the development of the manufacture of stonewares and porcelains in which China was to lead the world.

Methods of manufacture

Because valuable materials, particularly ceremonial bronzes, ceased to be buried in tombs, the objects which have survived from the Han dynasty differ somewhat from those which remained from the earlier dynasties. The two main types of object that were buried were items which could be manufactured in large numbers, often by a repetitive process, and luxury goods for personal use. This second group perpetuated a trend observed in connection with the Eastern Zhou period.

Already as early as the Shang dynasty, large workshops had existed for casting bronze or carving bone. By the Han period the scale of manufacture had greatly increased. Gradually, less attention came to be paid to individual items, and greater effort was put into methods of manufacture which could achieve spectacular effect by mechanical means, for example by using looms for weaving, or by division of labour. This point is best illustrated by examining first the well-developed crafts of bronze casting and jade carving, and then comparing them with silk weaving and lacquer production, two crafts which flourished especially in the Han period.

The changes in bronze casting provide an excellent example of a craft where the care given to each individual piece had significantly decreased since the Zhou period. Instead of the complex moulded designs of the Shang, or even the inlaid bronzes of the Eastern Zhou, many of the vessels made in the Han period were smooth and plain (187), or summarily ornamented with incised designs (164). Such vessels required much less work and skill than the earlier bronzes. The invention of parcel gilding illustrates another development designed to ease the ways of decorating bronze (188). By this method a bronze could be decorated in silver and gold. Mercury combines easily with most metals, and so pastes were made combining either gold and mercury or silver and mercury. These amalgams were applied to the bronze, outlining the required design. When the bronze was heated, the mercury evaporated, leaving the gold and silver pattern on the bronze. Such designs often consisted of cloud scrolls in silver against a gold background. This was a method of producing an enriched surface on the bronze without the effort or expense of inlaying the bronze with gold and silver in sheet form. Although such bronzes looked brilliant when first produced, the designs were often inaccurately executed and the gold and silver could be rubbed off. The inlaid pieces retained their bright decoration

187 Bronze wine flask, Han dynasty. Another flask of the same shape in the Shanghai Museum is decorated with fish scales. The two lines at the mouth indicating the jaws of the fish recall this theme. Height 32.8 cm.

for a much longer period. This is a feature that can be observed in many crafts: those items which were made by a complicated process were more enduring than those produced by a simplified method.

In jade carving exactly the same phenomenon can be observed. The technical methods of producing the carved surface decoration became even more simplified. The irregular spiral designs that had become regular in the late Zhou soon ceased to have much relationship to spirals at all (189). Simple raised dots were produced by making criss-cross lines across the surface of the jade. In the Western Han these were enhanced with an incised spiral. Alternatively this was abandoned and the raised design was left as a diamond pattern, its origin now forgotten. The effect was often exquisite, but it was probably popular because it was technically easy to produce.

While skills in bronze working and jade carving declined, lacquer, silks, and ceramics took their place. This change was probably hastened by the economic difficulties that made it necessary to use materials less intrinsically valuable

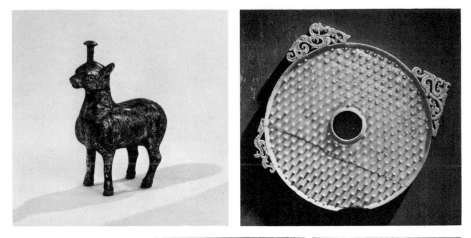

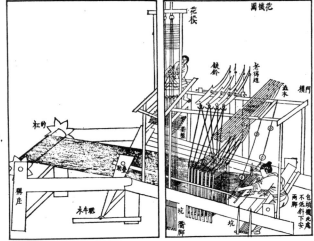

188 *above left* Qilin, bronze
with decoration of cloud
scrolls in gold and silver
(parcel-gilding), Han
dynasty. Height 7.6 cm.

189 *above right* Jade disc or
bi, Han dynasty, second-first
century BC. Diameter 14 cm.

190 Woodblock illustra-
tions from the *Tian gong kai wu*,
facsimile edition of AD 1637.
A small boy is seated at the
top of the loom to draw up
the warp. The heddles on
the right are operated by
pedals at the feet of the
weaver.

than bronze and jade. Fortunately the devices used for increasing the production in silk and lacquer did not, as in the case of bronze and jade, impoverish
the quality of items in these materials. Instead, methods were used that increased both production and the range of shapes and decorative styles.

In the case of silk this was done by means of the loom. The looms shown in
tomb bricks and stone slabs appear fairly simple in construction. However,
the actual silks which have been excavated at the oasis sites along the Silk
Route across Central Asia, and at Mawangdui in Hunan province, provide
additional information (166). Patterned silks had been woven as early as the
Shang dynasty. These regular patterns were formed by passing the wefts over
the warp in the scheme over-three under-one over-three, and so on. By the
Han dynasty, the twill, an important variant of such patterns, was widely
made. In a twill, the over-three under-one pattern is altered so that the first

weft starts its course over warps one, two, and three, and the next weft starts its course over warps two, three, and four. This causes the pattern to move diagonally across the cloth. The damask probably arose out of the twill. The patterned areas were produced by the twill system in different combinations. Alternating with this was a ground weave of over-one, under-one produced by means of two heddles, which lifted the warps. In a damask, the pattern appears in the positive form on one side, and in the negative form on the other.

The polychrome silk was evolved to produce an equal pattern on both sides. In a polychrome silk, every warp was part of the pattern and the pre-selected design was set up with alternating warp-threads of two different colours. A damask or a polychrome silk would need about 3000 warps of silk. It would have been impossible to select by hand the groups of threads to rise at each stage of the pattern, as the warps were not only so numerous but so fine. Therefore, before weaving the pattern, the combinations to which a warp belonged were determined, and then it was tied to a bundle with the others of the combination, by vertical strings. These bundles were then pulled up in the correct sequence by a boy sitting on the loom. Although most illustrations that survive of such looms, known as draw-looms, are late (190), the repetition of errors in Han weaves, at exactly the same point in the pattern, indicate that they must have been made mechanically by a draw-loom. The introduction of more mechanical processes for the working of bronze and jade made for a decline in the artistic level. The development of the loom for silk weaving had the reverse effect. Silk weaving could be improved by increased mechanisation.

Lacquer production likewise did not suffer with an increase in the level of production. Unlike silk, lacquer was not produced mechanically; but the numbers and types of items could be increased by division of labour. An inscription on a lacquer cup provides valuable evidence (191):

The fourth year of the Yuan Shi reign period (AD 4). Made at the western factory in Shu commandary, Imperial pattern. A lacquered carved and painted wood cup with gilt (bronze) ears [handles]. Capacity one *sheng* 16 *yue*. Priming by Yi; lacquering by Li; outercoat by Dang; gilding of the 'ears' by Gu: painting by Ding, [inscription] engraved by Feng; cleaning [and polishing] by Ping; passed by Zong. Officer commanding the Factory Guard, Zhang; Manager, Liang; Deputy, Feng; Assistant, Long; Chief clerk, Bao.

These named individuals were probably responsible for their process, and each must have had several apprentices. Lacquer making was a highly specialised craft and practised only in certain areas, principally Sichuan and southern Henan provinces. During the Western Han, lacquer vessels were very popular as a substitute for bronzes. In southern Henan, lacquered vessels, in bronze forms, have been excavated from many tombs. Such was the success of the lacquer factory.

Lacquer painting and silk textile designs were particularly important artistic influences during the Han period, and patterns and styles developed in these media were often applied to other materials. Many mirrors for example, incorporated textile designs (115), and fine chased decoration on some bronze vessels was copied from incised patterns on lacquer (164). Large pole ornaments, possibly parts of chariot umbrella supports (colour XII), are decorated with designs which combine the qualities of both lacquer painting and textile patterns. The areas of silver, which seem to outline faces, resemble the lacquer painting seen on sumptuous textiles excavated at Mawangdui in Hunan province. Small floral motifs on the other hand copy embroidery. These developments gave renewed vitality to bronze decoration. Indeed by contrast with the Eastern Zhou when lacquer painting had also been influential (see p. 159), but when the existing bronze styles had been modified rather than transformed by such contact or example, completely new styles were now brought into being following the model provided by the invention in both lacquer and silk. For example lacquer painting may have stimulated the use of the new technique of parcel gilding, for by using gilding rather than inlay the fine sweeping lines, so effectively produced on lacquer, could also be rendered on bronze.

This use of expressive flowing line was consonant with and perhaps brought about by the concern with calligraphy, an interest inevitable in a land where a soft supple brush was used for writing among the educated who prized the skills it demanded. The Han period saw, therefore, the first stages of the widespread adoption of calligraphic line as an important feature of much of Chinese art. A small pendant in jade of a lady dancing, showing her long sleeves flowing so

191 *left* Oval wine-cup in lacquer with decoration of confronted birds, Han dynasty, dated AD 4. The inscription, which lists the workmen involved in the production of the cup, is incised around the foot. Length 17.6 cm.

192 *right* A flat jade pendant in the shape of a dancing woman, Han dynasty, first century AD. The sleeves of the dress are elaborated into a flowing pattern.

that they curled upwards as she moved (192), is an example of the way this new decorative approach was used. Jade is a hard and intractable material and smooth lines are difficult to achieve. Further, at an earlier time, when bronze had provided the dominant artistic influences, decoration on jade had often been angular and symmetrical (60). Thus the fluid curving lines represent a new style and are evidence of the importance of the linear treatment of designs. This development had great implications for the future. In the immediately succeeding centuries the influence of this tradition is seen in the fine designs on moulded tomb bricks, and later in the low relief sculptures carved in the Buddhist cave temples of the sixth century AD. Painting was undoubtedly an important force by this time. However, the application of the styles appropriate to painting in sculpture was made possible because, from as early as the Han period, such calligraphic designs had been used in the decoration not only of lacquer but also of ceramics, bronzes and jades.

Conclusion

The Han period saw the fulfilment of much of the promise of the Neolithic, Shang and Zhou periods. At the same time, the formation of a unified empire marked the beginning of a new era in Chinese history.

The main theme of this book has been the development of the arts of bronze casting, jade working, ceramics, silk weaving, and lacquer. The high level of manufacture in these materials was, and indeed still is, one of the major features of Chinese culture. The beautiful ceremonial cups of the Neolithic were a significant pointer for the future, for the skill of craftsmen had been exceptionally developed even at that early date. The contribution of the intervening centuries was the development of semi-industrial methods of production, dependent on large numbers of people and a large market. These methods made possible in later times the silk-weaving industry, to be envied and emulated by the Byzantines, and the manufacture of porcelain. This porcelain or china – the bowls and the country are synonymous – was carried to every quarter of the world and made China famous.

In the creation of these ceramics or bronzes, with their exquisite decoration and technical accomplishment, the great size of the country, with its regional diversity, was an asset. China was relatively isolated from the outside world. Little in the way of innovation and change can be directly attributed to outside influence. In the place of external stimulus, the interchange of designs between different materials, or interaction between the different regions of China, was a fertile source of invention and change. Pottery designs were cast in bronze, and bronze designs incised on pottery. Silk and lacquer in turn were taken as models for other materials. Southern China was, even in the Han period, an alien world, yet its longstanding ties with metropolitan China made it simultaneously familiar and easy to assimilate, and also exotically attractive.

The character of Chinese art was further moulded by a consciousness of the traditions of the past. As has been shown in the discussion of the Western Zhou bronzes, artistic styles and forms were at that time deliberately preserved and reinterpreted. Such an approach could only reinforce the very distinctive nature of Chinese art. The importance of literate men to record matters of state, from as early as the Shang dynasty when scribes were employed to carve the divinations on the oracle bones, probably stimulated this awareness of the achievements of the past. Indeed the attitudes and the taste of the educated man, the official and the scholar, were to have an important influence on the future development of Chinese art.

Finally the unification of the country, and the conquests in Asia, established China as the most important power in eastern Asia. With political power came economic power and the export of Chinese textiles, ceramics, and lacquer ware, so that in the Han period Chinese art became known to large areas of the world.

Appendix

Appendix: Museum registration numbers for the illustrations and references to comparative material.

The following abbreviations are used:

BMFEA   *Bulletin of the Museum of Far Eastern Antiquities*
KG   *Kaogu*
KGXB   *Kaogu Xuebao*
KGTX   *Kaogu Tongxun*
WW   *Wenwu and Wenwu Cankao Ziliao*

Black-and-white illustrations

1   **1959.2—16.13,** acquired by exchange from the Institute of Archaeology of the Chinese Academy of Sciences, Peking.
2   After *Xian Banpo*, p. 19, fig. 19.
3   **1959.2—16.5,** acquired by exchange from the Institute of Archaeology of the Chinese Academy of Sciences, Peking.
4   Compare *Xian Banpo*, pl. cxxii:1.
    1959.2—16.4, acquired by exchange from the Institute of Archaeology of the Chinese Academy of Sciences, Peking.
5   After *Xian Banpo*, p. 184, fig. 130.
6   **1959.2—16.3 and 1,** acquired by exchange from the Institute of Archaeology of the Academy of Sciences, Peking.
7   After *KG* 1973/5, p. 292, fig. 1.
8   After *KGXB* 1973/1, p. 16.
9   After *KG* 1962/6, p. 319:6.
10 After *KG* 1962/6, p. 319:4.
11 See *KGXB* 1978/2, p. 193, pls. 1—12.
    1966.2—23.1.
12 For excavated examples compare *KGXB* 1962/1, p. 49, fig. 15; *KGXB* 1973/2, p. 47, fig. 10:6; *KGXB* 1957/2, p. 23, pl. 4.
13 After *KGXB* 1964/2, p. 9 ff, figs. 23, 30, 36.
14 See *KG* 1963/7, p. 347, pl. 1:1.
15 After *Dawenkou*, p. 27, fig. 19.
16 Compare *WW* 1978/4, p. 47, fig. 1.
    1945.10—17.115, Raphael Bequest.
17 Compare *WW* 1978/7, p. 3, fig. 4:4.
    1950.10—21.57, given by W. Weinberger.
18 **OA+ 453 (S.41.1),** found by Professor J. L. Shellshear.
19 See *KG* 1963/7, p. 347, pl. ii:6, 4.
20 Compare *KGXB* 1958/1, p. 25, pl. iii:4.
    1937.4—16.16.
21 After *WW* 1972/10, p. 13, fig. 14.
22 Compare *KGTX* 1957/2, pl. 11:9.
    1937.4—16.8.

23   Compare *WW* 1978/7, p. 15, fig. 34.
      1945.10–17.157, Raphael Bequest.
24   **1937.4–16.102.**
25   For shape compare *Dawenkou,* fig. 83:4; from Guangdong, *WW* 1978/7, p. 15, fig. 29; from
      Yunnan, *KGXB* 1977/1, p. 61, fig. 12. A *zong* with this combination of two different faces is in
      the Norton Gallery, Palm Beach, Florida. See H. H. F. Jayne: *A Handbook of the Chinese Collec-
      tions in the Norton Gallery and School of Art,* no. 55.
      1947.7–12.457, Oppenheim Bequest.
26   ——
27   After *KG* 1972/4, p. 57, fig. 2.
28   After *WW* 1976/2, p. 26, pl. 6.
29   Compare *Hui xian fajue baogao,* pl. 13:4.
      Early *jue* with spouts attached to the side have been found in pottery at Erlitou (*KG* 1965/5,
      p. 219) and in metal at Zhejiang Changxing (*WW* 1960/7, p. 49). In the next stage this spout
      was incorporated in the lip of the vessel as in a *jue* from Panlongcheng (*WW* 1976/2, pl. 4:1).
      Lastly the spout was cast open, as in the Museum's vessel.
      1960.10–14.1, Brooke Sewell Fund.
30   **1960.10–14.1.**
31   Compare a *jia* from Panlongcheng, *WW* 1976/2, p. 35, fig. 39:1.
      1959.10–20.1.
32   After *WW* 1972/8, p. 17, figs. 2, 10.
33   Compare the axe from Panlongcheng, *WW* 1976/2, p. 33, fig. 34, and later Shang axes from
      the tomb of Fu Hao, *KGXB* 1977/2, p. 57, pl. 13:2 and 3.
      1947.7–12.413, Oppenheim Bequest.
34   Compare *KGXB* 1977/2, p. 57, pl. 14:2, 4, 5.
      1932.10–14.9; 1937.4–16.179; 1953.12–15.1, given by P. T. Brooke Sewell.
35   Compare *Shangdong wenwu xuanji,* pl. 62; *Fengxi fajue baogao,* pl. XLIX:3, 5; *KG* 1964/3,
      p. 132, fig. 22; *Hui xian fajue baogao,* pl. 21; *KGXB* 1956/4, p. 1, pl. 3:3.
      1952.10–29.15; OA+ 298; 1880.8–2.91, given by Sir A. W. Franks; **OA+ 297; 1880.8–
      2.97,** given by Sir A. W. Franks.
36   After *KG* 1972/4, p. 25.
37   For a discussion of the use of this type of bronze and a number of excavated examples, see *KG*
      1973/3, pp. 178–184.
      1947.7–12.416, Oppenheim Bequest.
38   Compare *KGXB* 1977/2, p. 57, pl. 15:1.
      1955.5–19.1, given by P. T. Brooke Sewell.
39   **1959.2–16.9, 10,** acquired by exchange from the Institute of Archaeology of the Chinese
      Academy of Sciences, Peking; **1950.11–17.306.**
40   For bronze-casting moulds excavated at Anyang, see *KG* 1961/2, p. 63, pls. 1&2.
      1939.6–16.1, 2, 3.
41   After Shi Chang-ju, *Bulletin of the Institute of History and Philology,* Academia Sinica, vol. 26,
      p. 117.
42   For impressed pottery of Neolithic date from Shandong, see *Guo Moruo; 'Zhongguo shigao',*
      p. 100. For pottery from Jiangxi, see *WW* 1975/7, p. 62, fig. 5:5; from Zhengzhou, *KGXB*
      1957/1, p. 69.
      1959.2–16.24, acquired by exchange from the Institute of Archaeology of the Chinese
      Academy of Sciences, Peking.
43   ——
44   **1973.7–26.12,** Seligman Bequest.
45   **1973.7–26.12,** Seligman Bequest.
46   Compare *WW* 1976/2, p. 32, fig. 31:13.
      1953.12–14.1.
47   See Li and Wan, *Studies of fifty-three ritual bronzes,* pl. XIX; *WW* 1977/11, pl. 3:1.
      1973.7–26.13, Seligman Bequest.
48   **1953.7–14.1.**
49   **1959.10–20.1.**
50   **1973.7–26.13,** Seligman Bequest.
51   **1973.7–26.13,** Seligman Bequest.
52   **1954.10–19.1,** given by P. T. Brooke Sewell.

53 **1954.10–19.1,** given by P. T. Brooke Sewell.
54 Compare *WW* 1972/6, p. 29, fig. 9.
    1947.7–12.419, Oppenheim Bequest.
55 **1968.4–22.1,** Sedgwick Bequest.
56 After *Museum* no. 301, p. 5, fig. 1. Other examples of the decoration of bronzes from Panlong-
    cheng are illustrated in *WW* 1976/2, p. 32, fig. 31:4, 9.
57 After *KG* 1976/4, p. 262, fig. 6:1.
58 Compare *KG* 1976/4, p. 262, fig. 6:1.
59 See *KG* 1975/5, p. 302, pl. 8:9; *KG* 1978/4, p. 270, pl. 12:3.
    1945.10–17.144, Raphael Bequest.
60 See *KGXB* 1977/2, p. 57, pl. 33:3, 4.
    1945.10–17.85, Raphael Bequest.
61 **1947.7–12.446,** Oppenheim Bequest.
62 See *KGXB* 1977/2, p. 57, pl. 21:1.
    1945.10–17.114, Raphael Bequest.
63 **1947.7–12.468.**
64 **1935.7–24.13.**
65 Compare *KGXB* 1977/2, p. 57, pl. 34:1.
    1968.4–22.14, Sedgwick Bequest.
66 See *WW* 1960/1, pp. 32–33.
    1940.4–13.33, 34, 39, 64–70, given by Mrs Eumorfopoulos.
67 **1945.10–17.144,** Raphael Bequest.
68 Compare *WW* 1978/10, p. 91, pl. 3:4.
    1943.2–15.2, bequeathed by Mrs M. K. Coldwell.
69 After *WW* 1963/3, p. 45, fig. 2 and pl. 5:2.
70 After *KG* 1974/5, pl. 312, fig. 5.
72 This type of dagger-axe was perpetuated in Sichuan long after it had disappeared from metro-
    politan China. *WW* 1976/3, p. 41, fig. 2:5. For Western Zhou examples, see *Fengxi fajue
    baogao*, pl. LXIX:1, 2.
    1940.12–14.287, given by Mrs B. Z. Seligman.
73 See *WW* 1972/7, p. 8, fig. 11. For a bronze decorated with a dragon created from one half of a
    taotie see *WW* 1976/7, pl. 1.
    1945.10–17.195, Raphael Bequest.
74 See *KG* 1976/4, p. 257, fig. 18:5:6.
    1973.7–26.33, Seligman Bequest.
75 Compare *KG* 1976/1, p. 36, fig. 9:9.
    1973.7–26.35, Seligman Bequest.
76 See *WW* 1977/12, p. 28, fig. 8 (1–3).
    1936.11–18.35.
77 **1973.7–26.3,** Seligman Bequest.
78 Compare Shaanxi sheng bowuguan: *Qingtongqi tushi*, pl. 5.
    1973.7–26.4, Seligman Bequest.
79 **1945.10–27.219,** Raphael Bequest.
79a The Arthur M. Sackler Collection, New York.
80 Compare *WW* 1977/12, p. 28, fig. 9. For antecedents of the thread-relief triple band, see *WW*
    1977/12, pp. 86–87; *WW* 1978/10, pp. 91–92, pl. 3. The survival of the *li* can also be traced
    at these sites.
    1973.7–26.10, Seligman Bequest.
81 **1947.7–12.429,** Oppenheim Bequest.
82 Compare Shandong sheng wenwu guanli chu: *Shandong wenwu xuanji*, pl. 74.
83 Compare Shaanxi sheng bowuguan: *Qingtongqi tushi*, pl. 18, *KGXB* 1977/2, p. 107, fig. 7:1.
84 The ceramic vessel can be seen in *KG* 1964/3, p. 164, fig. 3. A bronze version, earlier in date
    than the Museum's example, has been excavated near Peking, *KG* 1974/5, p. 313, fig. 8.
    1973.7–26.8, Seligman Bequest.
85 Compare *KGXB* vol. VIII (1954), p. 116, fig. 8.
    1959.2–16.1, acquired by exchange with the Institute of Archaeology of the Chinese Academy
    of Sciences, Peking.
86 **1947.7–12.329,** Oppenheim Bequest.
87 Compare *WW* 1976/6, p. 51, pl. 7:2.

1958.5–16.1, given by P. T. Brooke Sewell.

88   Compare the S-shaped dragon on a *ding* excavated at Mawang cun near Xian, *KG* 1974/1, pl. 4:2.
1957.7–15.1, given by P. T. Brooke Sewell.

89   See *WW* 1976/5, p. 26, pl. 4:6, *WW* 1976/6, p. 52, fig. 4.
1955.5–19.2, given by P. T. Brooke Sewell.

90   After *KGXB* 1957/1, p. 81, fig. 7.

91   After *WW* 1976/5, p. 43, figs. 30, 32.

92   Compare a pottery *gui* from Peking, *KG* 1974/5, p. 317, fig. 15:7.
1936.11–18.66.

93   After *KG* 1974/6, p. 365, fig. 2:3.

94   Compare *Xinzheng yiqi*, pl. 55.
1959.10–20.2.

95   Compare *KGXB* 1977/2, p. 57, pl. 12:1.
1953.10–24.1, given by P. T. Brooke Sewell.

96   **1961.2–14.2**; **1973.7–26.22**. Seligman Bequest.

97   Compare *KGXB* 1957/1, p. 75, pl. 6:4.
1945.10–17.62, Raphael Bequest.

98   Compare *KGXB* vol. VIII, 1954, p. 109, pl. 17:4.
1937.4–16.151.

99   Compare crudely executed jade birds excavated at Peking, *KG* 1974/5, p. 318, fig. 16.
1947.7–12.465, Oppenheim Bequest.

100   **1911.4–7.6.**

101   The inscription is discussed by B. Karlgren, 'Yin and Chou', *BMFEA* 8, p. 64.
1936.11–18.5.

102   After *KGXB* 1974/2, p. 65, fig. 3.

103   **1933.10–25.1**, given by Oscar Raphael.

104   Compare a string of eye-beads from Langjiazhuang, Shandong province: *KGXB* 1977/1, p. 73, pl. 7:3.
1940.12–14.5, 35, 46, given by Mrs B. Z. Seligman; **1938.5–24.753**; **1940.12–14.34, 43**, given by Mrs B. Z. Seligman.

105   Compare *Shangcunling Guo guo mudi*, pl. xx:2, *ge* with openwork dragon from Luoyang, *Luoyang Zhongzhou lu*, pl. 74:12; for fine inlay, see bronzes from Hebei Mancheng *KG* 1972/1, pp. 1–8; *KGXB* 1957/4, p. 33, pl. 4:1.
1911.4–7.3; **1937.5–19.6**; **1945.10–17.197**, Raphael Bequest; **1949.5–18.1, 2.**

106   Compare *KG* 1963/5, p. 241, fig. 14:1; *KGXB* 1959/1, p. 52, fig. 4:2; *WW* 1977/3, p. 51, fig. 19; *KG* 1962/12, p. 624, fig. 15:8.
1932.10–14.13; **1973.7–26.36**, Seligman Bequest; **1962.5–19.1**; **1932.12–15.32.**

107   Compare *KG* 1965/5, p. 256.
1947.7–12.426, Oppenheim Bequest.

108   For swords from Sichuan, compare *WW* 1974/5, p. 71, fig. 9; for the hollow hilt type, see *Luoyang Zhongzhou lu*, pl. 67:1; and for the sword with solid hilt, *KGXB* 1972/1, p. 59, pl. 14:1. For knives from Sichuan which were antecedents of the single-edged sword, see *WW* 1976/3, pl. 1:5.
1940.12–14.276, 286, 274, given by Mrs B. Z. Seligman; **1968.4–24.1**, Brooke Sewell Bequest.

109   For Eastern Zhou triggers, see *WW* 1974/5, p. 71, fig. 11.
1927.6–17.1; **1927.6–17.1.**

110   **1934.2–15.1, 2**, given by the National Art Collections Fund.

111   After *KG* 1974/3, p. 177, fig. 7.

112   For a jade example of the Shang period, see *WW* 1966/1, p. 58. The bronze from Erlitou is illustrated in *KG* 1976/4, p. 260, fig. 3:2. For the jades from Houma, see *WW* 1972/4, p. 34, fig. 6.
1937.4–16.149.

113   Compare *Luoyang Zhongzhou lu*, pls. 48:2, 57:4.
1945.10–17.152, 153, Raphael Bequest: **1935.1–15.9, 10.**

114   **1934.6–12.1**, given by Edgar Gutmann; **1973.5–15.1**, given by H.M. The King of Sweden; **1932.3–16.13.**

115   Compare *WW* 1976/9, p. 51, pl. 1:1, dated to the Qin period (third century BC).

1962.2–14.2, Brooke Sewell Bequest.
116 Compare *WW* 1977/3, p. 36, pl. 1:5.
     1935.1–15.1.
117 See *Quan guo jiben jianshe gongcheng zhong chutu wenwu,* pl. 144:1; compare also the dragons on a *xian* from Hubei Jingshan, *WW* 1972/2, p. 52, fig. 8.
     1973.7–26.24, Seligman Bequest.
118 After *WW* 1973/5, p. 16, fig. 4.
119 After *KGXB* 1959/4, pp. 72, 73, figs. 7, 10.
120 For a more elaborate version, see *KG* 1976/2, p. 124, figs. 6, 7; also *KG* 1959/12, pl. 1:2.
     1973.7–26.25, Seligman Bequest.
121 ——
122 For lacquer fragments, see *KGXB* 1974/2, p. 74, fig. 12:6, 7.
     1973.7–26.23, Seligman Bequest.
123 For related moulds, see *WW* 1960/8–9, p. 9, fig. 9.
     1949.7–11.1.
124 Compare moulds from Houma, *KG* 1962/2, p. 55, pl. 1.
     1965.6–12.1, Brooke Sewell Fund.
125 Compare moulds from Houma, *WW* 1960/8–9, p. 9, fig. 12.
     1936.11–18.53.
126 **1960.7–24.1,** Brooke Sewell Fund.
127 **1936.11–18.32.**
128 See *WW* 1966/5, p. 53, fig. 25.
     1955.2–17.1, given by P. T. Brooke Sewell.
130 Compare *Changsha fajue baogao,* pl. 13.
     1970.11–4.3, Brooke Sewell Bequest.
131 **1969.7–24.1,** Brooke Sewell Fund.
132 **1957.7–17.1,** given by P. T. Brooke Sewell.
133 See *Hui xian fajue baogao,* pl. I.
     1934.2–16.3, given by the National Art Collections Fund.
134 Compare *KGXB* 1959/1, p. 49, fig. 2:1.
     1954.2–20.1, given by P. T. Brooke Sewell.
135 Compare similar dragon heads on pendants from Liulige, *Shanbiaozhen yu Liulige,* pl. 112:1.
     1945.10–17.6, Raphael Bequest.
136 For decoration of irregular raised scrolls, see dragon pendants from Liulige, *Shanbiaozhen yu Liulige,* pl. 113:1, 2.
     1937.4–16,250.
137 For this decoration, compare *KGXB* 1956/4, p. 1, fig. 19:1.
     1947.7–12.517, Oppenheim Bequest.
138 Compare pendants from Shou xian Wafuhu in Anhui province, *Chu wenwu zhanlan tulu,* p. 28, nos. 54–55.
     1938.5–24.185.
139 **1947.7–12.512,** Oppenheim Bequest.
140 Compare *Honan Xinyang Chu mu chutu wenwu tulu,* pls. 99, 100; and *Changsha Mawangdui yi hao Han mu,* vol. I, p. 16, figs. 17–22.
     1950.11–15.1.
141 See *WW* 1978/4, pl. 7:2.
     1945.10–17.59, Raphael Bequest.
142 Compare *WW* 1977/3, p. 51, fig. 19; *WW* 1976/10, p. 92, fig. 3.
     1932.12–15.44; 1966.12–23.11.
143 Compare *WW* 1974/5, p. 71, fig. 10.
     1960.12–14.5.
144 Compare *WW* 1974/5, p. 73, fig. 21.
     1936.11–18.84.
145 See whole drums from Shizhaishan, *Yunnan Jinning Shizhaishan gu mu jun fajue baogao,* pl. 61.
     1948.10–13.3.
146 For other bronzes decorated with well-modelled oxen, see *KGXB* 1975/2, p. 97, pls. 12, 13.
     1950.4–5.1.
147 Compare *KGXB* 1975/2, p. 107, fig. 10.
     1948.10–13.7.

148   Compare *WW* 1957/8, p. 42.
       W.G. 940.
149   Compare *KGXB* 1975/2, p. 108, fig. 11.1.
       1948.10–13.4.
150   Compare *WW* 1978/7, p. 13, fig. 22.
       1934.11–12.4.
151   Compare *WW* 1975/8, p. 55, fig. 23.
       1937.10–14.1.
152   **1973.7.–26.167.**
153   Compare *Wenwu ziliao congkan*, no. 1 (1978), pl. 14:2.
       1963.10–14.22, given by W. Schofield.
154   Compare *Wenwu ziliao congkan*, no. 1 (1978), pl. 14:2.
       S.83, given by Professor J. L. Shellshear.
155   After W. Meacham, 'Double-f; a reinterpretation', *Journal of the Hong Kong Archaeological Society*, vol. v (1974), p. 79.
156   Compare *Wenwu ziliao congkan*, i, no. 1 (1978), pl. 14:4.
       1963.10–14.5, given by W. Schofield.
157   Compare knives discussed in *KG* 1978/5, p. 324 ff, fig. 2:14.
       67.12–13.7; 1950.11–17.215.
158   **1950.11–16.6.**
159   Han dynasty life as seen in such decorated bricks and tiles is discussed in *WW* 1975/4, pp. 45–55.
       OA CR 249, 1947.2–11.1(19), given by Professor Luo Zhongsun.
160   See *WW* 1978/5, pp. 1–19, pls. 1–4.
161   ——
162   To date the most remarkable lacquer-painted wooden carving found in China is a small open-work screen excavated at Jiangling in Hubei province: *WW* 1966/5, p. 33, pl. 2.
       1978.12–18.1, Brooke Sewell Fund.
163   ——
164   Compare a group of bronzes from Guangxi province, *KG* 1972/5, p. 20, and *WW* 1959/11, p. 14, fig. 14.
       1947.7–12.332, Oppenheim Bequest.
165   For a bronze version, see *KG* 1972/5, p. 23, fig. 316; for an earthenware vessel, see *KG* 1966/1, pl. 7:3.
       1937.4–13.1.
166   Compare *Changsha Mawangdui yihao Hanmu*, vol. ii, pls. 139, 140.
       Stein M.A. 900.
167   **1973.7–26.28,** Seligman Bequest.
168   Compare *Sichuan Handai huaxiang xuanji*, pl. 72.
       OA CR 236, 1947.2–11.1(6), given by Professor Luo Zhongsun.
169   **OA CR 163, 1939.7–8.43.**
170   Compare *KGTX* 1955/2, p. 37, pl. 12:2.
171   Compare *KGXB* 1965/1, p. 107, pl. 6:1.
       1929.7–16.1, given by Mrs Chester Beatty.
172   Compare stamped bricks from a hollow brick tomb at Zhengzhou, *WW* 1972/10, p. 41.
       1914.5–12.1.
173   **1909.5–12.29.**
174   The most magnificent of Han dynasty incense burners was excavated at Mancheng from the tomb of Liu Sheng: *KG* 1972/1, p. 8, pl. 4.
175   **OA CR 209, 1941.9–1.24,** given by Lt. D. Mills (1886).
176   From **1934.3–13.1–369.**
177   Compare *KGXB* 1964/2, p. 127, fig. 23:1, fig. 22:2.
       1945.10–17.25, Raphael Bequest; **1937.4–16.114.**
178   **1938.5–24.694.**
179   Compare *KGXB* 1963/2, p. 1, pl. ix:4.
       1973.7–26.53, Seligman Bequest.
180   Compare *Zhejiang chutu tongjing xuanji*, pls. 11, 12.
       1954.2–20.3, given by P. T. Brooke Sewell.
181   After *Changsha Mawangdui yihao Han mu*, vol. i, p. 36.

182   After *KG* 1972/1, p. 9, fig. 2.
183   After *KGXB* 1964/2, p. 110, fig. 4; p. 108, fig. 2.
184   After *WW* 1972/10, p. 50, fig. 2.
185   Compare *Chuka jimmin kyowakoku shutsudo bumbutsuten*, no. 102; *KGTX* 1957/3, pl. 6: 1–4.
     1955.11–14.1; 1910.4–18.19.
186   Compare *WW* 1958/10, p. 71; *KK* 1962/8, pl. 5:7.
     1973.7–26.173, Seligman Bequest.
187   Compare *Shanghai Bowuguan cang qingtongqi*, no. 94.
     1973.7–26.40, Seligman Bequest.
188   Compare *Zhongguo gu qingtongqi xuan*, no. 92.
     1936.11–18.257.
189   Compare *KGXB* 1964/2, p. 145, fig. 20:2.
     1937.4–16.163.
190   ——
191   **1955,10–24.1,** given by P. T. Brooke Sewell.
192   Compare *WW* 1973/4, p. 21, fig. 8.
     1947.7–12.492, Oppenheim Bequest.

Colour plates

   I   Compare Li and Wan, *Studies of fifty-three ritual bronzes*, pl. XIV.
     1975.7–26.1, Seligman Bequest.
  II   Compare *WW* 1959/10, p. 4.
     1936.11–18.1.
 III   **1977.4–1.1,** Brooke Sewell Bequest, Brooke Sewell Fund, Planelles-Granell Bequest.
 IV   See *Zhongguo gu qingtongqi xuan*, no. 27; compare *KG* 1979/1, pl. 8:4.
     1936.11–18.2.
   V   For more complicated plumed bird decoration, see *WW* 1976/6, p. 59, fig. 28; for large S-shaped dragons, see *WW* 1955/8, p. 21, fig. 7.
     1957.11–18.1, given by P. T. Brooke Sewell.
 VI   Compare *Fufeng Qijia cun qingtongqi qun*, pl. 3.
     1970.11–14.1, Brooke Sewell Bequest.
VII   See *WW* 1976/4, pl. 9. Compare also jades from Pudu cun, *KGXB* 1957/1, p. 75, pl. 6; and Gaojiabao Shaanxi, *WW* 1972/7, p. 7, fig. 9.
     1945.10–17.13, 45, 118, Raphael Bequest; **1947.7–12.462,** Oppenheim Bequest.
VIII   See *The Freer Chinese Bronzes*, pl. 88. For moulds used for casting bronzes with similar decoration found at Houma, see *KG* 1962/4, pls. 1–3.
     1972.2–29.1 a & b, given by Mrs U. E. K. Cull in memory of her husband.
 XI   **1945.10–17.215,** Raphael Bequest.
   X   Compare *KG* 1963/9, p. 469, fig. 9.1, 2; for a shield-shaped belt hook, *KG* 1964/3, p. 111, fig. 26:2; *WW* 1960/8–9, p. 15, fig. 4; chip-carved belt hooks from Fenshuiling, *KG* 1964/3, p. 111, pl. 5:17.
     1932.12–15.26; 1936.11–18.113; 1932.12–15.33; 1936.11–18.127.
 XI   Compare *KGXB* 1957/1, p. 141, pl. 5.
     1940.6–5.1, given by the National Art Collections Fund.
XII   See *Changsha Mawangdui yihao Hanmu*, vol. II, pl. 131.
     1932.10–14.45; 1936.11–18.13; 1973.7–26.46, Seligman Bequest.

Bibliography

ABBREVIATION
BMFEA   Bulletin of the Museum of Far Eastern
        Antiquities.

GENERAL SURVEYS
Akiyama Terukazu et al. Arts of China I.
   Neolithic Cultures to the T'ang Dynasty.
   Recent Discoveries. Tokyo/Palo Alto, 1968.
Bachhofer, L. A Short History of Chinese Art.
   New York, 1946.
Chang Kwang-chih. The Archaeology of Ancient
   China. London, 1963, revised and enlarged
   edn 1968 and 1977.
Cheng Te-k'un. Archaeology in China. Vol. I:
   Prehistoric China, Cambridge, 1959. Vol. II:
   Shang China, Cambridge, 1960. Vol. III:
   Chou China, Cambridge, 1963.
Fontein, J. and Hempel, R. China, Korea, Japan
   (Propyläen Kunstgeschichte, Bd XVII).
   Berlin 1968.
Sickman, L. and Soper, A. The Art and Archi-
   tecture of China. 3rd edn, London, 1968.
Sullivan, M. Chinese Art: Recent Discoveries.
   London, 1973.
Tregear, M. Chinese Art. London, 1980.
Watson, W. China Before the Han Dynasty.
   London, 1961.
Willetts, W. Foundations of Chinese Art, From
   Neolithic Pottery to Modern Architecture.
   London, 1965.

SITE REPORTS
Chang Kwang-chih. Fengpitou, Tapenkeng and
   the Prehistory of Taiwan. Yale, 1969.
Chavannes, E. Mission Archéologique dans la
   Chine Septentrionale. Paris, 1913.
Chōsen Kōseki Kenkyūkai (The Society of the
   Study of Korean Antiquities). Rakurō saikyō-
   zuka (The Tomb of Painted Basket of Lo-lang).
   Seoul, 1934.
Chōsen Kōseki Kenkyūkai (The Society of the
   Study of Korean Antiquities). Rakurō Okō-bo
   (The Tomb of Wang Kuang of Lo-lang). Seoul,
   1935.

Finn, D. J. Archaeological Finds on Lamma Island.
   Hong Kong, 1958.
Guangxi Zhuangzu Zizhiqu wenwu guanli
   weiyuanhui. Guangxi chutu wenwu. Peking,
   1978.
Guo Baojun. Shanbiaozhen yu Liulige. Peking,
   1959.
Harada Yoshito et al. Rakurō (Lo-lang) (A
   Report on the Excavation of Wang Hsü's Tomb
   in the 'Lo-lang' Province, An Ancient Chinese
   Colony in Korea). Tokyo, 1930.
Hebei sheng wenhuaju wenwu gongzuodui.
   Wangdu erhao Han mu. Peking, 1959.
Henan sheng wenwuju wenwu gongzuodui.
   Henan Xinyang Chu mu chutu wenwu tulu.
   Zhengzhou, 1959.
Janse, O. R. T. Archaeological Research in Indo
   China. 3 vols. Cambridge, Massachusetts,
   1947.
Nanjing Bowuyuan et al. Yinan gu huaxiang
   shimu fajue baogao. Nanjing, 1956.
Rakurō Kambo kankōkai (Lo-lang Han Tombs
   Publishing Society). Vol. I: Rakurō Kambo
   (Report of Excavation Conducted in 1924).
   Nara, 1974. Vol. II: Rakurō Kambo (Report
   of Tomb No. 219 at Souk-am-li). Nara, 1975.
Sekino Tadashi et al. Rakurō-gun no iseki
   (Archaeological Researches in the Ancient
   Lo-lang District). 3 vols. Korea, 1925–27.
Shaanxi sheng bowuguan et al. Shaanbei Dong
   Han huaxiang shike xuanji. Peking, 1959.
Shaanxi sheng bowuguan et al. Fufeng Qijiacun
   qingtongqi qun. Peking, 1963.
Shandong sheng wenwu guanliju, Jinan shi
   bowuguan. Dawenkou. Xinshiqi shidai mu
   fajue baogao. Peking, 1974.
Shansi Provincial Library and the Freer
   Gallery of Art. Excavation of a Western Han
   Dynasty Site at Yen-tzu Ko-ta Wan Ch'üan
   Hsien, Southwestern Shansi. Shanghai, 1932.
Shanxi sheng wenwu gongzuo weiyuanhui.
   Houma meng shu. Shanghai. 1976.
Sichuan sheng bowuguan. Sichuan chuanguan
   zang fajue baogao. Peking, 1960.

Xinjiang Weiwuer Zizhiqu bowuguan. *Xinjiang chutu wenwu*. Peking, 1975.

Yunnan sheng bowuguan. *Yunnan Shizhaishan gumu qun fajue baogao*. Peking, 1959.

Zhejiang sheng wenwu guanli weiyuanhui *et al. Zhejiang xinshiqi shidai wenwu tulu*. Peking, 1958.

Zhongguo kexueyuan kaogu yanjiusuo. *Hui xian fajue baogao*. Peking, 1956.

Zhongguo kexueyuan kaogu yanjiusuo. *Shou xian Cai hou mu chutu yiwu*. Peking, 1956.

Zhongguo kexueyuan kaogu yanjiusuo. *Changsha fajue baogao*. Peking, 1957.

Zhongguo kexueyuan kaogu yanjiusuo. *Jiangsu Xuzhou Han huaxiang shi*. Peking, 1959.

Zhongguo kexueyuan kaogu yanjiusuo. *Luoyang Shaogou Han mu*. Peking, 1959.

Zhongguo kexueyuan kaogu yanjiusuo. *Luoyang Zhongzhou Lu*. Peking, 1959.

Zhongguo kexueyuan kaogu yanjiusuo. *Miaodigou yu Sanliqiao*. Peking, 1959.

Zhongguo kexueyuan kaogu yanjiusuo. *Sanmenxia caoyun yiji*. Peking, 1959.

Zhongguo kexueyuan kaogu yanjiusuo. *Shangcunling Guoguo mudi*. Peking, 1959.

Zhongguo kexueyuan kaogu yanjiusuo. *Zhengzhou Erligang*. Peking, 1959.

Zhongguo kexueyuan kaogu yanjiusuo. *Fengxi fajue baogao*. Peking, 1962.

Zhongguo kexueyuan kaogu yanjiusuo *et al. Xian Banpo*. Peking, 1963.

Zhongguo kexueyuan kaogu yanjiusuo. *Xun xian Xin cun*. Peking, 1964.

Zhongguo kexueyuan kaogu yanjiusuo. *Changan Zhangjiapo Xi Zhou tongqi qun*. Peking, 1965.

Zhongguo kexueyuan kaogu yanjiusuo. *Changsha Mawangdui yihao Han mu*. Peking, 1973.

CATALOGUES OF COLLECTIONS AND
EXHIBITIONS

Bunker, E. C. *The Art of Eastern Zhou*. Chinese Art Society of America, New York, 1962.

Bunker, E. C. *et al. 'Animal Style' Art from East to West*. The Asia Society, New York, 1970.

Catalogue of the International Exhibition of Chinese Art, 1935–6. Royal Academy of Arts, London, 1935.

Chongqing shi bowuguan. *Sichuan Han huaxiang zhuan xuanji*. Peking, 1957.

Chūgoku bijutsu (Chinese Art in Western Collections), Vol. IV: Bronze and Jade. Tokyo, 1973.

Chūka jimmin kyōwakoku shutsudo bumbutsuten (Archaeological Treasures Excavated in the People's Republic of China). Tokyo/Kyoto, 1973.

Chūgoku kodai no bijutsu. Catalogue of an exhibition of Ancient Chinese Art, held at the Idemitsu Art Gallery, Tokyo, 1978.

Chu wenwu zhanlan tulu. Catalogue of an exhibition of Chu antiquities held at Peking Historical Museum, 1954.

Fontein, J. and Wu Tung. *Unearthing China's Past*. Museum of Fine Arts, Boston, 1973.

Fux, H. and Janata, A. *Ausstellung Archäologische Funde der Volksrepublik China*. Vienna, 1974.

Gyllensvärd, B. and Pope, J. A. *Chinese Art from the Collection of H. M. King Gustav VI Adolf of Sweden*. The Asia Society, New York, 1966.

Jayne, H. H. F. *A Handbook of the Chinese Collections in the Norton Gallery and School of Art*. West Palm Beach, Florida, 1972.

Katz, L. *Selections of Chinese Art from Private Collections in the Metropolitan Area*. China Institute of America, China House, New York, 1966.

Kyōto University. *Catalogue of the Archaeological Collection in the Museum of the Faculty of Letters*. Kyoto, 1963.

Lee, G. J. *Selected Far Eastern Art in the Yale University Art Gallery*. New Haven and London, 1970.

Leth, A. *Chinese Art (A Selection of the Exhibits Shown at the Museum of Decorative Arts, Copenhagen, 1950)*. Copenhagen, 1953.

Loehr, M. *Relics of Ancient China from the Collection of Dr Paul Singer*, The Asia Society, New York, 1965.

Mostra d'Arte Cinese — Exhibition of Chinese Art. Venice, 1954.

Nanjing bowuguan *et al. Jiangsu sheng chutu wenwu xuanji*. Peking, 1963.

Or des Scythes, Trésors des Musées Soviétiques. Catalogue of an exhibition held at the Grand Palais, Paris, Oct.-Dec. 1975.

Palmgren, N. *Selected Chinese Antiquities from the Collection of Gustaf Adolf, Crown Prince of Sweden*. Stockholm, 1948.

Relics of Han and Pre-Han Dynasties. The Imperial Household Museum, Tokyo, 1932.

Schloss, E. *Art of the Han*. Catalogue of an exhibition held at the China Institute in America, New York, 1979.

Shaanxi sheng bowuguan *et al. Shaanbei Dong Han huaxiang shike xuanji*. Peking, 1959.

Shandong sheng wenwu guanlichu, Shandong sheng bowuguan. *Shandong wenwu xuanji*. Peking, 1959.

Shang Chengzuo. *Changsha chutu Chu qiqi tulu*. Shanghai, 1955.

Tenri Sankōkan zuroku, Chūgoku hen. Tokyo, 1967.

Trubner, H. *Arts of the Han Dynasty*. Chinese Art Society of America, Asia House, New York, 1961.

Trubner, H. *The Far Eastern Collection*. The Royal Ontario Museum, Toronto, 1968.

Visser, H. F. E. *Asiatic Art in Private Collections of Holland and Belgium*. New York, 1948.

Watson,W. *Handbook to the Collections of Early Chinese Antiquities*. The Trustees of the British Museum, London, 1963.

Watson,W. *The Genius of China*. An Exhibition of Archaeological Finds of the People's Republic of China, London, 1973.

Wenhua dageming qijian chutu wenwu. Peking, 1972.

Wu sheng chutu zhongyao wenwu zhanlan tulu. Peking, 1958.

Xin Zhongguo chutu wenwu (Historical Relics Unearthed in New China). Peking, 1972.

Young, J. J. *Art Styles of Ancient Shang from Private and Museum Collections*. China Institute in America, China House, New York, 1967.

Zheng Zhenduo. *Quanguo jiben jianshe gongcheng zhong chutu wenwu zhanlan tulu*. Peking, 1954.

Zhonghua renmin gongheguo chutu wenwu xuan (A Selection of Archaeological Finds in the People's Republic of China). Peking, 1976.

SPECIALISED STUDIES

Akatsuka, Tadashi. *Chūgoku kōdai no shūkyō to bunka. In'ochō no saishi*. Tokyo, 1977.

Bagley, R. W. 'Pan-lung-ch'eng: A Shang City in Hupei', *Artibus Asiae*, 39:3/4, 1977, pp. 165–219.

Barnard, N. 'The First Radiocarbon Dates From China', *Monographs on Far Eastern History*, no. 8. Canberra, 2nd edn, revised and enlarged, 1975.

Barnard, N. (ed.) *Early Chinese Art and its Possible Influence in the Pacific Basin*. A Symposium Arranged by the Department of Art History and Archaeology, Columbia University, New York, 1962. 3 vols. New York, 1972.

Chang Kwang-chih. 'Early Chinese Civilisation, Anthropological Perspectives', *Harvard-Yenching Institute Monograph Series*, Vol. XXIII, 1976.

Cheng Te-k'un. *Archaeological Studies in Szechuan*. Cambridge, 1957.

Cheng Te-k'un. *New Light on Prehistoric China*. Cambridge, 1966.

Creel, H. *The Origins of Statecraft in China*. Chicago, 1970.

von Dewall, M. 'Pferd und Wagen im Frühen China', *Saarbrücker Beiträge zur Altertumskunde*, Bd I. Bonn, 1964.

von Dewall, M. 'New Data on Early Chou Finds. Their Relative Chronology in Historial Perspective', *Symposium in honour of Dr Li Chi*, Part II. Taiwan, 1966.

von Erdberg Consten, E. *Das alte China*. Stuttgart, 1958.

Fairbank, W. *'Adventures in Retrieval'*. Harvard-Yenching Institute Studies, XXVIII. Cambridge, Massachusetts, 1972.

Garner, Sir Harry. *Chinese Lacquer*. London, 1979.

Goodrich, L. C. 'Archaeology in China: The First Decades', *Journal of Asiatic Studies*, Vol. XVII, no. 1, 1957, pp. 5–15.

Guo Moruo. *Zhongguo shi kao*. Vol. I. Peking, 1976.

Hansford, S. H. *A Glossary of Chinese Art and Archaeology*. London, 1954.

Hayashi Minao, (ed.) *Chūgoku Inshū-jidai no buki. (Weapons of the Yin and Chou dynasties)*. Kyōto University, Institute for Humanistic Research, 1972.

Hayashi Minao. *Kandai no bumbutsu*. Kyoto University, 1976.

Hayashi Minao. 'Seishū kimbun ni arawareru shaba kankei goi', *Kokotsugaku* no. 11, 1976.

Ho Ping-ti. *Cradle of the East*. Chinese University of Hong Kong and University of Chicago, 1975.

Hsü Cho-yun. *Ancient China in Transition. An Analysis of Social Mobility, 722–222 BC*. Stanford, 1965.

Jettmar, K. *Art of the Steppes*. London, 1967.

Jia Lanpo. *Jiushiqi shidai wenhua*. Peking, 1957.

Kane, V. C. 'A Re-examination of An-yang Archaeology', *Ars Orientalis*, Vol. X, 1975, pp. 93–110.

Keightley, D. N. 'Legitimation in Shang China'. Paper prepared for the Conference on Legitimation of Chinese Imperial Regimes, Asilomar, California, 1975.

Keightley, D. N. 'Shang Divination: The Magico-Religious Legacy'. Paper prepared for the Workshop on Classical Chinese Thought, Harvard University, 2–13 Aug. Mimeographed, 1976.

Keightley, D. N. 'The Bamboo Annals and Shang-Chou Chronology'. *Harvard Journal of Asiatic Studies*, Vol. XXXVIII, no. 2, Dec. 1978, pp. 423–38.

Keightley, D. N. 'The Late Shang State: When, Where and What?; The Late Shang State; Its Weakness and Strengths'. Papers presented to the Conference on the Origins of Chinese Civilisation, University of California, Berkeley, 26–30 June 1978.

Li Chi. *Anyang*, Seattle, 1977.

Lion-Goldschmidt, D. and Moreau-Gobard,

J-C. *Chinese Art, Bronze, Jade, Sculpture, Ceramics.* London, 1960.

Liu Zhiyuan. *Sichuan Handai huaxiang zhuan yishu,* Peking, 1958.

Loehr, M. 'The Stratigraphy of Hsiao-t'un (Anyang)', *Ars Orientalis,* Vol. II, 1957, pp. 439–57.

Loewe, M. *Crisis and Conflict in Han China.* London, 1974.

Loewe, M. *Records of Han Administration.* Cambridge, 1967.

Loewe, M. 'Man and Beast, The Hybrid in Early Chinese Art and Literature', *Numen,* Vol. xxv, Fasc. 2, 1978, pp. 97–117.

Maspero, H. *China in Antiquity.* Translation by Frank A. Kierman Jr. of *La Chine Antique.* Folkstone, 1978.

Nagahiro Toshio (ed.) *Kandai gazō no kenkyū. (The Representational Art of the Han Dynasty).* Tokyo, 1965.

Needham, J. 'The Development of Iron and Steel Technology in China'. *Publications of the Newcomen Society.* London 1958.

Pirazzoli-t'Serstevens, M. *La Civilisation du Royaume de Dian à l'Epoque Han.* Paris, 1974.

Poor, R. 'Notes on the Sung Dynasty Archaeological Catalogs', *Archives of the Chinese Art Society of America,* XIX, 1965, pp. 33–44.

Prusek, J. *Chinese Statelets and the Northern Barbarians,* 1400–300 BC. Prague, 1971.

Rudenko, S. I. *Die Kultur der Hsiung-nu und die Hügelgräber von Noin Ula.* Bonn, 1969.

Rudenko, S. I. *Frozen Tombs of Siberia, The Pazyryk Burials of Iron-Age Horsemen.* London, 1970.

Rudolph, R. C. *Han Tomb Art of West China.* Los Angeles, 1951.

Seligman, C. G. and Beck, H. C. 'Far Eastern Glass: Some Western Origins', *BMFEA,* no. 10, 1938, pp. 1–68.

Soper, A. C. 'The Tomb of the Marquis of Ts'ai', *Oriental Art,* N.S. Vol. x, no. 3, Autumn 1964, pp. 152–7.

Umehara Sueji. *Kanan Anyō ihō (Selected Ancient Treasures Found at Anyang, Yin Sites).* Kyoto, 1940.

Umehara Sueji. *Kanan Anyō ibutsu no kenkyū (A Study of Relics from Anyang, Honan).* Kyoto, 1941.

Umehara Sueji. *Rakuyō Kinson kobo shūei.* Kyoto 1937. Revised edn 1944.

Umehara Sueji. *Inbo hakken mokki in'ei zuroku (Illustrations of the stamped impressions of wooden objects discovered in Yin tombs).* Kyoto, 1959.

Umehara Sueji. *Inkyo Inbo no kotsuga yōki (Ivory and bone vessels in the Yin tombs of Anyang).* Taiwan, 1961.

Umehara Sueji. *Inkyo (Yin Hsü, Ancient Capital of the Shang Dynasty at An-yang).* Tokyo, 1964.

Watson, W. *Ancient China. The Discoveries of Post-Liberation Chinese Archaeology.* London, 1974.

Watson, W. *Archaeology in China.* London, 1961.

Watson, W. *Cultural Frontiers in Ancient East Asia.* Edinburgh, 1971.

Wen You. *Sichuan Han dai huaxiang xuanji.* Peking, 1956.

White, W. C. *Tombs of Old Lo-yang.* Shanghai, 1934.

Zhongguo kexueyuan kaogu yanjiusuo. *Xin Zhongguo de kaogu shouhuo.* Peking, 1962.

BRONZES

Bachhofer, L. 'The Evolution of Shang and Early Chou Bronzes', *The Art Bulletin,* Vol. XXVI, 1944, pp. 107–16.

Bagley, R. W. 'Shang Bronzes of Local Style from Shensi Province'. A paper given at the College Art Association Meeting, Washington, Jan. 1979.

Barnard, N. *Bronze Casting and Bronze Alloys in Ancient China.* Monumenta Serica Monograph, XIV, Canberra, 1961.

Barnard, N. and Satō Tamotsu. *Metallurgical Remains of Ancient China.* Tokyo, 1975.

Brinker, H. *Bronzen aus dem alten China.* Zürich, 1975.

Bulling, A. G. and Drew, I. 'The Dating of Chinese Bronze Mirrors', *Archives of Asian Art,* XXV, 1971–72, pp. 36–57.

Bulling, A. G. 'The Decoration of Mirrors of the Han Period, a Chronology', *Artibus Asiae Supplementum,* XX. Ascona, Switzerland, 1960.

Ch'en Meng-chia. 'Style of Chinese Bronzes', *Archives of the Chinese Art Society of America,* Vol. I, 1946, pp. 26–52.

Ch'en Meng-chia. 'Malcolm's K'ang-hou Kuei and its Set', *Oriental Art,* Vol. I, no. 3, Winter 1948, pp. 111–16.

Chen Mengjia. 'Xi Zhou tongqi duandai', *Kaogu Xuebao,* IX–XIV, 1955–6.

Chen Mengjia. *Yin Zhou qingtongqi fenlei tulu (A Corpus of Chinese Bronzes in American Collections).* Tokyo, 1977.

Chūka jimmin kyōwakoku kodai seidōki ten (Exhibition of Ancient Bronzes of the People's Republic of China). Nihon Keizai Shimbunsha, 1976.

von Dewall, M. 'Der Gräberverband von Wu-kuan-ts'un/Anyang', *Oriens Extremus,* VII, 1960, pp. 129–51.

Dohrenwend, D. 'The Early Chinese Mirror',

Artibus Asiae, Vol. xxvii: 1/2, 1964, pp. 79–98.

Ecke, G. *Frühe chinesische Bronzen aus der Sammlung Trautmann*. Peking, 1939.

Ecke, G. *Sammlung Lochow: Chinesische Bronzen*, i. Peking, 1943.

Elisseeff, V. *Bronzes Archaïques chinois au Musée Cernuschi*. Paris, 1977.

von Erdberg Consten, E. 'A Terminology of Chinese Bronze Decoration', *Monumenta Serica*, xvi: 1/2, 1957, pp. 287 ff; xvii, 1958, pp. 208 ff; xviii, 1959, pp. 245 ff.

von Erdberg, E. 'Chinese Bronzes from the Collection of Chester Dale and Dolly Carter', *Artibus Asiae Supplementum*, Ascona, 1978.

An Exhibition of Ancient Chinese Ritual Bronzes Loaned by C. T. Loo and Co. The Detroit Institute of Arts, 1940.

Fairbank, W. 'Piece-mold Craftsmanship and Shang Bronze Design', *Archives of the Chinese Art Society of America*, xvi, 1962, pp. 9–15.

Garner, Sir Harry. 'The Composition of Chinese Bronzes', *Oriental Art*, N.S. Vol. vi, no. 4, Winter 1960, pp. 130–35.

Gettens, R. J. *The Freer Chinese Bronzes*, Vol. ii: Technical Studies. Washington, D.C., 1969.

Gettens, E. J. *et al*. 'Two Early Chinese Bronze Weapons with Meteoritic Iron Blades', *Freer Gallery of Art Occasional Papers*, Vol. iv, no. 1, 1971.

Gugong tongqi tulu. Compiled by the Joint Administration of the National Palace and Central Museums. 2 vols. Taiwan, 1958.

Guo Moruo. *Liang Zhou jinwenci daxi tulu kaoshi*. Revised edn, Tokyo, 1935.

Hansford, S. H. *The Seligman Collection of Oriental Art*, Vol. i. London, 1957.

Hayashi Minao. 'In Seishū no aida no seidō yōki no hennen'. *Tōhōgakuhō*, Supplement to Vol. l, Feb. 1978.

van Heusden, W. *Ancient Chinese Bronzes of the Shang and Chou Dynasties*. Tokyo, 1952.

Higuchi Takayasu. 'Newly Discovered Western Chou Bronzes', *Acta Asiatica*, Vol. iii, 1962, pp. 30–43.

Higuchi Takayasu. 'Seishū dōki no kenkyū', *Kyōto Daigaku bungaku-bu kenkyū kiyō*, vii, 1963.

Ho Wai-kam. 'Shang and Chou Bronzes', *The Bulletin of the Cleveland Museum of Art*, Vol. li, no. 7, Sept. 1964, pp. 174–87.

Kane, V. 'The Chronological Significance of the Inscribed Ancestor Dedication in the Periodization of Shang Dynasty Bronze Vessels', *Artibus Asiae*, xxxv: 4, 1973, pp. 335–70.

Kane, V. 'The Independent Bronze Industries in the South of China Contemporary with the Shang and Western Chou Dynasties', *Archives of Asian Art*, xxviii, 1974–5, pp. 77–107.

Karlbeck, O. 'Anyang Moulds', *BMFEA*, no. 7, 1935, pp. 39–60.

Karlgren, B. 'Early Chinese Mirror Inscriptions', *BMFEA*, no. 6, 1934, pp. 9–79.

Karlgren, B. 'Yin and Chou in Chinese Bronzes', *BMFEA*, no. 8, 1936, pp. 9–156.

Karlgren, B. 'The Dating of Chinese Bronzes', *Journal of the Royal Asiatic Society*, 1937, pp. 33–9.

Karlgren, B. 'New Studies on Chinese Bronzes', *BMFEA*, no. 9, 1937, pp. 1–117.

Karlgren, B. 'Some Weapons and Tools of the Yin Dynasty', *BMFEA*, no. 17, 1945, pp. 117–20.

Karlgren, B. 'Once Again the A and B Styles in Yin Ornamentation', *BMFEA*, no. 18, 1946, pp. 367–82.

Karlgren, B. 'Bronzes in the Hellström Collection', *BMFEA*, no. 20, 1948, pp. 1–38.

Karlgren, B. 'Some Bronzes in the Museum of Far Eastern Antiquities', *BMFEA*, no. 21, 1949, pp. 1–25.

Karlgren, B. 'Notes on the Grammar of Early Bronze Décor', *BMFEA*, no. 23, 1951, pp. 1–80.

Karlgren, B. *A Catalogue of the Chinese Bronzes in the Alfred F. Pillsbury Collection*. The Minneapolis Institute of Arts, Minneapolis, 1952.

Karlgren, B. 'Some Characteristics of the Yin Art', *BMFEA*, no. 34, 1962, pp. 1–28.

Karlgren, B. 'Some Pre-Han Mirrors', *BMFEA*, no. 35, 1963, pp. 161–9.

Karlgren, B. and Wirgin, J. *Chinese Bronzes. The Nathanael Wessén Collection*. Stockholm, 1969.

Kelley, C. F. and Ch'en Meng-chia. *Chinese Bronzes from the Buckingham Collection*. The Art Institute of Chicago, 1946.

Kidder, J. E. Jr. *Early Chinese Bronzes in the City Art Museum of St Louis*. St Louis, 1956.

Koop, A. J. *Early Chinese Bronzes*. London, 1924.

Kümmel, O. *Chinesische Bronzen aus der Abteilung für Ostasiatische Kunst an den Staatlichen Museen Berlin*. Dritte Jahresgabe der Gesellschaft für Ostasiatische Kunst. Berlin, 1928.

Kuwayama, G. *Ancient Ritual Bronzes of China*. Los Angeles County Museum of Art, 1976.

Lefebvre d'Argencé, R-Y. *Ancient Chinese Bronzes in the Avery Brundage Collection*. San Francisco, 1977.

von Lochow, H. J. *Sammlung Lochow: Chinesische Bronzen*, ii. Peking, 1944.

Loehr, M. 'Bronzentexte der Chou-Zeit. Chou I: 1', *Sinologische Arbeiten*, II, 1940. 'Chou I: 2', *Monumenta Serica*, XI, 1946.

Loehr, M. 'The Bronze Styles of the Anyang Period', *Archives of the Chinese Art Society of America*, VII, 1953, pp. 42–53.

Loehr, M. *Chinese Bronze Age Weapons. The Werner Jannings Collection in the Chinese National Palace Museum, Peking*. Ann Arbor, 1956.

Loehr, M. *Ritual Vessels of Bronze Age China*. The Asia Society, New York, 1968.

Matsumaru, M. 'Seishū seidōki seisaku no haikei-Shū kimbun kenkyū Joshō', *Kiyō, Tōdai Tōyō bunka kenkyūjo*, LXXII.

Menzies, J. M. *The Shang Ko*. Toronto, 1965.

Mizuno Sei'ichi. 'Ancient Chinese Bronzes and Jades. Yin-Chou Culture and Bronzes', *Oriental Art*, N.S. Vol. V, no. 4, Winter 1959, pp. 132–56.

Mizuno Sei'ichi. *Inshū seidōki to gyoku*. Tokyo, 1959.

Mizuno Sei'ichi (ed.) *Tōyō Bijitsu – Asiatic Art in Japanese Collections*, Vol. V: Chinese Archaic Bronzes. Tokyo, 1968.

National Palace Museum (ed.) *Masterworks of Chinese Bronze in the National Palace Museum*, Taiwan, 1970. Supplement, 1973.

Plenderleith, H. J. 'Technical Notes on Chinese Bronzes with Special Reference to Patina and Incrustations', *Transactions of the Oriental Ceramic Society*, Vol. XVI, 1938–9, pp. 33–55.

Pope, J. A. *et al. The Freer Chinese Bronzes*, Vol. I: Catalogue. Washington D.C., 1967.

Rong Geng. *Shang Zhou yiqi tongkao – The Bronzes of Shang and Zhou*. Yenching Journal of Chinese Studies, Monograph Series no. 17, 2 vols. Peking, 1941.

Rong Geng and Zhang Weichi. *Yin Zhou qingtongqi tonglun*. Zhongguo kexueyuan kaogu yanjiusuo, Peking, 1958.

Rostovtzeff, M. *Inlaid Bronzes of the Han Dynasty in the Collection of C. T. Loo*. Paris/ Brussels, 1927.

Shanghai bowuguan cang qingtongqi. 2 vols. Shanghai, 1964.

Shih Chang-ju. 'Bronze Casting in the Shang Dynasty', *Bulletin, Institute of History and Philology*, XXVI. Taiwan, 1955.

Shirakawa Shizuka. *Kimbunshū I-IV*. Tokyo, 1963.

Shirakawa Shizuka. *Kimbun tsūshaku*. Vols. I–L. From 1962.

Smith, C. S. 'Bronze Technology in the East'. In Teich, M. and Young, R. *Changing Perspectives in the History of Science*, pp. 21–32. London, 1973.

Smith, E. A. 'Early Chinese Metallurgy', *The Metal Industry*, 10 Jan. 1936, pp. 27–31.

Soper, A. E. 'Early, Middle, and Late Shang: A Note', *Artibus Asiae*, Vol. XXXVIII: 1, 1966, pp. 5–38.

Stephen, B. 'Shang Bronzes with Ancient Repairs', *Royal Ontario Museum of Archaeology, Toronto, Annual*, 1961, pp. 8–14.

Stephen, B. 'Early Chinese Bronzes in the Royal Ontario Museum', *Oriental Art*, N.S. Vol. VIII, no. 2, Summer 1962, pp. 62–7.

Sugimura Yūzō. *Chūgoku kodōki*. Idemitsu bijutsukan sensho, 3, Tokyo, 1966.

Sun Haibo. *Xinzheng yiqi*. Kaifeng, 1937.

Trübner, J. *Yu und Kuang. Zur Typologie der chinesischen Bronzen*. Leipzig, 1929.

Umehara Sueji. *Henkin no kōkogaku-teki kōsatsu* (Etude archéologique sur le Pien-chin, ou série de bronzes avec une table pour l'usage rituel dans la Chine antique). (Memoir, Tōhō Bunka Gakuin, Kyoto Kenkyūjo, Vol. II). Kyoto, 1933.

Umehara Sueji. *Obei shūcho Shina kodō seika* (*Selected Relics of Ancient Chinese Bronzes from Collections in Europe and America*). 7 vols. Osaka, 1933.

Umehara Sueji. *Sengoku-shiki dōki no kenkyū* (Etude des Bronzes des Royaumes Combattants). Kyoto, 1936.

Umehara Sueji. *Kodōki keitai no kōkogaku-teki kenkyū (On the Shapes of the Bronze Vessels of Ancient China: An Archaeological Study)*. (Memoir, Tōhō Bunka Kenkyūjo, Vol. XV). Kyoto, 1940.

Umehara Sueji. 'Sensei-shu Hōkeiken shutsudo no daini no henkin' ('The Second Set of Ritual Vessels, *Pien-chin*, from Pao-chi-hsien, Shensi Province'). *Tōhōgaku kiyō* I, 1959, pp. iii-viii (English summary) and 1–15.

Umehara Sueji. 'In chūki to sarete iru Tei-shū (Chengchou) shutsudo kodōki no seishitsu', *Shigaku* 33/2, 1961, pp. 123–46.

Umehara Sueji. *Nihon shūcho Shina kodō seika (A Selection of Chinese Bronzes in Japanese Collections)*. 6 vols. Osaka, 1961.

Wang Shilun. *Zhejiang chutu tongjing xuanji*. Peking, 1957.

Watson, W. *Ancient Chinese Bronzes*. London, 1962.

Weber, C. D. 'Chinese Pictorial Vessels of the Late Chou Period', *Artibus Asiae* Vol. XXVIII: 2/3, 1966, pp. 107–54; XXVIII: 4, 1966, pp. 271–311; XXIX: 2/3, 1967, pp. 115–92.

Weber, G. W., Jr. *The Ornaments of Late Chou Bronzes: a method of analysis*. New Brunswick, New Jersey, 1973.

White, W. C. *Bronze Culture of Ancient China*. Toronto, 1956.

Yetts, W. P. *The Cull Chinese Bronzes*. Courtauld Institute of Art, London, 1939.

Yetts, W. P. *The George Eumorfopoulos Collection*. Catalogue of the Chinese and Korean Bronzes, Sculptures, Jade, Jewellery and Miscellaneous Objects. 3 vols. London, 1929–32.

Zhongguo gu qingtongqi xuan. Peking, 1976.

JADE

An Exhibition of Chinese Archaic Jades. Catalogue of a loan exhibition arranged by C. T. Loo, Inc. for the Norton Gallery of Art, West Palm Beach, Florida, Jan.–Mar. 1950.

Ayers, J. and Rawson, J. *Chinese Jade throughout the Ages*. Catalogue of an exhibition organised by the Arts Council and the Oriental Ceramic Society at the Victoria and Albert Museum, 1975.

Dohrenwend, D. *Chinese Jades in the Royal Ontario Museum*, 1971.

Dohrenwend, D. 'Jade Demonic Images from Early China', *Ars Orientalis*, Vol. X, 1975.

Hansford, S. H. *Chinese Jade Carving*. London, 1950.

Hansford, S. H. *Chinese Carved Jades*. London, 1968.

Hansford, S. H. *Jade, Essence of Hills and Streams: The von Oertzen Collection of Chinese and Indian Jades*. New York, 1969.

Hartman, J. M. *Chinese Jade of Five Centuries*. Rutland, Vermont and Tokyo, 1969.

Hartman, J. M. *Ancient Chinese Jades from the Buffalo Museum of Science*. Catalogue of exhibition held at the China House Gallery, China Institute in America, New York, 1975.

Hayashi Minao. 'Chūgoku no kodai saigyoku, zuigyoku', *Tōhōgakuhō, Kyoto*, Vol. XL, 1969.

Hayashi Minao. 'Haigyoku to jū'. *Tōhōgakuhō, Kyoto*, Vol. XLV, 1973.

Hayashi Minao. 'Sen-In shiki no gyokki bunka' ('Pre-Yin Jade Culture'). *Museum*, no. 334, Jan. 1979, pp. 4–16.

Kuwayama, G. *Chinese Jade from Southern California Collections*. Catalogue of an exhibition held at Los Angeles County Museum of Art, 1976–7.

Lefebvre d'Argencé, R-Y. *Chinese Jades in the Avery Brundage Collection*. Asian Art Museum of San Francisco, 1977.

Loehr, M. *Ancient Chinese Jades*. Fogg Art Museum, Cambridge, Massachusetts, 1975.

Na Chih-liang. *Chinese Jades: Archaic and Modern from the Minneapolis Institute of Arts*. London, 1977.

Pope-Hennessy, U. *A Jade Miscellany*. London, 1946.

Rawson, J. 'The Surface Decoration on Jades of the Chou and Han dynasty', *Oriental Art*, Vol. XXI, no. 1, 1975, pp. 36–55.

Salmony, A. *Archaic Chinese Jades*. Sonnenschein Collection, Chicago Art Institute, 1932.

Salmony, A. *Carved Jade of Ancient China*. Berkeley, California, 1938.

Salmony, A. *Chinese Jade through the Wei Dynasty*. New York, 1963.

Umehara Sueji. *Shina kogyoku zuroku (Ancient Chinese Jades)*. Tokyo and Kyoto, 1955.

CERAMICS

Andersson, J. G. 'Researches into the Prehistory of the Chinese', *BMFEA*, no. 15, 1943, pp. 1 ff.

Bylin-Althin, M. 'The Sites of Ch'i Chia P'ing and Lo Han T'ang in Kansu', *BMFEA*, no. 18, 1946.

Hochstadter, W. 'Pottery and Stonewares of Shang, Chou and Han', *BMFEA*, no. 24, 1952, pp. 81–108.

Huber, L. G. 'The Relationship Between the Painted Pottery and the Lung-shan Cultures'. Paper presented to the Conference on the Origins of Chinese Civilisation, University of California, Berkeley, 26–30 June, 1978.

Inshū no Toki. Ceramic Objects in the Yin (Shang) and Chou Dynasties (1300–221 BC) in the Collection of Tenri Sankōkan Museum. Tenri Gallery, Tokyo, 1978.

Koyama Fujio et al. *Sekai tōji zenshū*. (Ceramic Art of the World), Vol. VIII, From Ancient China to Six Dynasties. Tokyo, 1955.

Meacham, W. 'The "Double-*f*" Design: A Re-interpretation', *Journal of the Hong Kong Archaeological Society*, Vol. V, 1974, pp. 74–81.

Medley, M. *The Chinese Potter*. London, 1976.

Mino Yutaka. 'Brief Survey of Early Chinese Glazed Wares', *Artibus Asiae*, XXXVII: 4, 1975, pp. 39–290.

Shangraw, C. F. *Origins of Chinese Ceramics*. China Institute in America, New York. Catalogue of Exhibition, Oct. 1978–Jan. 1979.

Tregear, M. *Catalogue of Chinese Greenware in the Ashmolean Museum, Oxford*. Oxford, 1976.

Tsiang, K. R. 'Glazed Stonewares of the Han Dynasty. Part One: The Eastern Group', *Artibus Asiae*, XL: 2/3, 1978, pp. 143–76.

Umehara Sueji. *In yo shutsudo hakushokudōki no kenkyū* (Etude sur la poterie blanche fouillée dans la ruine de l'ancienne capitale des Yin). (Memoir, Tōhō Bunka Gakuin, Kyoto Kenkyūjo, Vol. I). Kyoto, 1932.

ORACLE BONES

Chang Tsung-tung. *Der Kult der Shang-Dynastie im Spiegel der Orakelinschriften. Eine paläographische Studie zur Religion im archaischen China.* Wiesbaden, 1970.

Chen Mengjia. *Yin xu buci zongshu.* Peking, 1956.

Hsü Chin-hsiung. *The Menzies Collection of Shang Dynasty Oracle Bones.* 2 vols. Royal Ontario Museum, Toronto, 1971, 1977.

Keightley, D. N. *Sources of Shang History, the Oracle-Bone Inscriptions of Bronze Age China.* Berkeley, Los Angeles, London, 1978.

Rao Zongyi. *Yindai zhenbu renwu tongkao (Oracle Bone Diviners of the Yin Dynasty).* Hong Kong, Hong Kong University Press, 1959.

Shima Kunio. *Inkyo bokuji sōrui.* Tokyo, 1967.

Tung Tso-pin. *Fifty Years of Studies in Oracle Inscriptions.* Tokyo, 1964.

SILK

Riboud, K., Vial, G. and Hallade, M. *Tissus de Touen-houang. Mission Paul Pelliot,* Vol. XIII. Paris, 1970.

Stein, A. *Serindia: Detailed Report of Explorations in Central Asia and Westernmost China.* Oxford, 1921.

Xinjiang Wuweier Zizhiqu bowuguan chutu wenwu zhanlan gongzuozu. *Sichou zhi lu: Han Tang zhiwu.* Peking, 1972.

PERIODICALS AND SERIES (Western)

Archives of the Chinese Art Society of America. New York, 1945–65. Later continued in: *Archives of Asian Art.* New York, 1966–.

Ars Orientalis. Freer Gallery of Art, Washington D.C., 1954–.

Artibus Asiae. Ascona, Switzerland, 1925–.

Arts Asiatiques. Paris, 1954–.

Bulletin of the Museum of Far Eastern Antiquities. Stockholm, 1929–.

Early China, Berkeley, California, 1975–.

Harvard Journal of Asiatic Studies. Cambridge, Massachusetts, 1936–.

Monumenta Serica. Peking, later Tokyo, 1935–.

Oriental Art. London, 1948–.

Transactions of the Oriental Ceramic Society. London, 1921–.

PERIODICALS AND SERIES (Chinese)

Archaeologia Sinica, Nanjing and Taibei, Institute of History and Philology, Academia Sinica.

Archaeologia Sinica, new series, Taibei, Institute of History and Philology, Academia Sinica.

Kaogu. Peking, 1959–.

Kaogu tongxun. Peking, 1955–8.

Kaogu xuebao. Peking, 1936–.

Wenwu. Peking, 1959–.

Wenwu cankao ziliao. Peking, 1950–8.

PERIODICALS AND SERIES (Japanese)

Archaeologia Orientalis, series A and B. Tokyo and Kyoto, Tōa kōko gaku kai.

Bijutsu kenkyu. Tokyo, 1932–.

Kōkogaku zasshi. Tokyo, 1910–. Originally published as *Kōko-kai,* Vols I–VIII. Tokyo, 1901–10.

Kokotsugaku. Tokyo, 1954–.

Museum. Tokyo, 1951–.

Tōhōgaku. Tokyo, 1951–.

Tōhōgakuhō. Kyoto, 1931–.

Tōhōgakuhō. Tokyo, 1931–40.

Tōkyō Shinagakuhō. Tokyo, 1955–.

Tōyō bunka kenkyūjo kiyō. Tokyo, 1943.

Index of Characters
Chinese Characters with pinyin and Wade-Giles Transliteration

Fufeng, Fu-feng, 扶風

Fu Hao, Fu Hao, 婦好

Fujian, Fukien, 福建

Fuling, Fu-ling, 涪陵

Funan, Fu-nan, 阜南

Gansu, Kansu, 甘肅

Gaocheng xian, Kao-ch'eng-hsien, 藁城縣

Gaojiabao, Kao-chia-pao, 高家堡

Gao Zu, Kao-tsu, 高祖

ge, ko, 戈

gengwu, keng-wu, 庚午

Gu, Ku, 古

gu, ku, 觚

guang, kuang, 觥

Guangdong, Kwangtung, 廣東

Guanghe, Kwang-ho, 廣河

Guangxi, Kwangsi, 廣西

Guangzhou, (Canton), 廣州

gui (pottery), kuei, 鬹

gui (bronze), kuei, 簋, 毀

Guizhou, Kweichow, 貴州

Guo, Kuo, 虢

Guwei cun, Ku-wei-ts'un, 固圍村

gu wen, ku wen, 古文

Han, Han, 漢

Handan, Han-tan, 邯鄲

Han Feizi, Han Fei-tzu, 韓非子

Han Shu, Han Shu, 漢書

hang tu, hang-t'u, 夯土

Hangzhou, Hangchow, 杭州

Han Shui, Han Shui, 漢水

Hao, Hao, 鎬

he, ho, 盉

Hebei, Hopei, 河北

Heilongjiang, Heilungkiang, 黑龍江

Hejia cun, Ho-chia-ts'un, 賀家村

Hemudu, Ho-mu-tu, 河姆渡

Henan, Honan, 河南

Hougang, Hou-kang, 後岡

Hou Ji, Hou Chi, 后稷

Houma, Hou-ma, 侯馬

hu, hu, 壺

Huai, Huai, 淮

Huaian, Huai-an, 淮安

Huai He, Huai Ho, 淮河

Huan Gong, Huan Kung, 桓公

huang, huang, 璜

Huangchi, Huang-ch'ih, 黃池

Huang He, Huang Ho, 黃河

Huating, Hua-t'ing, 花廳

Hua xian, Hua-hsien, 華縣

Hui xian, Hui-hsien, 輝縣

Hunan, Hunan, 湖南

jia, chia, 斝

Jialingjiang, Chia-ling-chiang, 嘉陵江

jian, chien, 鑑

Jiangling, Chiang-ling, 江陵

Jiangsu, Kiangsu, 江蘇

Jiangxi, Kiangsi, 江西

jiao, chiao, 角

Jilin, Kirin, 吉林

Jin, Chin, 晉

Jing Hou gui, Ching-hou kuei, 井(邢)侯簋

Jinning, Chin-ning, 晉寧

jin wen, chin wen, 金文

Ji xian, Chi-hsien, 汲縣

Jiu Gao, Chiu Kao, 酒誥

jue, chüeh, 爵

Kaifeng, K'ai-feng, 開封

Kang Gao, K'ang Kao, 康誥

Kang Hou gui, K'ang-hou kuei, 康侯簋

Kang Wang, K'ang Wang, 康王

Kexingzhuang, K'o-hsing-chuang, 客省莊

Kezuo xian, K'o-tso-hsien, 喀左縣

Langjiazhuang, Lang-chia-chuang, 郎家莊

Laozi, Lao-tzu, 老子

lei, lei, 罍

leiwen, lei-wen, 雷文

Lelang, Lo-lang, 樂浪

Li, Li, 立

li, li, 鬲

li, li, 禮

you, yu, 卣
You Wang, Yu Wang, 幽王
yu, yü, 盂
Yuanjunmiao, Yüan-chün-miao, 元君廟
Yuan Shi, Yüan Shih, 元始
yue, yüeh, 钺
Yuezhi, Yüeh-chih, 月支
Yunnan, Yünnan, 雲南
Zeng, Tseng, 鄫
Zhang, Chang, 章
Zhang Boya, Chang Po-ya, 張伯雅
Zhangjiapo, Chang-chia-p'o, 張家坡
Zhang Qian, Chang Ch'ien, 張騫
Zhanguo Ce, Chan-kuo Ts'e, 戰國策
Zhao, Chao, 趙
Zhao Hun, Chao Hun, 招魂

Zhe jia, Che chia, 折罳
Zhejiang, Chekiang, 浙江
Zheng, Cheng, 鄭
Zhengzhou, Cheng-chou, 鄭州
zhi, chih, 觶
Zhiyu, Chih-yü, 峙峪
Zhou, Chou, 周
Zhou Li, Chou Li, 周禮
Zhuang Gong, Chuang Kung, 莊公
Zhuangzi, Chuang-tzu, 莊子
Zong, Tsung, 宗
zong, tsung, 琮
Zou Yan, Tsou Yen, 鄒衍
zun, tsun, 尊
Zuo Zhuan, Tso Chuan, 左傳

Index of Objects

by reference number

Index